EXPOSED

THE HARROWING STORY OF A MOTHER'S UNDERCOVER
WORK WITH THE FBI TO SAVE CHILDREN FROM

INTERNET SEX PREDATORS

EXPOSED

THE HARROWING STORY OF A MOTHER'S UNDERCOVER
WORK WITH THE FBI TO SAVE CHILDREN FROM
INTERNET SEX PREDATORS

R. STEPHANIE GOOD

Published by
THOMAS NELSON
Since 1798
www.thomasnelson.com

Published in Nashville, Tennessee, by Thomas Nelson, Inc.

ISBN-13: 978-1-59555-062-0

Printed in the United States of America

This Dedication is divided into two parts; both were essential to the creation of this book.

First, I dedicate this book to children everywhere, for you have the power and imagination to create a future filled with love, laughter, and heart. Make it bright and happy and always strive to do what others think impossible. Stay safe and may you never know the pain that those written about in this book have inflicted upon so many. For those of you who do, remember that you are strong. Use your strength in the face of adversity to live a life that allows you to rise above the hurt and become the wonderful person that God intends you to be.

I am also dedicating this book to Supervisory Special Agent Austin Berglas, for your admirable work with the New York FBI's Squad C-20 (Crimes Against Children Squad), your endless devotion to making the world a safer place, and for allowing me the opportunity to work alongside you in such an important and fulfilling capacity.

Acknowledgments

THIS BOOK COULD NOT HAVE BEEN WRITTEN WITHOUT TWO competing factions, good versus evil. I wish there was no need for stories such as those in the following pages, but there is. And, with your help, we will chip away at the monsters who prey upon children until there are no more stories to tell and no more sexual predators to catch.

There are numerous people to thank for making this book possible, all of whom have my sincerest and deepest gratitude:

I would like to begin by thanking my husband, Ed, for your love and understanding, for allowing me the time and space to communicate with such an inhumane segment of society, and for recognizing the need for me to follow through with their cases.

I also extend my heartfelt thanks to my sons, Brian and Christian, and their beautiful wives and children whose presence in my life constantly inspires me to strive to make a difference. Christian, your contribution to this book was essential and is greatly appreciated. Thank you for your time, your effort, and your honesty!

I am especially grateful to my brother, Larry Garrison, "The Newsbreaker," whose support, friendship, and love mean so very much to me. Thank you for making this book possible by introducing me to the people at Thomas Nelson.

To my late brother, Jim Garrison, not a day goes by that I don't think of you and miss you. You will always be in my heart! Someday in Camelot!

I would like to extend a special thanks to my parents, Helen and Robert, who taught me the importance of making the world a better place for everyone, rather than merely being concerned with my own little corner of the universe. You are greatly missed.

I am also grateful to my extended family and friends, all of whom have shown so much love and support to Ed and me, especially recently, when we needed them the most.

To my friend, Dorothy Welch, thank you from the bottom of my heart for your help with our mission to take sexual predators off the streets.

To Carol, for your unwavering encouragement and support, I thank you.

A special thank you to the wonderful people at Thomas Nelson, especially David Dunham for taking a chance on such a controversial, yet essential book, and to my editors, Joel Miller and Alice Sullivan, for working so hard to make this book a reality.

I also want to thank my agent at Waterside Productions, Bill Gladstone, for watching over me and helping me to keep my focus, and to Ming Russell for all of your help and support.

To the very special woman who courageously contributed her personal story about being the victim of a child molester, I thank you from the bottom of my heart.

To Austin Berglas, there are no words. You have made a difference for so many people in so many ways, including me. I am truly grateful!

To Squad C-20, for your dedication to keeping children safe and for always being so gracious to me.

And finally, I want to express my gratitude to the Federal Bureau of Investigation for creating squads to protect children and for allowing me to work with the Special Agents of Squad C-20.

God bless you all!

Contents

ONE

White-Collar Capture

"BE TRUE TO YOUR WORK AND YOUR WORK WILL BE TRUE TO you." Those are the words inscribed on the seal of New York's famous and praiseworthy Pratt Institute. The school has a history that spans back in time to well over a century ago, which has left the campus adorned with many architectural landmarks. Distinguished faculty members take pride in what they have to offer their students. One such individual, Steven Dovas, whose expertise is in the area of animation, spent many hours in his office doing what most assumed was "being true to his work." However, that was not always the case. When Steven slipped into his office and closed the door behind him, sometimes work was his priority. Often he focused on his own needs, needs that had nothing to do with furthering his career or the needs and reputation of his employer.

Sitting at his desk, Steven booted up his computer hoping to find someone to his liking. He was looking for female companionship, someone who would fulfill his every desire. He must have believed that the Internet would be the place where those dreams could come true. So, he logged onto America Online in his quest to find that one special girl. One day, as Steven perused the chatrooms, scouring the profiles of those whose AOL screen names interested him, he came across one that immediately caught his attention. It was anything but subtle. It revealed the person's name, her age, her location, her likes and dislikes, as well as a full description of her: long blonde hair, blue eyes, 5'2". She was online; he could not resist. He instant messaged Julie hoping for a reply. To his delight, she responded and they chatted for quite awhile, revealing just enough details to hold each other's interest. He seemed excited about his new acquaintance and her eagerness to chat with him. And, she was just as excited about hers. It was obvious to Julie that Steven wanted to be more than friends.

As the days passed, Steven thought of Julie. He often booted up his computer and looked for her. As soon as he saw her name appear on his buddy list, he would instant message her right away. She always responded. At first, they talked mainly about Julie's interests and her family. He seemed more cautious than she was about revealing too much about himself. They traded pictures and exchanged some minor personal details about themselves.

As their chats became more regular, Steven began to open up and discussed subjects of a more intimate nature. He told Julie how much he had missed her since their last chat and how he was hoping to someday meet her. She liked hearing that. When he saw that she was flattered by his comments, and also interested in meeting him, the intimacy soon turned into sex talk. He asked her about past affairs. She hesitantly shared that she had never been with anyone. Steven expressed admiration for her, commending her for saving herself for that special someone. And, as time passed, he carefully described all of the things he wanted to show her someday. Julie responded that she was anxious to learn from him. He knew that their relationship had moved to the next level.

As the dialogue continued, Steven increasingly monopolized the chats with talk about sex. He appeared to be fixated on it, and the more responsive Julie was, the more descriptive he got. It wasn't long before their communications were mostly about sex.

When Steven felt that he had gained Julie's complete trust, he asked her if she would call him. She agreed. He gave her his office phone number and anxiously waited for her call. He quickly answered, and when he heard Julie's voice, he became excited. He talked casually at first, asking how she was and telling her how nice it was to finally talk to her. She was shy. It was easier for her to chat on the computer. She didn't really have any experience with the opposite sex. She tried her best not to let on to him how nervous she was. Eventually, she grew more comfortable and they had several phone conversations. There were times when Steven's voice grew low and the conversation would turn to sex. He would go into detail about all of the things that he wanted to do to her. Then, there were long periods of silence from him, followed by more details. During those times, Julie barely had a chance to respond. Steven's breathing would become heavy as he commented about how much he liked her voice and how excited he felt listening to her. He would often ask her to say certain seductive things to him. She hesitantly agreed. He would tell her what to say and she would repeat it. But, Steven would often abruptly end the call, saying that he had to get back to work. Julie was surprised to be cut off so quickly. Several similar phone calls took place until Steven asked her out on a date. They agreed to meet at City Hall Park in Manhattan. It was then that the situation moved beyond the point of no return.

Steven and Julie's story resembles that of a steamy romance novel—full of love and lust. But there is one crucial detail missing: two consenting adults. When Steven, using the AOL screen name RoyLpain, first made contact with Julie, he was a respected teacher, lecturer, and well-known filmmaker and commercial animator who had been praised for his work on various projects for children's television segments for Nickelodeon, HBO, and Sesame Street. But today, he is best described as a convicted sex offender. Steven Dovas is a child predator, an adult who desires sex with children. He went after Julie thinking that she was thirteen years old. But, Julie is made up of two people: FBI Special Agent Austin Berglas, known on AOL as "Julie13nyc;" and me—a concerned citizen, who uses the AOL screen name "Teen2hot4u."

In truth, the thirteen-year-old girl that Steven Dovas thought he was communicating with does not exist. She is one of a number of fictitious teenagers created for the purpose of weeding out Internet predators. The teen's voice on the other end of Dovas' phone conversations was mine. On the telephone, I usually portray Julie. Sometimes I speak to the predators as Lorie, also known as Teen2hot4u. I am not an FBI agent, nor am I a law enforcement officer. But, I am also not a thirteen-year-old girl. I am very good at what I do, which is why the FBI has allowed me into their circle of trust. On the Internet and on the telephone, I can convince anyone that I am a young teen. I know the lingo, and I can speak the part. So, while men like Steven Dovas occupy themselves trying to make young girls their victims, they had better be very careful that they don't run into me first, because it will be their last stop before a prison cell.

When Steven Dovas showed up at City Hall Park to meet Julie, he was greeted instead by a squad of FBI agents, and arrested.

The government's complaint against him stated that he had initiated over forty Internet chats and a number of telephone conversations with the girl he was trying to meet. All of those communications included graphic depictions of the sexual acts that he had planned to engage in with his young victim.

Steven Dovas' story is not unlike that of most convicted sex offenders who search for children online. He first came across Julie in an Internet chatroom while on a quest to find young girls to meet for sex. She seemed like just the right type for him. She was the only child of a single mom, and she had no experience with boys. Due to her mother's long working hours, she spent a lot of time alone at home on the Internet. His intention was to "groom" her, a maneuver that sexual predators use to gain a child's trust and reduce their inhibitions with the ultimate goal of initiating physical contact. He used the chats, emails, and phone calls to build up Julie's self-esteem and make her feel comfortable enough to talk to him about sex. He gently asked whether she had siblings, what her father was like, and whether her mother was home a lot. Was her mother strict? Did she give Julie a lot of freedom? He encouraged her to talk about school, what grade she was in, and where she lived. Her answers convinced Steven that he had found the perfect mark, because Julie had enough free time to sneak away and meet him without arousing her mother's suspicions. He spent many long hours chatting with her about how much he liked her and all the fun they would have if they ever met. When he felt the time was right, he brought up the subject of sex, and praised her for not having been with a boy yet. He said that he wanted to be the one to teach her everything, and when he thought he had that chance, he took it. Predators like this almost always have numerous victims while on their mission to seduce children.

Upon his arrest, Dovas' background with children's programming led to newspaper headlines that ran the gamut from "'Sesame' Prof Hit in Perv Sting" to "Brought to Jail by the Letters S, E, and X." He was charged with using the Internet to persuade, induce, entice, and coerce an individual younger than eighteen years old to engage in sexual activity. After pleading guilty, he was sentenced to five years in a federal prison; five years supervised release; a $10,000 fine; and attendance in a sex offender program. He was lucky. Based on the charges, he could have received thirty years.

Steven Dovas was a very prominent individual. He was married, successful, and well respected. A Google search yields pages of links to his many achievements. Yet, he succumbed to his desires and lost everything when he put his entire life on the line for a moment of sex with a child. Now he sits in a jail cell, and like most other incarcerated sexual predators, he probably wonders what he did that was so terribly wrong. After all, according to what many of them say, they are only giving the child the kind of love that they deserve. Unfortunately, these predators have the convoluted notion that if they do not force themselves on a child, the sex is consensual, and therefore, it should not be considered illegal. With over 550,000 sex offenders registered nationwide, you would think they would figure out that their opinion is not relevant. Their behavior is illegal and, if caught, they will go to jail. But they have an addiction, and these deviants stop at virtually nothing. And, I will stop at nothing to find them and turn them over to the FBI. The fact is that my odds are much better than theirs. While there is no doubt that the Internet has dramatically increased the access of child predators to their young prey, it has also increased the chances that law enforcement officials will catch them. Since the Internet is now one of the most commonly used methods by which sexual predators entice children into illicit sexual relationships, law enforcement agencies all over the country are forming squads for the sole purpose of catching them before they can victimize another child.

Unfortunately, most sexual predators have already left a trail of hurt and trauma behind them, so it is important that we do everything in our power to stop these criminals in their tracks. Just as sexual predators hide anonymously behind their computer screens, so do law enforcement agents, and so do I. Unfortunately for Steven Dovas, he sits among the throngs of sexual predators who have crossed my path while I continue to lie in wait for my next prey.

So, who am I? When it comes to catching sexual predators, I can best be described as two different people. Sometimes, I am Julie. Most of the time, I am Lorie. And, in my other life, the one that has nothing to do with deviant perverts, I am a wife, a mother, a grandmother, an attorney, a news producer, and an author. What I do on the Internet is the clandestine part of my life that stays hidden from most who know me. After all, it is not easy telling your friends that you spend most of your time searching for sexual predators. I also never know who might be within earshot. It could be a local Internet predator who might end up going offline to find victims after hearing about me. But, more importantly, up until now, I have shared my secret with only a few select people because what I do puts me in harm's way. I never made it public knowledge before because someone might retaliate against me for having caught one of their loved ones, or friends, or them. But this story must be told, regardless of the consequences.

Not too long ago, I received several threats when one of my screen names was revealed in a newspaper article after an arrest was made. People were instant messaging and emailing me nasty comments and warnings. Some said they would hurt me for what I do; one individual told me that I would "never be able to get them all." It is amazing that they do not realize how easy it is to find out who they are. I have no interest in those people yet. Their threats are as meaningless to me as the depraved individuals who hide behind their computer screens lurking around for children who cannot defend themselves. But, I do keep track of them. After each threat that I receive, I put their names on my buddy list, and it is not long before I recognize them as people who hang out in the same chatrooms that I frequent looking for sexual predators. They just haven't approached me yet. But, they will. People forget quickly.

When I sign onto the Internet, I transform into a different person—a curious, naïve child. As Lorie, I play the part of a teenage girl who goes online looking for older men who are interested in teaching me about grown-up things. I sit in chatrooms and wait for them to find me. Yes, you read that correctly. I frequent their loathsome hangouts and wait for them to make their move. I have developed Internet screen names and profiles that clearly reflect that I am very young, and they come in droves to pursue me, one instant message after another.

A screen name is like a tag. I use those that identify me as a child. For example, my most famous screen name, the one most responsible for the capture and conviction of several sexual predators, is Teen2hot4u. It clearly shows that I am a teenager. How young I am can be seen in my profile that states that I am thirteen. Agent Berglas' screen name was Julie13nyc. People familiar with the Internet chat world would easily recognize that to be Julie's name, her age, and her location. As with Teen2hot4u, many people don't use their real names in their screen name. Some use names that indicate a hobby, like Surfergrl or Tennisany1. While Lorie is not my screen name, it is one of the names that I use in my profile which is filled with all of the details that I think will attract child predators. All they have to do is click on my screen name, and my profile shows up on the screen. In it, I include my age and other information that makes me appear to be a young teen.

Using my screen names, I sign onto the Internet and go into chatrooms that most likely cater to sexual predators, otherwise known in the legal world as predicated chatrooms. Through experience, I have learned where to find them. They are easy to spot and are always filled with people who frequent the same types of rooms. These predators go from one chatroom to the next, checking out profiles to see who might be an easy mark.

Once I have myself situated in a room, it never takes more than a couple of minutes before I am bombarded with instant messages. I receive so many, in fact, that I have no choice but to weed some out. I do that by reading their profiles to see if I can spot people who live within traveling distance from Lorie. It is far more likely that a predator will look closer to home for a child rather than travel several hundred miles away. Some will travel, but it is less common. I look for indications of their age, because I don't want to chat with children. I eliminate those who state they are only interested in trading pictures, chatting online or on the phone, and not meeting in person. Those are the ones who are usually only interested in fantasizing and/or role-playing, and not meeting in real time, meaning outside of the Internet. I also avoid most people who do not have a profile, unless their screen name clearly indicates that they are from somewhere close enough for a meeting. For example, a screen name such as ChicagoJoe or Dallasman generally suggests the person's location. If it merely says Joe123htu and they have no profile, I sometimes skip over them by ignoring their instant message. But, if their screen name indicates that they are looking for younger girls, for example, Man4ynggrl, I might take a chance.

After going through the above process, I respond to some of the messages. The chats are live. In other words, we are typing back and forth and receiving the messages instantly. Most chats begin with "a/s/l" which means they are asking for an age, sex, and location. So, my answer might be "13/f/ny." That would mean I am a thirteen-year-old female from New York. Some of the chats that I have begin like this one:

Man4ynggrl: Hi. Are you into older men?
Teen2hot4u: yeah
Man4ynggrl: How old do you like them?

8

Teen2hot4u: I don't care so long as he's cute.

Man4ynggrl: So, you don't mind if I'm 57?

Teen2hot4u: no way that's cool with me. Is it cool that im 13?

Man4ynggrl: Sure. Have you had sex yet?

Teen2hot4u: I didn't really do so much yet but I wanna

Man4ynggrl: If you want to, why haven't you?

Teen2hot4u: just haven't found the right guy yet

Man4ynggrl: Maybe I can be that guy

Teen2hot4u: cool*

That chat is just the beginning. They often get extremely graphic later on. Some may even start out very sexual depending upon what the person is hoping to do with a young girl.

As I mentioned earlier, while playing the part of Lorie, I usually stay behind the computer screen. But as Julie, I am the voice on the telephone of the other young girl who, while chatting on the Internet with sexual predators, is in reality, Agent Berglas. When it comes time to call a predator, Agent Berglas contacts me. Calls are arranged when a child predator wants to hear the voice of the girl he has been chatting with online. We never suggest it first. The request usually comes after the predator has expressed an interest in meeting the girl and is looking for reassurance that she is not a law enforcement officer. However, occasionally the request comes from someone only looking for phone sex. We never comply with those.

When I make a call, I go into a room for complete privacy and put a sign on the outside of the door that reads, "Don't come in. I'm on the phone for the FBI." Everyone in my family understands what that means: no loud TV, nobody can pick up the extension, and no one can come into the room to talk to me. I have to take a few minutes to compose myself and I wait for Agent Berglas to let me know it's time.

*The screen name Man4ynggrl was invented for purposes of the previous example. I have not had contact with anyone using that screen name and have no information about anyone who may have used, may currently use, or may subsequently use that screen name.

Sexual predators never doubt Julie's identity once they hear my voice. They are completely convinced that they have been communicating with a thirteen-year-old, and this allows them to show up at a meeting place with few reservations. In the end, I believe their greatest fear is that my mom will find out. I reassure them that she would punish me if she knew what I was doing, so there is no way I would tell her.

Once a predator has seen the young girl's picture that Julie or Lorie provides, and chatted with us, showing up for a meeting is the final step that seals his fate. He will be charged even though there is no little girl waiting for him at the meeting place. The chats and phone calls, combined with the attempted meeting, provide more than the requisite intent for an arrest. The evidence is so clear and compelling that most of these predators plead guilty rather than risk going to trial and receiving longer sentences. That is not to say that they could not be arrested prior to a meeting. Many of them send obscene pictures or include enough sexual comments in their chats to warrant an arrest since they think they are communicating with children. However, if their ultimate goal is to have sex with a minor child, we would rather have them attempt to go all the way with their plans so they will receive the maximum sentence that those circumstances would warrant. If an enormous amount of time passes and they waiver on the meeting, but have sent incriminating pictures and said things that are not fit for minors, the evidence already collected is considered in making a determination as to whether there is probable cause for an arrest. But that part of the picture is totally within the hands of the FBI and the Justice Department. I am merely an observer in all of this.

I should explain that I work *with*—not *for*—the FBI. The FBI considers me a cooperating witness or a confidential informant. Defense attorneys have other names for me, including "government-employed vigilante," "dramatist," "zealot," "liar," "slippery person," "underage teenage vixen," "clever and cunning bounty hunter," "confidential witness doorman," and "walking, talking, reasonable doubt." But those are just fabricated out of sheer desperation in an effort to make a defendant look innocent.

I am not the usual cooperating witness, as they are generally either victims of a crime or were present while it was occurring. I am also not the typical informant, as (most of the time) those people are looking to make a deal to get out of trouble. I am just a citizen who wants to do something to help children. I know it might be a rarity today, but it is true.

To my knowledge, I am the only non-law enforcement person who the FBI allows to work alongside them on a daily basis in an online undercover operation to put Internet predators in prison. In fact, Agent Berglas has concurred that he knows of no one else who does what I do with the FBI.

It was a process for me to gain the complete trust of the agents, and my credibility is well established at this point. I recently asked Agent Berglas why he allowed me to work so closely with him, and this was his response:

You had a proven track record. You were reliable and always available. I remember any time I called you, no matter what you were doing, you would drop it to make a phone call. And that's something I didn't have available to me. Plus, you would be working on the Internet during the hours that I wasn't. When I went home at 5:00 or 6:00 at night, you were there chatting at 11:00 or 12:00 at night, and that was very useful for credibility of our story—to have a thirteen-year-old girl online that late at night. Not only that, but you were excellent at it: Your phone calls as a thirteen-year-old girl were clearly believable. We would play them in the office and nobody believed that you were a grandmother and could sound so young, or could engage in these types of conversations so well with a straight face. And, the added factor was that you were providing this information with no expectation of a reward. You didn't have a criminal record that you were looking for help with. And, it was a free source of valuable information for us, and I was careful not to abuse that. I never took you for granted.

I have never given the FBI any information that was not legitimate or could not be used as evidence. While I have no official FBI training, they have offered me guidance regarding the things that I should and should not do while pursuing sexual predators. There is no point in doing this work if I am performing it in a way that leaves the evidence tainted, so I am extremely careful never to cross the line that differentiates between attraction and entrapment, which would mean that I induced a person to commit a crime for which he or she had no propensity. I am also careful about who I turn over to the FBI. I do not want to jump the gun and implicate an innocent person who has come close to crossing a forbidden line that they have no real intention of crossing. I only alert the FBI about someone when it is clear that an adult person on the other end of the chat is interested in having a sexual relationship with a minor child.

There are those people who flirt and give the impression that they are interested but who may really just be lonely or bored men who are looking to chat with anyone who will respond. I have to admit that I haven't really come across many of them. Most of the time, they are fishing to see if they have found a young girl who would be willing to have sex with an older man. If someone says hello to me using my first name, I know they have read my profile, which gives them enough information right up front to know that I am a young teenage girl. It is doubtful that if they are merely lonely and bored, and not a sexual predator, they would go out of their way to chat with "Lorie," but I do give them plenty of time to prove to me what their real intentions are.

While the discussion of sex eventually comes up in a chat, I never bring it up first. It is always the predator that makes it clear he is interested in sex, and that he does not care that I am underage. I merely assume the role of a very willing and inexperienced child who is anxious to learn about what grown-ups do.

My goal is to identify sexual predators, not to trap innocent people.

I have no agenda, no ulterior motive other than to keep children safe. I do not get invited to ceremonies where special commendations are awarded. My name is never in the newspaper articles or news segments when an arrest is made. My ultimate reward is the satisfaction that I feel when Agent Berglas has called me to let me know that an arrest was successful and nobody was hurt.

In regard to the FBI agents who I work with, they too have no ulterior motives. Yes, they may at times receive commendations for their hard work, as they well should. Those brave men and women have dedicated their lives to keeping our children safe. They are the ones who go out onto the streets and risk their lives to arrest these criminals. I can close my laptop any time I want without having to explain my actions to anyone. The FBI agents are on the job all day and they do a great service to us all. I have a tremendous amount of respect for all of them. They have never once made me feel like an outsider, and I have been shown nothing but appreciation, friendship, and respect from them.

It is not easy spending the day talking to the most perverse elements of our population. But, when one of them is taken off the streets, it means that there are children who can rest easy because another predator is out of commission for a very long time. It took awhile for me to feel comfortable talking to sexual predators. It used to really get under my skin, and every once in awhile I had to pull back and take a break. They are a disgusting breed who will stop at nothing to get what they want. Lorie and Julie have been offered gifts, shopping sprees, dinners, fancy hotel stays, money, trips, and even marriage as enticements to meet a predator for sex. They have also been enticed with compliments and compassion. There are many methods by which these perverts gain favor with children, and there is no way to know what will really happen when one of them gets close to a young child. Some have been found with weapons and drugs. Others go as far as to commit murder. So, it is comforting to know that for every extra minute that I put up with their sick, demented comments, I am keeping them from contacting a real child.

I have been working with the FBI since spring 2003. At first, I assumed that I would remain behind my computer screen, never revealing my identity or the work that I do to identify predators. However, things have happened that were not part of my initial plan. I went online thinking that all I had to do was turn sexual predators over to the authorities, and that would be the extent of my involvement. However, as you will see later on, at times I have gotten in way over my head, even coming face-to-face with a couple of my Internet "boyfriends."

The teen in the chatrooms and the young voice on the other end of the phone line has evolved into the woman who might show up at an arrest scene, or the witness who testifies at a predator's trial. The dynamics have changed dramatically since I first started sitting at my computer and delving into the dark side of the World Wide Web searching for the deviants who court children. Along with those dynamics has come the revelation that there is a reservoir of sexual predators on the Internet, and it flows right into your home and onto your child's computer screen. In fact, statistics show that one out of every five children in the United States has been solicited online by sexual predators, and eighty-nine percent of them said they were solicited while in an Internet chatroom. An even more frightening statistic is that in the United States alone, over 2,500 children go missing every single day. Many meet their abductors online.

One problem is that the 550,000 registered sex offenders mentioned earlier are just the ones who have been caught. That number does not include those still getting away with molesting children, or those who have had their names removed from the sex offender registry. On top of that, add the number of offenders who move away and fail to report their new whereabouts. For instance, during the horrendous wrath of Hurricane Katrina that ravaged the south in the late summer of 2005, at least two thousand registered sex offenders apparently vanished from the area and also from the tracking system on which they are required to register. Some were found in other states applying for disaster assistance. While they had applied for relief, they had not put themselves onto a sex offender registry. It was reported that of the three hundred and four known sex offenders who had relocated to Texas, a mere fourteen were known to have registered.

Sexual predators are among us every which way we turn, and they are not who you often envision. Most of them are not walking around in trench coats or wearing ragged clothing and hiding around dark corners waiting to grab unsuspecting children. Of course, there are deviants who do that, but the norm is something that you do not quite expect. While our opinions may have evolved somewhat due to all of the publicity about the church scandals, many of us still do not associate what frocked priests have done with what goes on among the general population. Nobody ever suspects the well-dressed businessman who lives next door and buys your child's Girl Scout cookies, the soccer coach who pats a kid on the head after a great play, the school bus driver who pulls right up to a house to drop a child off in the rain, the teacher who stays after to tutor a failing student, the pediatrician, friends, siblings, parents, or even a spouse. But the truth is that sexual predators come from all walks of life. They are most often the people we least suspect, which is why you may see their friends and families coming forward in disbelief to stand by the accused.

As a matter of fact, when Steven Dovas went off to prison, supporters posted comments on message boards in his defense. One person claimed to know him well and considered the charges against him to be completely fabricated. While describing the misdeeds of many of those people on the Internet who claim to be young teens, but who are really adults, the blogger defended Dovas to the hilt, insisting that he was only kidding around and that he knew the girl he was chatting with was not really a child. Claiming that the whole thing was based on merely role-play, the writer seemed to have missed the most important part of Dovas' actions—after having spent an enormous amount of time chatting sexually on the Internet and the telephone with the girl, he showed up at the arranged meeting place to have sex with her. That exceeds role-play.

Other Dovas supporters considered the situation to be a sting, a set-up, the entrapment of a very nice, dedicated, and loving husband who would never hurt a child. This is exactly how he portrayed himself to his family and friends. He knew what he was doing, and he knew how to hide it from those close to him. If Julie had been a real child, Dovas might have gotten away with having sex with her and moved on to other victims.

An important point to clarify is that there is a big difference between a sting operation and entrapment. They are not one and the same. A sting operation is something set up to catch those criminals who have the propensity to commit a crime. This means that they are going to do it. Nobody is forcing them, convincing them, or going after them. The criminals enter the situation because they want to commit the act, they intend to commit the act, and, in fact, they show up to commit the act. Their big mistake is that they think they are talking to children, when they are really communicating with law enforcement officials or people like me. Entrapment happens when law enforcement lures someone who has no propensity to commit a crime into committing that crime. This is not what happened to Steven Dovas. Nobody contacted him first. He went after a young girl, enticed her with promises and compliments, brought up the subject of sex, asked for phone calls, and arranged a meeting with her. Nothing in the chats or phone calls indicated that the girl instigated any part of the situation at all.

Dovas obviously had the people in his personal life fooled. Predators are good at what they do. They work their way into our heads, our hearts, our homes, and then, our children's lives. And, our kids are often unaware of what is happening. They are taught not to talk to strangers. But, they are also taught to trust their parents' friends or the officer in a uniform, their physician, their religious instructor, or their teacher. They have a hard time trying to differentiate between the bad people they are warned about and the good people they think they can trust. When they meet someone online, they often believe that they are capable of making an informed decision based on their own judgment. They have long chats with people and, as far as they know, they are receiving enough true information about their new friend to decide how best to proceed. As an adult, I can honestly say that there are times when some of the predators I talk to do a great job of trying to gain my sympathy or making me feel as though I know who they really are. Of course, they do not fool me, but I can see how a young person would believe their lies.

I keep track of those I chat with, and it is fairly common to get different information from them each time. They instant message so many young girls that they forget what they say to them. One day, they say they are forty-three years old and the next, twenty-seven. Some send the same pictures under different screen names or different ones under the same name. I might chat with a person one day and answer all of his questions, only to be instant messaged by him a week later and asked the same things, as though we had never made contact. But, the substance of their chats is still consistent. They have an agenda, and they say whatever they can to entice young children into relationships with them.

Many of the child predators whose cases I have been involved with are people who work with children and/or have children of their own. They seemed like everyday respectable people. As in Dovas' case, those close to them—families, friends, employers—had no idea what they were doing online. Many hearts were broken, and lives were destroyed. The effects of a sexual predator's behavior reach very far, to their families, their friends, their colleagues, their neighbors, and their communities. Everyone is touched by what they do. It is not uncommon for those whose family member has been affected by a child predator to question his or her own judgment. "How could I not have known? Why didn't I recognize what he was doing? Was I in denial?" are all thoughts that run through the minds of those who think they knew the sexual predator well enough to have recognized what he or she was doing with children. It is important to note that just because a child predator has not molested his or her own children, a relative's children, or the kids next door, that does not mean he is not a sexual predator. These guys are not stupid, and just as a man who does not want to get caught cheating on his wife may go out of his circle of friends to have an affair, so may a child predator. They are sick deviants, but they are not necessarily too ignorant to keep their actions a secret. So, leave the blame where it belongs: on the perverts who destroy our children.

The following chapters will tell the stories of individuals who were living what their families thought were perfectly normal lives. They went about their days following their normal routines, according to what everyone assumed. In reality, they had deep, dark, well-hidden secrets, until they met Julie and Lorie. It was then that they came out of the closet, so to speak. It was with their young prey that they felt most comfortable to reveal who they really were. Everything they said and did was meant to lure a child out from behind the safety of their computers, away from home, and into the arms of perversion. I will take you into their chats, along for the busts, and even into the courtroom where the suspects attempt to defend their actions.

Some were even more deviant than I ever envisioned, like the slave master who was actually looking for underage girls to run away from home to live with him, or the dominant males and females looking for the submissive child who will go along with their every whim. There are also submissive men and women looking for young teenage dominants willing to control them. Another group of select perverts are the ones who expect young children to perform some extremely disgusting acts for them, acts that have shocked even the FBI agents. Then, there are the "daddies." They are the men who want young girls to dress like little girls, even younger than they actually are, and call them daddy. Some have asked me if I could bring along friends as young as eight or nine years old.

Steven Dovas was really just a run-of-the-mill sexual predator with nothing about him that stood out other than the fact that he had so much going for him and threw it all away. It is not surprising that he worked in a profession that was in many ways connected to children. That's the point, isn't it? Sexual predators do everything they can to get close to their victims!

TWO

The Road to the FBI

IT WAS A LONG ROAD FOR ME TO GET TO THE FBI. I NEVER expected to be involved with them—except maybe in the Sixties when they probably had a file on me for being a Beatles fan. Still, I am quite comfortable with what I do today, and I find it extremely rewarding. But, never in my wildest dreams would I have consciously chosen to hang around the Internet waiting for sexual predators to instant message me. And to clarify, I have used terms such as "lie in wait," "pursue," and "catch" to refer to what I do, but I use those words loosely here. I do not do anything more than create a screen name and profile, and I sit in a chatroom without saying a word until I'm invited to do so. I do acknowledge that I am there for one reason, and one reason only—to delete sexual predators from the Internet and also from the general population. It is my goal to find their haunts and stake them out.

You may ask why I dedicate much of my time to identifying Internet predators. My answer is simple: If a predator is searching for a child to victimize, I'd rather they find me instead. My reasons for doing this work started a long time ago. It was at a time in my life when I was still unsuspecting and naïve. I had always thought of myself as a good mother; loving, concerned, protective, and careful about to what and whom my children were exposed. My sons were good boys. They played sports, participated in the school band, and attended religious instruction, which was the one place where I took it for granted that

19

they would be the safest—and that could not have been further from the truth.

One of their religious instructors was Marc Gunning. The moment I saw his face, I recognized him from my college days. He had been the president of the student government organization at Stony Brook University, and he was involved with many of the same campus activities in which I participated. Marc was a fairly nice-looking, seemingly gentle man who fought for many worthy causes. Although I had never really gotten to know him personally, I naively assumed that he had to be an honorable guy to have been voted in as president.

At the place of worship where my family belonged, Marc was involved with the children. I thought his position there to be admirable. At the time, he had claimed that he was studying to become a child psychologist, but I was never really sure about that. He had a job as a local radio disc jockey where he often allowed young boys to intern for him, including my younger son, Christian. He would bring them to the radio station and teach them how to use the equipment. He also taught karate and tai chi, and worked part-time in a nearby comic book store. Marc even found the time to frequent a local arcade to play various games, such as paint ball and laser tag, with the young teen boys there. It was just amazing how well he appeared to get along with kids. So, I had no qualms about the fact that he took a special interest in my son. In fact, I was somewhat grateful since my older boy, Brian, had left for college and Christian seemed lonely without him. When Marc confided to me that Christian seemed a bit withdrawn, I just assumed that he was troubled about Brian's absence.

Over the next few months, Marc's efforts to hang out with Christian increased. He often stopped by the house to shoot some hoops, drop off comic books, or show him some karate moves. It seemed pretty innocent, but I noticed that Christian continued sinking deeper into what I perceived as a depression. I was concerned and kept hoping that Marc's presence in the boy's life would pull him out of it. As time passed, Christian became resistant to attending church and began to stay home on Sundays. I worried that he was dwelling too much on his older brother's absence.

In the meantime, Marc apparently had been battling some personal demons and surprised everyone one Sunday when he made the bold move of revealing to several people at the congregation that he was gay. He considered it to be his moment of truth. He explained how very isolated he had felt growing up in a home where his sexual orientation was completely unacceptable. He said his parents were ashamed of him, and he had experienced the same kind of rejection from his peers as he went through school. He could not stand the thought of other young boys having to suffer the way he did. He was determined to help them accept themselves for who they really are, no matter what their sexual orientation was, so they would never have to go through the type of ridicule and humiliation that he had endured. Thus, whatever else we all thought, he had sold us on the idea that he had nothing but the best of intentions towards our children. Due to Marc's background, it seemed only natural that he counseled young boys who had problems, and that he taught karate and tai chi, calming disciplines that helped to ensure self-protection and confidence. He obviously wanted to do everything in his power to bolster the youngsters' self-esteem.

Marc always had a smile on his face, but his eyes had a sense of loneliness about them. I assumed that he simply had the remnants of his past lingering in his expression, the pain of a difficult childhood. That was something that I understood all too well. I knew what it felt like to be different and not fit in. Although in my case, it was not about sexual orientation.

My own innocence was shattered by the sudden death of my father when I was nine years old. He died of a heart attack right in front of me. What was once a secure and happy childhood quickly turned dark with the loss of the center of my family's universe. It was a difficult trauma that took years to overcome. I was suddenly thrust into a world where I felt different from all of my friends who had fathers and financial security, and mothers who were waiting for them with milk and cookies when they arrived home from school. I had become a latchkey kid when there was no such thing. The other children did not understand. Too young to deal with a friend's tragic loss, many drifted away from me. Not only was my father gone, but so too was my emotional security. Like Marc, I often felt out of place and lost, so when I heard his speech that day, I understood about all of those things I imagined he had experienced as a gay teenager trying to fit into a "normal" world where it seemed that everyone had rejected him. And, having been a child of the Sixties, I was open to diversity. It was always my nature not to judge people before I got to know them. Since I had already allowed him into our lives and assumed I knew all about his background, I was comfortable with Marc. I thought I understood where he was coming from, or where he *had* come from. And, the idea that he might be anything other than a decent human being who was struggling with his own issues was beyond me. For the longest time, it did not occur to me that there was anything strange about his behavior, at least, not that I ever noticed. Everyone spoke so highly of him. The fact that they trusted him with their children left me completely devoid of any suspicions.

Marc was quite intelligent and interesting. Our conversations were always stimulating. He was well educated, and he was an activist in college, as was I. We had even participated in some of the same demonstrations. I never had access to his private life, but since the minister had hired him to teach the children about spirituality, I had no serious concerns about his motives for hanging out with my son. Up until that point, I had walked through life trusting people and looking for the best in them. It was the last time I would ever trust first and ask questions later.

It turned out that Marc Gunning was a child molester. He was a member of the same club as Steven Dovas—part of the lowest level of society—those who prey upon children. My son Christian was the perfect victim for him. He had a hard time when Brian left home, and he missed his companionship. The brother who had always paid so much attention to him, taking him places, playing games with him, including him when his own friends came over, was now living far from home. But, not only did Marc think he found the perfect victim, he thought he had chosen the optimal parents, too, in that he was able to walk right into our home and go after our son without us suspecting a thing. "How did that happen?" I wondered. I needed to know. I suppose he knew that there was a void in our home. One of our sons had moved on to the next phase of his life, and I was recovering from a serious car accident. We were ripe for Marc to try to fill the gap. It was only after looking back that the picture became crystal clear. While it was happening, we were totally clueless to what he was up to. Here is how the events unfolded:

One evening Marc stopped by for dinner. Right after eating, he headed straight into Christian's room and closed the door behind him. It shouldn't have concerned us. He was just another guy. We were used to our other son's friends, all much older than Christian, coming over and hanging out here. But, that particular night something just didn't feel right. I'm not sure what it was. Call it a mother's instinct: Remember, at this time I had no idea what kind of a monster Marc Gunning really was.

My gut told me to get out of my chair and check on Christian. Feeling uneasy, I headed down the hallway towards his room. It was as though my sixth sense had kicked in to let me know that I had better intervene. As I approached his bedroom door, the silence was deafening. Without knocking, I practically burst the door open. Christian and Marc were startled, but thankfully, nothing unusual was going on. They were just reading comic books and sitting across the room from each other. I was relieved. "I must have been watching something on television that made me feel so paranoid about Marc," I thought. I'm not sure exactly why, but I remained a little more vigilant after that. I still permitted Christian to help out at the radio station, but I drove him there and picked him up, often arriving back early and walking inside, so Christian would never be left alone with him after the show had ended.

I also listened to the show each time my son was there to make sure that Marc was actually working the entire time. However, my discomfort took even deeper roots one night as I sat by my radio.

What I heard was truly unbelievable. Marc was defending a man who had been arrested for kidnapping and molesting a young girl. She was a local child who had been missing for several weeks before police finally rescued her from a bunker that the kidnapper had built under his house. Marc was actually complaining about how unfair the system was. He defended the man, saying that he probably meant well, and that people should not judge him too harshly, because the kind of love he had for the little girl was obviously misunderstood.

The kidnapping story had been all over the news. A child was missing and this man had finally confessed to hiding her in a bunker under his house. She was held prisoner for weeks in a dark, dreary dungeon. She had been kept down there inside a box, with a thick chain around her neck. Nothing like that had ever happened in our community before, and it was hard to understand how Marc could have sided with the kidnapper, defending his motives, making excuses for his crimes, and actually praising him. I was outraged! It was at that very moment that I knew I had to dig deeper into Marc's background. Something was obviously very wrong with this man, and I had missed it for far too long!

After thinking back over the past few months, I suddenly realized that I had never seen Marc hanging around with men his own age. All of the males he associated with were young teenage boys. I don't know why I hadn't noticed it sooner, but I really did not have any experience with sexual predators. I had nothing to go on. Marc was a trusted member of the congregation. He tried to be nice. He said he cared about kids. He also said he was gay. I tried to be open-minded. I didn't really know anything about homosexuality either, but at that point, I doubted that this was really his issue. I no longer believed that he was gay. He was clearly interested in being with young boys, very young boys. He was very devious and manipulative, and he knew exactly how to discourage suspicion. By declaring himself gay, he had slipped himself into a category that was so sensitive that most people would not question his actions for fear of appearing homophobic. I finally recognized the truth, but I was very careful about checking Marc out, not because of the homophobia issue, but because I didn't want to make a mistake and ruin his life over my suspicions.

The first person I turned to for information was a mutual friend who had known Marc in college. I was able to track him down, and I called and asked him if he remembered Marc. His response was truly disturbing to me. "I sure do," he said. "He always had young boys walking around in their underwear in his dorm room." As though that wasn't bad enough, what he said next floored me. "I remember hearing a rumor that he had been run out of his hometown while still a teenager for molesting several young boys." He continued, "I figured it was true because he rarely hung around with anyone his own age at college unless it was school-related." This information was more than I could handle. I hung up and sat for a moment in complete shock. I didn't expect such a blatant response. The information had me reeling. If what my friend said was true, then what about my son? Was I finding all of this out too late, or did I uncover the truth just in time? I had to talk to Christian!

I was truly at a loss as to how to approach him. I knew that it had to be with great hesitation, because how could I ask my eleven-year-old son if the man who I had welcomed into our lives had done the unspeakable? I was determined to keep Christian away from him, but what if Marc had already done something to forever change Christian's life?

I immediately headed into Christian's room to talk to him. This was a first for me. I generally knew how he would handle most issues, but on that day I was concerned that he might become angry and resentful that I was coming between him and his friend. "What if he rebelled and tried to run away—or worse?" I wondered.

When I entered Christian's room, I could barely speak. "How could

I talk about Marc's alleged motives knowing that my son might already be one of his victims?" I wondered. Christian was sitting by his computer. I asked for his complete attention, and he gave it to me. Even though the words were not yet in my head, I began talking. "I know you like hanging out with Marc, but I have a terrible feeling that he has more than a friendly interest in young boys." Before I could continue, Christian cut me off, "Yes mom, I *know* he does!"

I was taken aback. I wanted to know what he meant, yet, I didn't really want to hear it. I was so afraid that things had already gone beyond the point of no return. In an angered tone, Christian continued, "Marc has been bothering me for months. He's always trying to figure out ways to get me to take my shirt off or to get near me. He's so gross. I can't stand being around him. That's why I don't go to church anymore." Christian told me that while Marc was teaching him tai chi, he had tried to convince him that, to do it effectively, he had to take his shirt off. Then, Marc tried to put his hands on him to show him the moves. At first, the contact was in places that would not have caused concern: his back, his shoulder, and his arm. Then, Christian said that Marc had made certain suggestions to him, and when Christian became repulsed, Marc would change the subject. Marc continued to try to do things to get physical with Christian, and he said he knew that Marc was way out of line. Christian became more distant with Marc, often making excuses to avoid being around him. He was disgusted by Marc's behavior and frustrated by his own inability to do anything about it. He said that even when Marc patted him on the shoulder, it made his skin crawl.

I was relieved. But, I wondered, why then, didn't Christian tell me about Marc's behavior? He said he didn't think anyone would believe him due to Marc's position in the church, and that everyone respected Marc so much he thought it best to keep it a secret. He added that because Marc was my "good friend" from college, he didn't know how to tell me that he was trying to hurt him. Now that I had confronted him, the issue was out in the open.

Marc had done everything he could to be alone with my son and to try to have physical contact with him. He wanted to convince this young, eleven-year-old boy that any confusion he may have had about his sexuality most likely meant that he was gay and that he, Marc, would be the perfect mentor to help him understand his homosexuality. Marc was trying to put ideas into Christian's head, telling him that he was too young to already know about his own sexual orientation. When Christian protested, saying that he liked girls, Marc confided to him that even *he* had crushes on girls when he was young. Marc also told Christian that I would be disgusted with him if I thought he was gay. Christian said he didn't care what Marc said because he knew he wasn't gay. Marc continuously applied pressure to try to make Christian unsure of what I would believe about him. Christian tried his best not to be around him, and he felt compelled to keep the whole thing a secret. I would later learn that this was Marc's modus operandi— trying to convince a boy that the youngster was gay in order to open the door for a relationship.

Christian and I spoke for a long time. I think it was the longest conversation we ever had up until that point. He was very open about Marc, and he seemed relieved that he didn't have to put up with him anymore. As a matter of fact, he looked more relaxed than he had in months. And I was angrier than I had ever been.

After hearing about Marc's actions in college, it was obvious to me that my son was not Marc's only intended victim. The following day, I went to the church to discuss with the minister what I knew. She was shocked. She said she had not run a background check on Marc because she did not feel the need. To be honest, back then, nobody would have thought it necessary, especially with Marc's credentials. But I needed to understand how this had happened. "How could everyone have been so wrong?" I wondered. I needed to know that I wasn't the only one he had fooled.

The minister was obviously shaken. She called in one of her assistants to discuss the information that I had brought to her attention. The assistant was a social worker who had a lot of knowledge about sexual predators. It was she who first educated me as to how Marc was able to get away with what he had been doing. I learned that these predators do everything they can to gain a child's trust. Often, this involves winning the trust of the child's parents as well. I began to understand the scenario. Marc had been grooming my son. He was trying to ease Christian and several other boys into feeling comfortable with whatever advances he was planning to make. He started this process by convincing them that what he was doing was perfectly normal and for their own benefit.

The assistant also told me that Marc's behavior had nothing to do with homosexuality. She said that homosexuals were no more prone to child molestation than heterosexuals, and she felt that he used the term homosexual to keep everyone's suspicions in check. She continued, explaining that sexual predators gain a child's trust by doing various things, such as bringing gifts, taking them to fun places, playing games with them, sharing common interests, and even discussing problems that the child might have with a parent, then offering sympathy and advice. They justify their behavior by calling it love, and they claim that they would never hurt the child—they just want to love them. They often convince the child that they are the only one who understands them. This was sounding a little too familiar. What the woman was describing to me was exactly what Marc had done to get close to our son.

Marc was summoned to the church for a meeting with the minister, the social worker, and my husband, Ed, and me. I had made up my mind that I wasn't going to let on about what I had heard about him from my friend. I wanted to sit there quietly and let him try to explain his behavior to us. He sat there sheepishly, denying any wrongdoing. He apologized profusely for anything he might have done to give the impression that he had improper motives for hanging around with children. Then, he went into his story about being gay and how he was used to being chastised for nothing at all. He put on a pretty convincing act, tears in his eyes, sorrowful look on his face, all meant to make us feel as though his comments were genuine. This time, I wasn't sympathetic. I was angry, although I didn't let him know it yet. Marc had gone too far, and according to my college friend, there was a pretty clear history. There was also his current behavior to consider. Everything he did involved young boys.

Shortly after the meeting, Marc called. He asked if he could meet with me. Not wanting him in my home anymore, but also not ready to tell him that yet, I agreed to meet him at a nearby diner. I pulled into the parking lot with a knot in my stomach. I put a mini tape recorder into my pocket, pressed the record button, and entered the diner. Marc was waiting for me inside. We were seated across from each other in a booth, and as he held his coffee, he tearfully apologized to me for who he was. He admitted that he had serious problems. He used several different excuses to explain away his behavior, but still maintained that he had done nothing wrong with children. In fact, he tried to convince me that my son had imagined the whole incident. I tried as hard as I could to remain composed, but made it clear to Marc that I didn't believe that Christian had imagined what happened, especially considering that the boy had not come to me in the first place. He did not even want to tell me about it.

Marc continued, telling me that he had medical and psychiatric problems, including a thyroid condition, and a dissociative disorder that took him away from reality at times. He said that it was possible that he had done something while in one of his detached states, but he had no way of knowing if that was true. I sat quietly and listened. I let him go on. I was not rude, but I wasn't nice either. The relationship had definitely changed, and Marc could sense it. I didn't listen intently with a concerned look on my face as in the past when he had talked about his childhood and his issues of alienation. Instead, I stared at him with disdain and he knew what my expression meant. I listened for as long as I could before finally excusing myself to go home.

As I got up to leave, Marc grabbed my arm. I swung around, feeling like slapping him for touching me. As our eyes met, he blurted out, "I didn't do anything wrong! I would never hurt a child! I love children—I love them. It's the kind of love that you will never understand." His words pierced my heart. "It's the kind of love that *no one should ever have to* understand," I shot back. I pulled away from him in disgust. As I walked away, I slowly reached down into my pocket and turned off the tape recorder. "I got what I came for. Where I go from here is up to Christian," I said to myself.

When I arrived home, I went into Christian's room to talk to him again. I found him reading comic books, and as I sat at the edge of his bed, I suddenly envisioned the tiny infant that I was so lucky to have been blessed with eleven years earlier. Christian was my miracle baby in the true sense of the word. He was born from my ninth, and last, pregnancy. He was my second surviving child. Brian was my first. They were born eight years apart. I had lost five other pregnancies due to late miscarriages, and I had given birth to two other babies, but much too early for either of them to survive for more than a couple of weeks in those days. Christian arrived nine weeks early, at thirty-one weeks, and Ed and I were thrilled. We had two beautiful sons! As the years passed, Christian and Brian became best buddies, with Brian always watching out for his little brother. And now, eleven years later, there I was sitting with that miracle baby, wondering if I could ask him the question that could change everything.

I told Christian about the conversation I had with Marc. I also explained what my college friend had said about Marc's past, and I asked Christian if he was willing to tell his story to the police. He was apprehensive. He was afraid of what people would think of him. I didn't want to force him, but I also didn't want Marc to go after another child and succeed. I hated to do it, but I asked Christian how he would feel if that happened. He said he would feel terrible. He didn't want something like that on his conscience. He knew that not every boy would be able to resist Marc the way he had. We got in the car and drove to the local police precinct. The first officer we met with put Christian through a tedious interview. It was only the first of many times that he would have to recount the events that occurred with Marc. After we left, an officer was assigned to investigate Marc further. She treated the situation very seriously and came to my home to interview Christian. She had done a background check on Marc and confirmed what my college friend had told me, but there was much more.

She said that when Marc lived in another state, he had molested a few young Boy Scouts while he was a volunteer as a teenager. He had disrobed with the boys and showed them how to fondle him, as well as each other. Subsequently, he moved to New York where he was tutoring young boys through his college program. He was caught molesting one of them during a tutoring session in the boy's bedroom. He was arrested, convicted, and ordered into treatment, something he obviously didn't take very seriously because he had also been ordered to stay away from children. He moved to the next county and, according to him, was studying to be a child psychologist. And, he was doing all of those other things to be near children: working in a comic book store, teaching religious education to young teenagers, instructing boys in karate and tai chi, allowing them to intern for him at his radio show, and playing laser tag with them at a local kid's hangout. As the police officer continued, my mind raced. I had been putting the pieces together, learning about sexual predators, trying to understand their mindset, hoping to figure out how this had happened. All I could absorb was that I had allowed a monster to infiltrate our lives. Christian was just a child, but *I* should have known better.

The officer appeared deeply concerned. I was surprised when she asked if I wanted to accompany her on a stakeout at Marc's house. Of course, I agreed. The next night, she picked me up, and we sat in her unmarked car for hours talking about the situation and waiting for Marc to come home. I had visions of him pulling up with a young boy in the car and watching as he led the child into his house. I was hoping he would and at the same time, I was hoping he wouldn't because I didn't want him to even come close to hurting another child. The night passed, and he didn't return, so the officer brought me home. A few days later, I received a call from her informing me that Marc had moved, and in spite of the apparent interest that the police had demonstrated, the district attorney decided that based on what my son had told them, there wasn't enough evidence to make an arrest. I was appalled. The only reason that no molestation had occurred was because Christian had resisted. But Marc tried, over and over.

I called the district attorney's office and, after pleading my case, I was told that they would investigate further. I felt sure that they would take some action, but before long they notified me that no crime had been committed and, therefore, nothing could be done. I was infuriated that Marc could keep trying to hurt children and nothing could stop him until he was actually caught having sex with a child. I couldn't let this go.

I responded to the assistant district attorney with the following statement, "This man has been grooming my son for over three months. If he had solicited a prostitute just one time, you would arrest and prosecute him. So, how can you allow this man to repeatedly go after a child and continue on with his life without stopping him?"

The assistant district attorney was unsympathetic. He continued to maintain that he could do nothing because no crime had been committed. I interrupted him, "This man must be molesting other children. My son can't be the only one he went after. He has a history. I won't stop until he is stopped. If you do not arrest him, I will do everything in my power to catch him in the act and when I do, I will go to the newspapers with the headline, 'Mother Catches Sexual Predator Molesting Another Boy after D.A. Refuses to Arrest Him.'"

I hung up feeling angry and frustrated. My son had the courage to come forward and his efforts were going to be for nothing. The day wasn't yet over when I received another call from the assistant district attorney. He had changed his mind. They were going to arrest Marc the next day.

As soon as Marc was taken into custody, I notified the local papers. I knew that was the only way to find out if there were other victims. A few days later, an article with Marc's picture appeared in the paper. Five more boys came forward to press charges.

Not long after that, I received a call from the investigating officer saying that she had been contacted by a man who said that Marc had molested his younger brother nine years earlier. He wanted to talk to me, so the officer gave me his number. I called him. The man had gone to college with Marc and, over a holiday weekend, he had brought Marc home with him for a family get-together. During the day, he realized that his younger brother had disappeared from the gathering. While searching for him, he noticed that Marc was also nowhere to be found. He immediately ran up to his brother's room, and upon finding the door locked, pounded on it until Marc opened it. Standing there with a sheepish expression on his face, Marc made up a story about the door locking by itself. The man told me that he was horrified when he noticed his little brother in the background struggling to zip up his pants. The youngster denied that anything had happened as he looked away to hide his tears. Apparently, years had passed and the boy had never revealed what truly happened to him that day—until now. It was only when the man on the phone had seen the article about Marc's arrest and contacted his brother, who was now grown and away at college, that the younger sibling finally admitted being molested by Marc that day in his room.

That was what Marc had counted on, that the boy would never come forward. In fact, I learned that teenage boys rarely come forward to admit that a man has molested them. Just as Marc had tried to do with my son, predators convince their young victims that their parents would blame them and be disappointed.

Due to the length of time that had passed since Marc had molested the caller's younger brother, the statute of limitations had run out and there was nothing that law enforcement officials could do to prosecute him for that particular offense.

But other boys had come forward.

The case was a difficult one. My son was interviewed over and over. The investigators kept being transferred, the assistant district attorneys (ADAs) kept changing, and even the judges were replaced. Christian had to endlessly repeat his story, almost to the point where I was ready to have him withdraw the charges.

I wondered what had hurt my son more, Marc's attempted molestation or the constant barrage of questions from authority figures. For example, there was an incident in the courthouse when I brought Christian there for an Order of Protection after Marc had threatened him. The ADA insisted on questioning him in the hallway, near onlookers. It was obvious that Christian was uncomfortable talking about Marc in front of strangers, but the ADA continued as though my son was on the witness stand. I pulled Christian away and told the ADA that he had to find a private room or forget questioning my son. He told me that the boy would be asking for his Order of Protection in open court with no privacy at all. He said that Orders of Protection must be done that way, even though the boy's name had not been released when Marc was arrested due to the sensitive nature of the attempted crime. That was the last straw.

I demanded that the ADA go back inside and ask the judge to see us in chambers. He agreed. Once there, I explained that my son's case involved an attempted molestation, a charge that made his anonymity a necessity. I reasoned that by asking him to request the Order of Protection in open court, the judge would, in effect, be forcing him to reveal who he is and what had almost happened to him. The judge readily agreed and the proceedings were held in chambers. The judge was wonderful; he made Christian feel completely at ease and issued the Order of Protection without hesitation.

Over the next few months, I received numerous threatening phone calls. Unfortunately, it was before caller ID, so there was no proof of who it was. My car was vandalized. My garbage was strewn all over the street, and my mail was stolen. I couldn't help feeling that it was Marc or someone doing it on his behalf, but I was never able to catch them in the act. Whoever it was knew my schedule down to the minute.

The only thing I could do was to keep a close eye on Christian.

THREE

The Search Begins

WHEN THE TIME CAME FOR MARC'S CASE TO GO TO TRIAL, I expected him to be charged with endangering the welfare of a child for trying to groom my son. But, the ADA called to notify me that, in my son's case, he had decided not to prosecute Marc since he had not succeeded in molesting Christian. I was disappointed and feared that all of Christian's efforts were for nothing. That night, I had a difficult time sleeping. I drifted off shortly before my alarm rang, but in that small space of time I had a dream that left me quite shaken.

I was young again, around fourteen years old, and living in the small seaside town where I grew up, Long Beach, New York. It was summer and my friend's "Uncle" Frank offered me a job as a model for his swimming pool company. I begged my mother for permission to go with him to the pool place for an audition and she agreed. Frank told me to bring my bikini bathing suit along. He picked me up early one evening, and on the way to the audition he stopped at a local bar in Lido Beach to make a phone call. He brought me in with him through the back door and sat me on a bar stool with a Coke to wait while he made the call. I had never been in a bar before. I sat there feeling quite grown up. Frank made his call, got me a soda to go, and headed for the door. I followed him out to his car all excited about the possibility of becoming a bathing suit model.

We traveled along the Meadowbrook Parkway that ran parallel to the Long Island Sound. As I stared out at the water, imagining my future as a model, I felt myself growing tired and my vision became fuzzy. I told Frank how strange I felt. He said that it was just my nerves acting up. He handed me the other soda and told me I would feel better after I drank it, but I didn't feel better. Instead, I fell asleep. The next thing I remembered, Frank was driving down a long gravel road towards the entrance to the swimming pool company. I noticed that there were no cars in the parking lot, and I could see that it was dark inside the building. There wasn't anybody else there. It was just Frank and me. When I asked him about it, he said that it was he whose job it was to choose the model, so no one else's presence was necessary. He instructed me to go into the restroom and put on my bikini. I was just a naïve kid, so I complied.

When I came out, Frank commented on how pretty I was and what a nice body I had. He told me he knew that I would be perfect for the modeling job. Then, he began putting me into different poses. He watched me intently as I tried to stand still. Each time he moved me into another position his touch was that much stronger and more personal. At first, he just seemed to be helping me to stand a certain way or to straighten my bathing suit straps. But he went further, and I didn't like the way he made me feel. He stroked my arm and then my back.

I felt uncomfortable and finally worked up the courage to tell him that I wanted to go home. He reassured me about how much he wanted me to get the job, but I insisted that we leave. He grew angry and argued with me, threatening to hire a different model. But, I stood my ground and demanded that he take me home. Thankfully, he complied. On the long ride back, Frank apologized and said that I had misunderstood his intentions. I didn't believe him and I began to realize that I might have been tricked into the whole situation. I started to wonder about the modeling job. I just wasn't sure what was happening, but I foolishly still hoped to get the job.

When we got back to Long Beach, Frank stopped at his apartment saying that he had to go to a meeting and needed to pick up some paperwork on the way. He told me that he rented part of a house and he wasn't supposed to leave his car in the driveway, so he parked down the street. He said I wouldn't be safe alone in the car and convinced me to accompany him inside. I hesitantly followed, not knowing which was more dangerous, going with Frank or being in the car by myself.

We entered Frank's apartment and I noticed that his part of the house was nothing more than a room with a bed and bathroom. I could hear people talking through the walls, so I felt more comfortable knowing that I wasn't completely alone with him. He instructed me to sit down while he used the bathroom. There was only one place to sit, on the bed, so I positioned myself at the very edge.

He emerged from the bathroom, pants hanging open. I was startled and started to stand up, but he blocked me. He sat down next to me and started whispering to me about sex. He tried to convince me to take off my clothes. He said he wanted to make me feel good. Again, I tried to get up, but he held onto me saying that he would like to perform oral sex on me, and it wouldn't hurt. I tried to pull away, but he held me tight.

At that point, I became frightened and insisted on leaving. He yanked me closer. I began to cry, and remembering that there were other people in the house, I raised my voice. Frank immediately let me go and agreed to take me home. I just wanted to get out of there. I didn't want to get into his car, but he convinced me that I would have a lot of explaining to do if I showed up at home without him. "What would your mother think?" he asked. Then, he told me that he had put alcohol into my sodas, and that my mother would immediately notice it on my breath. He said she would never believe me if I told her the truth, and he insisted on driving me home.

I got into Frank's car. On the way to my house, he stopped at a drug store and bought breath mints. He shoved one into my mouth and told me to suck on it and not talk directly to my mother. I was confused. I knew that I hadn't willingly consumed the alcohol, but I also felt ashamed because I began to realize that there wasn't really any model-ing job. The man just wanted to have sex with me. Being so young, I didn't fully comprehend the implications of someone his age attempt-ing to seduce a young girl. I had no idea about things like that. Nobody ever talked about child predators back in the early Sixties. I vaguely recall hearing about a man who used to drive around the neighborhood exposing himself to young girls, but nobody was that concerned. We were all just warned not to get too close to any strangers calling out to us from inside of their cars.

When Frank and I arrived at my house, my mother rushed out to meet us. I sheepishly exited the car, bathing suit in hand. I quickly walked past her without saying a word for fear of alerting her to the alcohol. Frank told her that I did a great job, but that there were other girls to consider, and he would let her know. My mother smiled and thanked him. She followed me inside and tried to talk about my excit-ing night, but I just wanted to go to bed. "How could I ever tell her the truth—that I was just made a fool of and almost molested by that man?" So, the incident was put into the back of my memory bank and tucked away for many years, until now.

My son had almost been molested—almost. And Marc was going to get away with it. Christian had gone to the police and told them everything, but it didn't seem to matter. It gnawed away at me. I was frustrated, angry. I ached for someone to listen, to understand, to want to stop Marc so he wouldn't get away with hurting kids like "Uncle" Frank probably did.

I guess that was why the memory came back to me at that time in my life. Somewhere deep inside of me, there was a feeling that was wait-ing for just the right time to come to the surface. It had been hidden away for so many years. I knew what it was like to have somebody try to molest me and get away with it. In my case, I hadn't told on the man. I had held on to it for too many years. But Christian had the courage to tell his story, and I wanted him to know that it had made a difference.

When the trial drew near, I received a phone call from the arresting officer. He told me that the charges against Marc for one of the other boys who had come forward would stick. Marc had victimized the boy in his car, and the boy's father had caught them having sexual contact. The other claims made against Marc were either past the statute of limitations or pleaded away. While the one boy's charges did stick, they were reduced to a single misdemeanor due to Marc's insistence that, not only was he mentally ill and suffering from thyroid problems, but that he would kill himself in prison. He even brought in a psychiatrist to testify on his behalf about it.

When the trial ended, Marc was found guilty. Due to my son's initial involvement in the case, I was offered the opportunity to make a statement before the court at Marc's sentencing. I accepted and walked to the front of the courtroom.

Marc was standing with his attorney on the left side of the bench as I faced the judge and talked about his consistent deviant actions towards children and how he had continued to do everything he could to be near them, in spite of past orders from the court. I felt some satisfaction in letting Marc hear exactly what I thought of him. As I continued talking, he stood there, head hanging down, silent, and expressionless. It was clear that he did not see the damage he had done.

Even though a number of boys had told their stories to the authorities, and in spite of the prior convictions and Marc's continued attempts to be with children, a deal was made that allowed Marc to spend only fifteen days behind bars. That was not nearly enough compared to the wounds of all of the children he had hurt.

A woman who Marc had rented a room from attended his sentencing to show her support for him. She became quite agitated when he was led away in handcuffs. She belted threats at me. The ADA took note of her outburst, and I was escorted safely from the building to my car.

In spite of Marc's past crimes and his propensity for molesting children, he was able to manipulate the system and gain enough sympathy to go right back out on the street, and against a court order, move back into the home of the woman from whom he had been renting a room.

Her five young children lived in the house with her, which made Marc's presence there a violation of his probation.

Shortly thereafter, I received a phone call from the children's father. He told me that one of his sons had come forward and told police that Marc had molested him. Marc was brought in for questioning, but according to the boy's father, the boy recanted after being pressured by his mother and Marc.

Needless to say, I was frustrated with Marc's ability to roam free. "How could the system fail children in such a blatant way?" I wondered. I didn't realize at the time that my anger was not only fueled by the events involving Christian, but also the circumstances of my own childhood. I wanted to spare Christian the suffering that I had gone through. I wanted to give him something that I never had—someone to shield me from harm, to step in and save me.

Not long after Marc was released from jail, I received a notice that he had brought a complaint against me with the local bar association. He claimed that I had violated the attorney/client privilege when I brought my son to the police to make a complaint against him, and also when I spoke at Marc's sentencing. According to the notice, Marc claimed that I had been his attorney and he said that the privilege was in place because of that. He actually had the audacity to claim that he had retained me to represent him against my son in his criminal case. I am not sure how he expected anyone to believe him, but it made me realize how seriously deranged he was.

The bar association dismissed Marc's claim, and I was left concerned that this man would seek revenge in some other way. I had no idea where he was or whether he still lived nearby. I tried to keep track of him. I did not want him to hurt my family or any more children. Knowing that he had never taken the court's restrictions seriously, I kept my eyes and ears open thinking that I might run into him again in my neighborhood. Unfortunately, due to the circumstances of his plea bargain, Marc was not put onto the sex offenders' registry. Therefore, it was easy for him to conceal his whereabouts. Needless to say, I realized that there was something very wrong with the then-current system of justice, in that a man like Marc could virtually get away with what he had done. Even though he was ordered to stay away from children, there had never been anybody keeping tabs on him to make sure that he did.

Years passed after Marc's brief confinement. My focus had shifted to other issues, but Marc remained in the back of my mind. I often wondered where he was and who he might be hurting. I occasionally performed online searches for his address hoping to find out whether he lived in my community. And, I thought about all of the places he might be hanging out in order to be close to kids. I finally had to let it go.

Several years later, in April 2003, I was sitting alone at home working on my laptop when I suddenly thought of Marc again. I can't put my finger on what brought him to mind, but I decided to do an Internet search to see if I could find him. I had heard about chatrooms and thought that I would enter a few to see what they were about. I had never been in a chatroom and didn't even know how to maneuver my way around. I invented a screen name that made me appear to be a young girl of fifteen and started scanning through the different AOL chatrooms looking for Marc. I thought that even if I couldn't find him, I might be able to come across some children who knew him. If they thought I was another kid, they might confide in me if they knew Marc. I didn't want to portray a boy, because I didn't know how to act like one. Besides, Marc had a habit of warming up to people to get to their siblings, so I felt that there was a chance that he might even make friends with me to see if I had a brother.

I found some interesting chatrooms that appeared to be aimed at older men looking for young people for sex. I joined a few and sat there watching what was going on. There was a lot of sex talk, and it appeared to be transpiring between young girls and older men. I scanned some more rooms in search of Marc and came across one called "I Love Older Men." That was where my focus changed. I suddenly found myself sitting in a room being bombarded with instant messages from people openly asking me if I was interested in having sex with them. I was still trying to spot Marc, so I didn't really care what those other men were saying.

I tried one more general search for him and when I couldn't find anything under his first name, I began searching for some of the names he used to make up when he played laser tag with the boys. Still, nothing showed up, but I did gain some experience learning my way around the chatrooms. At that point, I still wanted to find him, so when I came up empty in the chatrooms, I did a search on the Web for him under his first and last names. What I found truly shocked me.

There was a link to a newspaper article about him. I opened it up and came face to face with his picture. There he was, right in front of my eyes after all that time. I got a sick feeling in the pit of my stomach. I sat there wondering what he had done this time to warrant him being in the newspaper. I prayed that he hadn't hurt another child. As I began to read, I realized that the purpose of the article was to discuss a loophole in the sex offender laws that had previously shielded criminals like Marc. The article detailed an indictment against him for several counts of sex crimes against children, including sodomy. I was sickened by this news. He had molested several more boys between the ages of eight and fourteen. He had done it again, and the legal system had allowed him to do it. After all, he had been afforded more protection than his victims. But, the information that followed really floored me. Marc was never convicted of the numerous charges in the indictment because he did what most would consider the unthinkable: he committed suicide. The article said that he hanged himself.

I was stunned.

Marc must have come to the realization that he had finally gone too far. He wasn't going to get away with his crimes anymore. There were too many convictions and too many boys who had come forward claiming to have been hurt by him. He also knew what would happen to him in prison while he sat on the lowest rung of the jailhouse ladder. He took the only way out that he thought was feasible for him.

Months later, I found another article entitled "Jail Suicide/Mental Health Update," jointly published by the National Center on Institutions and Alternatives and the National Institute of Corrections for the US Department of Justice, that said that Marc died after taking an overdose of psychiatric medications that he had been accumulating in his cell when he was supposed to be swallowing them. He was taken to a hospital where he reportedly died two days later. It also said that "the charges against Marc shocked people who knew him and the parents of his victims." Not surprisingly, it continued, "Several neighbors had him baby-sit their children and teach them martial arts."

That was the way Marc operated. I had seen it many times already, and yet, he was able to do it all again because the system had failed more children. Here was a man who had apparently achieved a master's degree in human development from the State University of New York (SUNY) at Stony Brook. He was able to fool everyone around him for years in order to get close enough to children to molest them. And yet, his suicide "prompted jail officials to re-examine how they treat 'high risk' inmates." They changed the way they handled offenders at the jail. How about changing the way they let child molesters prowl amid our children? If Marc Gunning wasn't coddled in court and sent for a whopping fifteen days in jail the last time he was incarcerated, the trail of hurt he left behind would be a lot smaller!

When I first found out about Marc's death almost four years had already passed, and I could not believe that I hadn't heard about it sooner. I know it sounds harsh, but, in a sense, I was relieved. He was obviously not going to stop on his own. At least this predator would not take advantage of any more children. I knew where he was now, and I knew that children were safe, at least from him, and so was I.

While searching for Marc online, my eyes were opened to things that I had never known existed. The chatrooms were full of adults who were hunting for children with whom to have sex. I decided to continue with my online identity, but now I had a broader search in mind. Surely, the persona I was using could be put to good use. I had already seen that there were people on the Internet trying to talk to children about having sex. I decided to go back into the chatrooms that I visited in looking for Marc and see what would happen. Maybe I could do something to save another child from going through what Marc's victims had endured.

I used the screen name that I had created, Teen2hot4u, as well as the profile that clearly reflected that I was a young teen girl. According to the terms of AOL, profiles can contain anything that a person wants as long as it does not violate the terms of the Internet provider's service. Many include catchy sayings, personal quotes, and photographs. They generally list a person's name, location, gender, marital status, hobbies, occupation, and anything else that the creator wants others to know or to think they know about them. Often, much of the information is fabricated so as not to reveal the true identity of the creator.

The first night that I signed onto the Internet, I really thought it a remote possibility that I would accomplish anything. I suppose finding out about Marc was some type of accomplishment, but I had also stumbled into a world that I never knew existed. I scanned the chatroom names until I found the ones that I thought would contain sexual predators; in other words, adults looking for children to meet for sex. I signed into a chatroom that was created by members of AOL and I sat there. My name appeared on the room's list, but I never entered into the public chat in which everybody in the room participated. In barely a minute, I began receiving instant messages from people identifying themselves as older men.

The first guy to really catch my attention was from California. He was in his mid-forties and he instant messaged me by typing "a/s/l." I had no idea what that meant. I now recognize it as the standard introductory question to find out someone's age, sex, and location. Then he immediately went into a deep conversation about sex. Through my answers, I made it clear that I was a young teenage girl with no sexual experience. He wanted to see what I looked like, but I did not send him a picture. That did not deter him.

The following is part of a chat that I had with him. Since he was not one of the men who were subsequently arrested, his screen name is altered.

> HotXXXinCal: Would be nice to see you in bikini . . . you sound really pretty
> Don't have to of course
>
> Teen2hot4u: i have to c if i can find one [c: "see"]
>
> HotXXXinCal: If you ever wanted to see more of me you can . . . does it bother you when I am sexual? Please be honest
>
> Teen2hot4u: no. what dya mean see more [dya: "do you"]
>
> HotXXXinCal: I have pics of me undressed, to be honest [pics: "pictures"]

I did not realize it at the time, but most guys want to see the girl's picture before becoming too sexually explicit or sending nude pictures of themselves. They don't generally offer theirs up as easily as this guy did. However, I have since learned that many of those who do are merely looking to send lewd pictures of themselves out to young girls because the girl's reaction arouses them. For example, read on:

> HotXXXinCal: Have you seen a guy's cock before? Is it OK to use the word cock, btw? [btw: "by the way"]
>
> Teen2hot4u: in magazines. i guess so
>
> HotXXXinCal: Never in person tho, right?
>
> Teen2hot4u: no
>
> HotXXXinCal: Has any guy sent his online?
>
> Teen2hot4u: no
>
> HotXXXinCal: k . . . just wanted you to know I would if you want me to. I'm open sexually. You want to see? [k: "okay"]
>
> Teen2hot4u: k
>
> HotXXXinCal: Could not share, tho could save on disc & put in purse if want

47

Teen2hot4u: what dya mean share? show it to someone?

HotXXXinCal: Some people show others. yeah . . . please don't

Teen2hot4u: k

This man was so eager to have a young girl see him naked that he started emailing the pictures almost immediately. He had no idea who I was or what I really looked like. In reality, I doubt he even cared. I didn't know much about how all of this Internet chatter worked yet, but looking back, I can honestly say that he was probably just an exhibitionist. That's not to say that he wasn't also a child molester, but I doubt he intended to fly all the way across the country to see me. However, he appeared to have a sick need for a young girl to *see* him naked and listen to his sexual stories.

HotXXXinCal: I once chatted with a young woman who stripped and another who even fingered, both on condition no one would see . . . no one has or will NO ONE EVER sees your pics unless you asked me to share em

HotXXXinCal: I sent mail [mail: "email"]

Teen2hot4u: k

HotXXXinCal: 2nd pic. Please let me know if you like at all

Teen2hot4u: is that really u or a magazine?

HotXXXinCal: Its me. Here . . . let me do something. Gimme a minute

Teen2hot4u: what r u doin

HotXXXinCal: Takin a pic. I'm downloading into computer & will send.

Teen2hot4u: k

HotXXXinCal: Took just for you. Did you like the ones I sent already?

Teen2hot4u: yeah but i didnt get anotha pic

HotXXXinCal: mail

HotXXXinCal: See, its really me. Did you see it?

Teen2hot4u: how come u dont show me your face. r u really the one who sent the pix

HotXXXinCal: yes. I'll take digital pic right now

Teen2hot4u: k
HotXXXinCal: I just don't take full nudes until with someone
Teen2hot4u: its weird seeing jus that
HotXXXinCal: Just my cock?
Teen2hot4u: yeah
HotXXXinCal: k . . . let me take another . . . I'll take one of face & then one naked but without face, k?
Teen2hot4u: how come u dont want me to c yur face
HotXXXinCal: I do. Just not full nude . . . no offense, but til REALLY know one another, people sometimes share pics . . . we are just learning about each other
Teen2hot4u: i dunno
HotXXXinCal: Here . . . let me share pics
Teen2hot4u: if yur sendin me pix of it why cant i see its really yur face
HotXXXinCal: I am. Mail. 2 more just took in bathroom

At this point, I was beyond horrified. Here was a man who assumed that he was communicating with a fifteen-year-old girl, and he thought nothing of talking explicitly about sex and sending nude pictures of himself to her. I needed a break!

Teen2hot4u: k.have to let my dog outside.brb [brb: "be right back"]
HotXXXinCal: k [after some time away]
Teen2hot4u: i got em
HotXXXinCal: I would not lie . . . its really me
HotXXXinCal: If was gonna send fakes, would send one in better shape . . . LOL [LOL: "laughing out loud"]
HotXXXinCal: You like what you see?
Teen2hot4u: yeah
HotXXXinCal: What think might want to do if I was there? You can save any, all or none of em, btw
Teen2hot4u: i dunno
HotXXXinCal: Have ever wanted to touch one or stroke a cock?

Teen2hot4u: i guess
HotXXXinCal: This is kinda personal and you don't have to say, but ever touch self?
Teen2hot4u: maybe
HotXXXinCal: k . . . its OK if don't want to chat about it
Teen2hot4u: i feel funny
HotXXXinCal: k . . . no prob. Honestly. I just was wondering if had ever had orgasm was all. I had my first when your age
Teen2hot4u: i dunno
HotXXXinCal: Masturbating that is. Oh, you'd know if you did. Its rather intense. Feels awesome

Again, I needed a diversion. This subject was not one that I discussed freely, especially with total strangers on the Internet!

Teen2hot4u: wait moms on phone
HotXXXinCal: k
Teen2hot4u: shes comin home soon i have to get ready
HotXXXinCal: k . . . I understand . . . can I ask one q before go? Did seeing me excite you? [q: "question"]
Teen2hot4u: yeah i guess
HotXXXinCal: cool
Teen2hot4u: i gotta go now before she gets home
HotXXXinCal: Hope you can scan your pic soon & email . . . great chatting & will chat more soon
Teen2hot4u: what if u don like my pic
HotXXXinCal: I will. No doubt
Teen2hot4u: even if im just a kid not like in a magazine
HotXXXinCal: Thats what I prefer
Teen2hot4u: really how come
HotXXXinCal: I don't want done up pics . . . just you
HotXXXinCal: I just like natural. Look at me, I'm not a model. I'm just me

Teen2hot4u: but im not like a grownup like my mom
HotXXXinCal: Thats cool . . . you sound really gorgeous to me

I "sound" really gorgeous? On the computer?

HotXXXinCal: I'm serious
Teen2hot4u: i dunno did u see someone my age before
HotXXXinCal: yes
HotXXXinCal: One of the girls who took naked pics was your age . . . I
                  don't expect yours to be naked tho of course
Teen2hot4u: yur just sayin that cause yur nice to me
HotXXXinCal: She started with dressed pics
HotXXXinCal: No . . . I'm not just saying that
Teen2hot4u: and you liked it
HotXXXinCal: yes. a LOT
Teen2hot4u: did she meet u
HotXXXinCal: She would have. Dad caught her as going out
Teen2hot4u: o-was she in trouble
HotXXXinCal: yeah, kinda. Nothing serious
Teen2hot4u: did she live in cal
HotXXXinCal: yes 10 miles away
Teen2hot4u: how did he know where she was goin
HotXXXinCal: He didn't . . . he just knew she was ready to go out at 1AM
                  or so. Mighta been 2
Teen2hot4u: did she tell that she was goin to c u
HotXXXinCal: No
HotXXXinCal: He grounded her anyway
Teen2hot4u: i guess he was jus mad cause she was sneakin out
HotXXXinCal: yeah
Teen2hot4u: yeah my mom doesnt like me to go out late but she works
                  alot
HotXXXinCal: cool

Teen2hot4u: i gotta get ready
HotXXXinCal: k
HotXXXinCal: Glad you liked me naked
Teen2hot4u: k*

This guy had just told me that he makes plans to meet young girls, and he gets naked pictures of them. "What kinds of girls do that?" I wondered. They must really talk about sex with him. But, thinking it through, I realized our chat was obviously one-sided. I barely said anything to him except that I didn't believe the pictures were of him and that I had to go. But, that didn't stop him from talking sexually and sending me nude pictures of himself.

The man never saw a picture of Lorie. He hadn't heard her voice yet. But, because she was a young impressionable child, he knew he could make her feel special with his compliments.

His first pictures were innocent. Then, he sent a few showing his genitals. It took only a matter of minutes before he sent full-length nude photos of himself. Some even showed him masturbating. Others depicted women and men performing sexual acts together.

I was outraged, not only because he was exposing himself on the Internet without caring who saw him, but because he thought he was sending the pictures to a child. I never expected that. I thought that I might come across some people who wanted to chat with young girls and possibly even meet them for sex. I never expected to be faced with visuals. This man was obviously using his webcam, as I came to learn that many of the Internet predators do, to send instant images of himself. I wanted to tell him what a disgusting pervert I thought he was, but I realized that he would just sign off, maybe create a new screen

---

*The screen name HotXXXinCal was created for purposes of the previous example. While the content of this chat is authentic, I have not had contact with anyone using that screen name and have no information about anyone who may have used, may currently use, or may subsequently use that screen name.

name, and then move on to find another young girl. I couldn't let that happen. I had to do something to stop him from finding a real girl to meet. I had to notify the authorities.

Due to the fact that the man lived out of state and was using the Internet, I thought it appropriate to notify the FBI rather than the local police. I decided to contact them to see if they were interested in investigating the man.

My initial reaction after communicating with him was that I had caught the big, Internet predator! I felt so lucky to have come across him as quickly and easily as I had. After all, I was signed on for only a few minutes, and somehow I managed to attract who I perceived as this infamous criminal. I thought it would make such a huge difference to get him off the Internet.

The next morning, I called the Manhattan FBI office. I was asked several questions and left my phone number. The following day, Special Agent Austin Berglas called me. He asked if I would send him the man's photos and we discussed the chats. Then he suggested that we set up an appointment to meet at my home. I assumed that he wanted to see if I was a crazy woman trying to get revenge against an old boyfriend. And, my assumption was pretty much correct. Much later, Agent Berglas shared with me that when I first called, he was skeptical about me and wondered what type of person I was because they do get calls from some questionable people. But, he added that he was interested in talking to me because it is important for the FBI to have sources outside of law enforcement. He said that it's difficult to have a good source of information because individuals who report these kinds of crimes are generally involved with them, and most agents aren't willing to give those types of people a break. Since I didn't have an ulterior motive, he was excited to talk to me because I already had an in.

Agent Berglas was the Coordinator of Squad C-20, also known as the Crimes Against Children Squad, which is a violent crime squad in the New York FBI's criminal division. At the time, Squad C-20 did not have the authority to go online to do proactive investigations. They were reactive, meaning that they were reacting to tips from citizens and leads from other agencies or field offices. So Agent Berglas was glad to have a person who was already talking to sexual predators and could provide the squad with valuable information.

Agent Berglas arrived at my home with another agent, most likely for protection, I thought. I invited them in and led them into my living room where we all sat down. There was a moment of silence during which I felt quite awkward. "They work for the FBI and I sit home talking to perverts on my computer," I thought. "What must they really think of me?" They began asking me various questions.

"What made you go into these chatrooms?"

"Did you know the man you called us about?"

"Did you instigate the conversations?"

"Did you bring up sex first?"

"Did you ask for his pictures?"

At first, I felt somewhat defensive. They were shooting questions at me, and I began to feel as though I was on the witness stand. But, then I realized that I would have been asking the same questions if positions were reversed. So, I just continued to answer them to the best of my ability and soon, I had a reason to exhale. It wasn't long before Agent Berglas commented that what I was doing was wonderful, because for every sexual predator that is arrested, several children are being saved from getting hurt. I was relieved. The agents had validated what I was doing. They didn't consider me to be a perverted weirdo. Whew!

Much later, Agent Berglas shared with me that when he showed up at my home, he was pleasantly surprised to find someone who was intelligent, well spoken, and willing to help. He added that he was impressed because I had no ulterior motive other than to help.

At our first meeting, Agent Berglas suggested that I save my chats if I continue chatting with sexual predators. I didn't know how to save chats, so he instructed me. He also explained what entrapment was, a term that I was already familiar with due to my legal background. But, he needed to make certain that what I was turning over to him would not be tainted evidence, in other words, evidence that would be inadmissible in court. He then gave me some instructions regarding how to avoid entrapping anyone. I knew what he was going to say, but I also knew that he had to say it, so I remained quiet. He said that I was never to begin an instant message chat with anyone the first time. And, once a chat had been initiated, I was never to bring up sex the first time.

We talked for quite awhile longer, during which time Agent Berglas informed me that if I continued reporting predators to the FBI it would be of my own free will and that I would not be an employee of the agency. He added that I should not be under the assumption that I work for the agency in any capacity and that I could not expect to receive any type of compensation from them. However, he did clarify that last statement. He said that there is a reward fund set aside and that, on occasion, he is sometimes able to give people money for various reasons. He said that he couldn't promise anything. I understood that before they had arrived. I never expected to get anything in return. Frankly, I never expected most of what has transpired since that meeting.

Before our meeting ended, the agents got down to business and discussed the man I had called them about. Since he had given me his phone number and asked me to call him, Agent Berglas decided to set up a monitored phone call. I had always sounded young, especially on the phone. Callers still often ask if my mother is home. So, the agents agreed on a time and day for me to make the call and our meeting ended. Unbeknownst to us all at the time, that was the beginning of a very long and unique relationship between two good friends—Lorie and Julie.

I was excited. I felt as though I was finally doing something worthwhile, something that would give me back a purpose in my life. I had been home for a long time recovering from a car accident. I had planned to be out in the world working on a great career, but it was derailed by a motorist who ran into the back of my car, pushing it into and under the vehicle ahead. The accident caused injuries serious enough to put my plans on hold.

Not long after our first meeting, Agent Berglas and a colleague of his returned to my house with some telephone monitoring equipment. They hooked it up to my phone and we called the man I had met on the Internet. It was awkward sitting there in front of two strangers, making myself sound coy and so much younger and talking about things I normally didn't discuss on the phone or in front of strangers. The man freely talked about all of the sexual things that he wanted to do to "me," the little girl he thought he had been chatting with online. I didn't know yet just how typical the call was for a conversation with a sexual predator.

Over the next few weeks, I had many more chats and calls with the man. He was more than explicit about his intentions. He told me that he was going to fly 3,000 miles to see me and we would get a hotel room and spend a few days having sex. After each call, he would send more obscene pictures and chat more openly about what he wanted to do with me when we met.

As I have learned, there comes a point when we have to make a decision about whether to continue communicating with certain people. At times, it becomes clear that a person is not really interested or is too afraid to meet. Then, the agents have to decide if there is enough evidence to make an arrest without a meeting or if they should just let the person go until something more happens.

As time passed, it was obvious that this particular person did not really intend to do more than chat, at least not with me, a "girl" 3,000 miles away. So, his name was passed on to local agents in his area. Thus, a meeting with him and Lorie never took place, but the experience sparked the beginning of a long relationship for me with the world of Internet predators and the FBI that has led to many arrests and convictions.

FOUR

Looking into the Eyes of a Sexual Predator: "Daddy Dearest"

DURING THE SPRING OF 2003, I BEGAN COMMUNICATING online with a Connecticut man named Jason Corso. He was in his late thirties, and I later learned that he worked as a manager at Mutual of Omaha. On the Internet, one of Corso's AOL screen names was Profphoto j. He claimed to be a photographer. He was one of the first few sexual predators that I became involved with back when Teen2hot4u was still a fifteen-year-old girl. At the time that I created the name, I was looking for Marc Gunning and I thought the age was a good fit. But, I continued to use it, naively assuming that no grown man would go after anyone much younger.

Corso was quite friendly and had a different approach than many of the others I had previously chatted with online. He told me that he had a son, but that he wanted a daughter to spoil and treat like a princess. He said all of the things that you would expect someone to tell a young girl who he was trying to lure into a relationship. But, he wasn't another teenager and she was a vulnerable, young teen who told him that she had no experience with boys. He moved slowly. He was more careful than the others I had encountered. He seemed to be well aware of how dangerous his behavior was because he made every effort to be sure that he was really talking to a young girl rather than the authorities. However, he still made his intentions crystal clear.

The following is part of one of the earlier chats that I had with Corso.

> Profphoto j:　does idea of having me as a friend and "daddy" and all that bother you? sound nice?
> Teen2hot4u:　i guess its cool
> Profphoto j:　you arent very talkiative . . . lol
> Teen2hot4u:　but whadya mean daddy [whadya: "what do you"]
> Profphoto j:　just some one you can confide in, someone who takes you shopping, someone you look up to
> Profphoto j:　some one who treats you like "his special" girl

Corso didn't talk about sex right away. This let me know that he was interested in more than merely chatting online or doing what is known as "cybersex." When people are engaging in cybersex, they come on strong and get right to the point. They don't waste time with small talk because, as crude as it sounds, their motive is to find someone to talk to them while they are masturbating. There are probably more of those people on the Internet than the ones who want to actually meet. The cybersexers generally begin with something similar to these standard lines:

Are you home alone? What are you wearing? Take off all your clothes. Can anyone see what you're typing?

Corso wasn't one of those. He tried to gain Lorie's trust and make her feel safe with him. As with the other child predators who contacted Lorie, Corso's goal was to make the girl feel comfortable enough chatting with him to allow him to move on to the next step. He was also apparently searching for a young girl who would call him "Daddy." He asked Lorie about her home life. By the time we had that particular chat, he already knew that Lorie lived alone with her mom. This appeared to be exactly what he wanted. A father figure to a young fatherless girl could be a real blessing, especially to a teen that didn't get along very well with her mother. Corso could move right in and fill that void in her life by making her feel *special* with him. That way, she might eventually give in to what he really wanted.

By the time we had been chatting for several weeks, Corso made it clear that he wanted to take control. He did this gradually, first asking Lorie to redo her profile to indicate that she was "taken," so she would not chat with anyone else. Teen2hot4u's profile was pretty standard back then. It was clear that this was a young teen and that she lived in New York. But, he wanted something more. So, Lorie made a small change.

Profphoto j: muahh . . . i really hope we hit it off, thursday princess (Muah: kiss)
Profphoto j: i will make you sooo happy
Teen2hot4u yur so nice
Profphoto j: bet youd look so hot in the teddy you saw too
Teen2hot4u: muah
Profphoto j: if i give you money for it, will you model it for me?
Teen2hot4u: yeah but u dont wanna pick out the color or anything?
Profphoto j: nope you will suprise me
Teen2hot4u: k
Profphoto j: i will like the curves in it baby . . . not the color
Teen2hot4u: ty [ty: "thank you"]
Profphoto j: will you let me take pics of you in it?
Profphoto j: you know i love photography, right?
Teen2hot4u: sure so yul bring ur camera
Profphoto j: actually i am in between cams
Profphoto j: broke my fav . . . hoping my son will get me one for fathers day. . .
Teen2hot4u: cool
Profphoto j: in the mean time i been using throw away ones . . .lol

Teen2hot4u: thats cool

Profphoto j: they take pretty good pics as long as your subject is close up

Profphoto j: so lets make this profile baby girl

Teen2hot4u: k

Profphoto j: are you gonna mention your "special man"? in it?

Profphoto j: so the other men know to leave you alone?

Teen2hot4u: if u want me 2 i sure wuld like 2

Profphoto j: well i dont want to tell you what to say . . . so you do it now,
             then i will look at baby girl. so get started baby..i am right
             here . . . just ask if you need to.

Profphoto j: but tell me when your done, ok?

Teen2hot4u: k

Profphoto j: kisss me first sexy

Profphoto j: with tounge . . . lol

Teen2hot4u: muah

Teen2hot4u: :-P [:-P: smiley face sticking tongue out]

Profphoto j: mmmmm yummy i bet

Profphoto j: now get busy young lady

Profphoto j: i promise you alot if you are what you seem

Teen2hot4u: well i am

Profphoto j: you will be the princess of queens

Teen2hot4u: cool

Profphoto j: all your friends will be so jealous..and want a "daddy" too

Profphoto j: :-) [:-) : smiley face]

Teen2hot4u: but u don want me 2 tell anyone right

Profphoto j: noooo

Profphoto j: our secret baby

Profphoto j: ok?

Teen2hot4u: k

Profphoto j: maybe down the road we can trust a friend of yours but not
             right away so you must be quiet about it

Profphoto j: now get busy, sexy girl. just do it and get it over with baby, girl

Teen2hot4u: k

Profphoto j: muahhhhhhh
Teen2hot4u: muahhhhh
Profphoto j: now go reboot..i want a profile baby girl

I had to change my profile to please Corso, but what I wrote could have applied to any of the guys I was talking to, so it didn't make much of a difference. I put the following comment in there next to "Location," "NYC an anywhere as long as its with u." Corso was pleased, and I was able to continue chatting with everyone else. Nobody suspected a thing. They all just thought the profile comment was meant for them.

Corso and I had several more chats, emails, and some phone calls before a meeting was finally arranged. First, he had to make it crystal clear to me that he wanted to meet for the purpose of having sex.

As it sometimes happens, Corso had insisted on hearing Lorie's voice before the meeting, so Agent Berglas arranged the phone calls when Corso requested them. An interesting thing occurred during one of the attempted calls. Agent Berglas made the arrangements for the call and after dialing Corso's number, he called to patch me through. Corso didn't answer, but unbeknownst to us, his machine came on. After Agent Berglas thought he had disconnected the call to Corso, he began to talk to me starting with, "Are you still there?" Apparently, the call to Corso was still alive and his answering machine picked up Agent Berglas' question to me. Boy, did I have some explaining to do! The next time I spoke to Corso, he was all bent out of shape about the guy on the other end of the phone. But, this young, inexperienced, naïve, fifteen-year-old girl was able to convince him that my mom's boyfriend must have come into the apartment when I was in the other room and picked up the phone to make a call. When he realized that he had interrupted my call, he asked me if I was still there because he wanted to use the phone. Corso bought the story and we continued communicating.

Corso was cautious at first, but he soon discussed his intentions to have sex with Lorie. During one of the calls, a meeting was arranged where Corso planned to cross state lines in order to be with the young girl with whom he thought he had been chatting. He was going to meet her at the Queens Center Mall in Queens, New York. Everything seemed like a go as the agents planned the arrest. But, a small problem arose which could have put an end to our plans. Corso insisted on having his young princess call him several times from the meeting place to help direct him to where she was waiting. I did my best to convince him to change his mind about the call, but he just would not budge. This is how the chat went:

Profphoto j: if you get there and i am not there within 15 minutes of time i said, call me. i could be stuck in traffic or something

Profphoto j: sound good?

Teen2hot4u: well k but i hope ur not gonna be late

Profphoto j: well I wont be on purpose

Profphoto j: and if i was, it wouldnt be long

Teen2hot4u: k so don worry if ur a little late ill jus hang out an wait

Profphoto j: thats why i said . . . if i say like 7 and i am not there by 715, call and ask me how close i am, so you know i am close and not standing you up, or broke down or something

Teen2hot4u: k but im not worried bout it

Profphoto j: well good . . . you shouldnt i am definitely coming

Profphoto j: just call me and let me know your there, if i am 15 minutes late

Teen2hot4u: like if ur not there in like half hour or more ill call theres lots a traffic round there i culd jus walk round an all

Profphoto j: right. . . but dont wait a half hour to call . . . wait like 15 minutes . . . cause if you dont call for a half hour and i am 20 minutes late and you are walking around, i might show up when your walking around

Teen2hot4u: so its gonna be fun

Profphoto j   yes it will be

Profphoto j: ok, or better yet, just call when you get there, if i am not already there . . .

Teen2hot4u: well i wont walk far theres lots round there its not a big place
              just a high one

Teen2hot4u: im sure ill cya. i know ur comin [cya: "see you"]

Profphoto j: baby, can you just call me when you get there? why is this
              such a big deal. . .

Teen2hot4u: i guess but u mite even be there

Profphoto j: when you get there go to the pay phone and call my cell

Profphoto j: if i am there already i will say hey cutie i am right here . . . lol

Teen2hot4u: i jus know ur comin and if ur late its no big deal

Teen2hot4u: k an i hope im not late 2 cause i don have a cell or anythin

Profphoto j: i understand, but lets just say you'll call me when you arrive . . .
              so either i am there already and you'll see me in a minute or i
              can tell you where i am and how long i will be, then neither of
              us is just waiting around

Teen2hot4u: well if ur so worried bout it

Profphoto j: make sense? i am not worried. jeez honey

Teen2hot4u: i know u said it already

Profphoto j: ok . . . lol. but you havent agreed yet

Teen2hot4u: well if u really need me 2 call i will

Profphoto j: thank you:-)

Profphoto j: i dont ask for much . . . lol

Profphoto j: and i just want this to go smoothly

Teen2hot4u: i don have 2 be home at a certain time an all so im not gonna
              be upset if ur a little late so don think im leavin

Profphoto j: i wasnt worried you'd leave . . .

Profphoto j: just do me a favor, and call me when you get there

Profphoto j: ok?

Teen2hot4u: well u seem 2 be scared bout me showin up or not waitin
              round

Profphoto j: no i am not scared i just dont want to be looking around for
              you and i dont want you to be standing around waiting for me
              thats all please just call me when you arrive

Teen2hot4u: im jus not use 2 havin someone be so well stressin

Teen2hot4u: k

Profphoto j: ok . . . whew . . . lol

Profphoto j: and i am not stressin, after tommrow, everything will be
              different ok?

Teen2hot4u: yeah cause u seem so intense an all bout it

Profphoto j: i am nervous and like i said i will be better after we meet. just
              call me when you get there . . . pleassssseeee . . . lolo we
              will either both be there or i will be close by and say i will see
              you in 10 minutes . . . lol

Teen2hot4u: i guess its somethin u do i jus never get bugged if my freinds r
              late

Profphoto j: baby what is this?? why are you being like this? all i said is
              give me a call when you arrive so i can tell you where i am.
              thats all . . . dont read anything into it

Teen2hot4u: i said ok i jus don get u thats all

Teen2hot4u: so if u get there an i get there its gonna be cool

Profphoto j: yes it wil be great!!!!

The chat was much longer than that, with me trying my best to get him
to give in to not wanting a phone call, but he didn't budge. He insisted
that Lorie call him when she got to the mall and there was no way
around it. That presented a problem. I had to somehow call Corso and
make him think I was at the mall. Agent Berglas was concerned regarding how the call would actually work. Since the agents would all be at
the meeting place waiting for Corso, the calls could not be monitored
as they are from FBI headquarters. Further, if I called Corso from my
home and he asked me where in the mall I was calling from, I would be
taking the chance that he would be near that particular pay phone and
see that nobody was there, or that somebody who was obviously not a
young girl was using that phone. The mall was very far from my house
and nobody expected me to drive all the way there for an arrest. Agent
Berglas had discussed the problem with me, but it didn't seem feasible

to travel there. However, as the minutes passed and the meeting time grew closer, I began thinking about how everything could fall apart over a simple trip to the mall after all of the time and effort that was put into the meeting.

I couldn't sit home and take the chance that Corso would turn around and leave if he didn't get the call. I also didn't want to risk calling from home knowing that he might be right there where I said I was calling from. I had been chatting with him for quite awhile and I knew, as the agents did, that he was a sexual predator. I also knew that if the meeting fell through, he would move on to another child—a real one. I decided that I had no choice but to head to the mall. My husband, Ed, was home and against me going, but I was adamant, so he decided to take the ride with me. On the way there, I called Agent Berglas. He immediately began telling me what the agents were up to and how they were going to call me when they needed me to make contact with Corso. I interrupted, "I'm on my way there." He was silent for a moment. I continued, "I'm coming there. I'll make the call from there." He sounded glad, almost relieved. In my opinion, it was the only solution, but Agent Berglas would never have tried to talk me into doing anything with which I was uncomfortable.

This would be my first involvement with an arrest. Prior to arriving at the mall, several different scenarios played out in my head. Corso might not show up. That was always a possibility in any case. He might figure out that he was not meeting a real child and leave. He could also be carrying a weapon and put everyone in danger when he realized that he was about to be arrested. The most frightening thing that entered my mind was that while he was being arrested, he might somehow spot me in the crowd and know that I was the person responsible for what was happening to him. I was new at this, and I had visions of being retaliated against for reporting these guys to the authorities; I never expected to be present during an arrest. I had gone into this assuming that all of my communications would be done from safely behind my computer screen, or on the telephone in the privacy of my home. Now, I was about to come face to face with one of the men who I turned in to the FBI.

Ed and I arrived at the mall, parked our car in the garage, and went inside. Just after I walked through the entrance, my cell phone rang. It was Agent Berglas. He had been watching for Corso on the mall security cameras and saw me enter the mall. He instructed me to go through a set of closed doors right past the food court and wait. I followed his instructions, walking by the food stands and a set of pay phones. There were several people milling around and sitting at tables eating. I scanned the area for Corso. As my husband and I went through the doors, we found ourselves standing in an empty hallway. Thinking that we had gone the wrong way, we were about to return to the food court when the door opened and a mall security guard entered. He took us outside and through some passageways to the security office where the agents were waiting. I was introduced to everyone and told that Corso's car had already been spotted in the parking garage. We immediately headed back into the mall to find a pay phone from which to call him.

The agents escorted me to a phone in a secluded area on the second level where I wouldn't be seen. It was close to the restrooms behind a wall where nobody could spot me unless they actually walked down there. I chose a phone that allowed me to keep my back against a wall, and an agent kept me within his site from the entrance to the hallway.

I have to admit that once I was there, the whole situation became very exciting for me. There I was, a lawyer-turned-housewife-turned-Internet-predator-catcher actually participating in an FBI sting operation out in the real world. It was an incredible feeling. The blood was rushing through my body, and I felt alive for the first time in years. I picked up the phone and dialed Corso's cell number. After a few rings he answered and said he was still in his car, stuck in traffic, and lost. He insisted that I stay on the phone with him and he asked exactly where in the mall I was. I was concerned that he was already close by looking for Lorie. The agents were all around the area, and I was safely hidden behind the phones. I could not possibly have been in Corso's line of vision if he was anywhere on that level of the mall. If he did come up there, he would have been caught before he got near me. But it was nerve-wracking not knowing where he was. I kept talking, but tried to get him off the phone. He didn't want to let me go, but I was finally able to hang up by promising to call him again soon. Wondering if he was already somewhere in the mall, I walked around with the agents and looked for him, hoping to recognize him from the picture he had emailed me. At one point, we thought we found him in a department store when we saw a man lurking through the girls' bathing suits by himself. He did look similar to the picture that Corso sent me, and he was acting very strange. But the agents decided that it was not him.

Once again, I went back upstairs to the pay phone and called Corso. This time, I tried to hold him off by saying that I was really hungry and that I wanted to get some fries. I was hoping that would put him off for a while and he would just come into the mall to find me. But then he insisted that I call him from down there. I was nervous about what to do next. The food court was out in the open and the pay phones were in full view of everyone. If I called and he was anywhere in that area, he would have immediately known that there was something wrong.

Once down in the food court, I slowly headed to the phones while scanning the tables for Corso. I still had to make that one final call, and now my heart was pounding so hard I could hardly think. I approached one of the phones knowing that Corso could be hiding among the dozens of people milling around or sitting at the tables eating. I slowly dialed his number, and as I waited for him to answer, I again scanned the area to see if anyone's cell phone was ringing. The agents were sitting close by at a table chatting, acting like any other mall shoppers. They were also listening for a cell phone to ring, hoping to catch Corso when he answered. Nobody in the area resembled Corso's picture or had a ringing phone. I was unnerved. Corso could have silenced his ringer or he may have been off in a corner where nobody would notice, but where he could watch a person use the phone. Maybe he had someone else with him who was watching out for me while he hid.

The phone rang a few times until Corso finally answered and told me that he was waiting right outside for me. He instructed me to come out to meet him. I wasn't sure what to say. Unlike the other calls I make, there was no agent instant messaging me to let me know what the next move should be if I was in a tight spot. They usually don't tell me what to say unless I need something like directions or street names, but this was different. I didn't think I should tell Corso that I was coming outside. How could I? Who would walk out there to meet him? He was waiting for a young girl. I certainly didn't fit that description. Finally, Agent Berglas nodded to give me the go ahead. So, I timidly agreed to leave the mall to meet him. After I hung up, Agent Berglas instructed me to sit down with my husband at a nearby table and wait. Everyone waited. I sat close to the mall entranceway and the agents were at a table in the center of the food court. They were sure that Corso would eventually enter the mall to find the girl he had driven so far to meet. This was my first time at an arrest scene. I was certain that Corso would leave if a girl didn't come outside soon. I couldn't imagine why he would come in if she didn't follow his instructions to go out to meet him. Time was passing and we waited—and waited. I watched the agents, hoping for some kind of sign. I was anxious for something to happen, anything. I was excited, yet scared. My mind was racing with all of my original fears.

"What if he leaves? What if we get the wrong guy? What if he has a weapon and uses it? What if he sees me and knows that I was the 'girl'?"

I was so anxious. The anticipation of what might happen was really starting to get to me. I kept looking towards the mall entrance and then back to the table where the agents were sitting. "Something has to happen!" I thought. Eventually, one of the agents decided to stroll outside to see if she could spot Corso. As I sat at the table waiting, my heart raced. I wanted it to be over already. Suddenly, the other agents jumped up from their table and ran towards the entrance. It happened so fast that I barely saw them swarm a man who had just entered the mall. They surrounded him and when one of the agents moved aside, I immediately recognized the familiar face from the picture in the email that Corso had sent me. However, this time, it was beet red and smashed up against a wall. I still knew that half-scrunched face. I had looked at his picture enough times to know that this was the man I had been chatting with on the Internet and talking to on the phone.

I stayed in my seat. I don't remember if it was by choice or if I was paralyzed with the excitement of the moment. But I didn't budge. I watched intently as the agents cuffed Corso, and from only about ten feet away, I looked right into his eyes. As he was led outside, he never looked directly at me, not even when I followed the group out to watch him being placed in an agent's car. I stayed far behind, blending in with the rest of the onlookers. There was a short staircase right outside of the mall entrance, and I stood there on the top step staring for a while, somehow briefly becoming lost in thought. I started to imagine a rerun of the scene in slow motion, and as I reflected on that for a moment, my mind drifted back to the beet-red face I had just recognized inside of the mall. I had caused this man to be arrested. "Could I really live with that?" I wondered. "What if I was somehow wrong? What if this destroys his life, his family? How will his young son react when he finds out his father was arrested? What if this gives his ex-wife the excuse to keep his son away from him? Is there any possible way that this whole thing could be a mistake?" I didn't want to hurt an innocent person.

Pulling my thoughts back to the scene, I had to remind myself of the events as they had unfolded over the past few weeks. I thought about the way Corso had contacted me first on the Internet and how he told me that he wanted a young girl to spoil. He said he wanted to make her his little princess. He offered to take the girl shopping and buy her anything she wanted. He was going to take her out to dinner and they would be like daddy and daughter in public, but they would have sex when he was alone with her. I didn't contact him first. I hadn't said anything to provoke his words. I never initiated sex talk. He was clearly a sexual predator, and instead of feeling guilty that I had been the catalyst for taking away a man's freedom, I began to feel proud for stopping him from going near any more children. I knew that I had done the right thing!

After Corso was arrested, my feelings of self-assurance were confirmed. When he was searched, the agents found crushed OxyContin, a very strong narcotic pain medication, in his pocket along with the key to a motel room. He immediately confessed everything about his plans to meet the teen girl, including the fact that there was another young girl, a real one with whom he had been meeting in Long Island, NY. When I heard that, I realized how very important this was—stopping people like him from preying on children.

Corso was released on $250,000 bail and confined to his home with an electronic ankle bracelet where he was to await trial. A newspaper article entitled, "Cybersex Tryst Twist" hit the stands and I was able to read about my first case. I cut it out and saved it, reading it several times before putting it to rest. I felt a strong sense of victory. One sexual predator was off the streets. Nobody was injured during the arrest. No children were involved. And I could rest easy knowing that Corso would not be victimizing any more kids for a long time.

Corso eventually pleaded guilty. On October 7, 2004, he was sentenced to three years in prison and three years probation.

FIVE

"Baker Nabbed in Sex-Slave Sting"

To THIS DAY, THERE IS ONE SEXUAL PREDATOR WHO STANDS OUT in my mind as the most disturbed individual that I have had the unpleasant experience to come across on the Internet. John Hamilton was a man much older than many of the others I had conversed with at the time, and he lived out-of-state in Kentucky. He was sixty-two years old when he first began instant messaging young, fifteen-year-old Lorie.

What was the most unsettling feature of our chats was that Hamilton had an extremely distorted view of the dynamics of a relationship between a male and a female. That's not to say that the other sexual predators I have communicated with don't, but with Hamilton, it didn't end there. His twisted ideas of life and love were so gross and so far removed from normalcy that I still have a hard time thinking back to my communications with him without getting a knot in the pit of my stomach.

Hamilton wanted much more than a young teen who would comply with his wishes like a good little girl. He was not planning to venture out on a certain day to meet Lorie at the local mall for a few hours of sex like many of the other sexual predators with whom I had communicated. He didn't even give the impression that he was looking for someone to have fun with or to fulfill his fantasies for a day or two. He was serious, very serious about what he wanted and what he expected, and he wasn't your every day, garden-variety child predator. As a matter of fact, Lorie's chats with Hamilton included things that were so far out of my realm of understanding, that I was almost susceptible to falling into his twisted trap, even as an adult with experience in the real world.

Up until I began communicating with Hamilton, my impression of sexual predators ran the gamut from the pervert in the trench coat who waits in the shadows to grab an unsuspecting child, to the seemingly nice guy who lives next door and makes friends with the neighborhood children hoping to scope out his next victim. I had absolutely no idea about guys like Hamilton. There was something about him from the start that made me realize that I was not dealing with what I had come to recognize as the typical child predator who was looking for sex. But I had no idea just how at odds with reality this man really was, and I doubt whether most people could even imagine the kinds of unbelievable things that John Hamilton was looking for from a young girl. His expectations opened my eyes to a whole new dimension of perversion, and it frightened me even more to realize that there were people like him trying to lure in kids over the Internet. In fact, he was so far out there in his thinking that, at one point, Agent Berglas suggested that I limit my chats with him. He thought it best that I only speak to Hamilton for a brief amount of time each day instead of the numerous hours that Hamilton insisted upon from Lorie. Agent Berglas was concerned that I was being subjected to too much of this man's disgusting behavior.

I hate to admit it, but Hamilton's chats did begin to envelop me. He was so insistent that I stay online with him most of the day that I started to get caught up in his sick demands. I had a hard time concentrating on anything else. I was also nauseated much of the time. And I knew what was really going on; I can only imagine what would have happened had I been an actual teenager and mentally unprepared for his barrage. He was increasingly demanding and very domineering. If I was having trouble detaching from this man and his sick comments, how difficult would it be for a real young girl to draw herself away from him? I would have cut off communications with him had it not been for my fear that he would move on to a real child.

Hamilton was what is sometimes referred to on the Internet as a slave master, but he had a seriously distorted and much more perverse idea of sexuality than most of the other slave masters that I had encountered online. There were times when I wondered if he was serious or if he was just trying to play with my head. After all, I was still fairly new at talking to child predators. I did know a lot, but since he was a new breed of predator for me, I didn't know what to think about the things that he expected. It was a real eye-opening experience.

At first, Hamilton gently manipulated his way into Lorie's young, naïve life, taking his time and slowly making subtle suggestions about how much power and control he wanted to have over her. He probably didn't want to scare her away by coming on too strong. Either that, or he just wanted to ease her into his way of thinking, assuming that her inexperience would allow him to convince her that his expectations about what he wanted from her were normal for a man and woman. But later, the unimaginable happened.

Hamilton sent his first instant message to Lorie sometime around the early summer of 2003. I was signed into a chatroom, but as always, I wasn't involved in any of the conversations going on in there. The screen name that I use for Lorie, Teen2hot4u, was on the list of people in the room and Hamilton, in his search for a young victim, obviously saw it and checked out Lorie's profile. The way I described her must have interested him, because he sent Lorie an instant message. This was the first chat that I had with John Hamilton as Lorie.

Jbham12141: Hello are you seeking an older man? and maybe more?
Teen2hot4u: hi
Jbham12141: how are you may i ask?
Teen2hot4u: ok
Jbham12141: are you looking for more than a date in an older man

Teen2hot4u: what dya mean

Jbham12141: would you consider a live in maybe?

Jbham12141: how old are you

Teen2hot4u: o . . .i never thought about it

Teen2hot4u: 15

Jbham12141: oh

Jbham12141: do you have an older man now?

Teen2hot4u: no

Jbham12141: do you date an older man?

Teen2hot4u: not yet

Jbham12141: may i ask you another question pls? [pls: "please"]

Teen2hot4u: yeah

Jbham12141: If i said do you want to serve an older man would you understand the question?

Teen2hot4u: no

Jbham12141: ok

Jbham12141: where are you located I am in Louisville

Teen2hot4u: ny

Jbham12141: ok

Teen2hot4u: where is that

Jbham12141: KY Kentucky

Teen2hot4u: thats far

Jbham12141: somewhat. are you looking for a place to go is that a thought

Jbham12141: do you like sex a lot?

Teen2hot4u: dont know yet

Jbham12141: ok

Jbham12141: well i wish i could help you i surly would

Teen2hot4u: so what did ya mean be4

Jbham12141: oh by the way what do you look like

Teen2hot4u: blonde, 5'5

Jbham12141: weight

Jbham12141: Teen2Hot4u: so what did ya mean be4 [Here Hamilton

74

cut and pasted my instant message from a few lines
earlier and sent it back to me to find out what I was
asking about]

Teen2hot4u: about serving an old man

Jbham12141: serve is a term for a sex slave basically

Jbham12141: you serve sexually

Jbham12141: is that what your looking for ?

Teen2hot4u: maybe not sure

Jbham12141: ok the rest of your looks

Teen2hot4u: new in here

Jbham12141: ok

Jbham12141: how much do you weight

Teen2hot4u: 118

Jbham12141: what is your cup size?

Teen2hot4u: c

Jbham12141: if you get an old man would you let him train you sexually . . .
             about what pleases him and obey him?

Teen2hot4u: i guess

Jbham12141: you would have to be before anyone will take you to live in
             if . . . that is where you go

Teen2hot4u: to live in kentucky?

Jbham12141: well if you wanted that

Jbham12141: if you stay on here you will get many offers

Teen2hot4u: really

Teen2hot4u: to live with one?

Jbham12141: my only thought is to get you before anyone mess you up . . .
             i want to train you to please me the way i want.

Jbham12141: are you a virgin

Teen2hot4u: yes i am

Jbham12141: well you keep this talk in mind and if you decide

Jbham12141: keep this in mind and email me if you want more information

Jbham12141: my name is john

Teen2hot4u: more info like what

Jbham12141: what your duties would be how would you be dressed and how you would be sexually used

Jbham12141: and many many more?

Teen2hot4u: but with who

Jbham12141: what do you mean?

Teen2hot4u: youd tell me all that stuff that i would do 4 who?

Jbham12141: I have to go now catch me about in an hour ok?

Jbham12141: most any Master you would serve

Teen2hot4u: k

Jbham12141: your name

Jbham12141: put me on your BL ok? [BL: "buddy list"]

Teen2hot4u: Lorie

Jbham12141: does aLL this sound like what you want Lorie

Teen2hot4u: i think so

Jbham12141: ok i will discuss it with you in an hour or sometime later

Teen2hot4u: k

Jbham12141: does it sound like exactly like what you want Lorie

Teen2hot4u: i think so

Jbham12141: Is this who you are really Lorie

Teen2hot4u: what dya mean

Jbham12141: don't you think

Jbham12141: this fits you to a tee i bet

Jbham12141: makes you feel good

Jbham12141: just thinking about doing it

Teen2hot4u: yeah

Jbham12141: must run now be here in an hour Lorie

Teen2hot4u: k

Jbham12141: understand

Jbham12141: good slave Lorie if you don't mind the title now

Teen2hot4u: i guess

Jbham12141: you must obey

Jbham12141: ok bye Lorie

Teen2hot4u: k bye

I was convinced that Hamilton was delusional. He appeared to believe that in a few brief minutes, he had found himself a girl who actually agreed to become his servant. This chat was my introduction into sex slavery. It was different, but not so awful that I could have ever foreseen what was coming. Hamilton's chats grew more obscene and crude, so much so that most of what he said to Lorie cannot even be put into this book.

The following instant message session was another one of the first few chats that Hamilton had with the person he believed to be fifteen-year-old Lorie. It goes much deeper than the previous exchange. I was uncomfortable with his earlier comments, but what came soon after bordered on the unbelievable, at least in my world of Internet predator experience.

Jbham12141: Hello Lorie
Teen2hot4u: hi
Jbham12141: how was your night
Teen2hot4u: ok
Jbham12141: did you masturbate more for me
Teen2hot4u: yes
Jbham12141: how many times
Teen2hot4u: a couple
Jbham12141: is it starting to feel good
Teen2hot4u: yes
Jbham12141: is someone there
Teen2hot4u: i thought someone was at the door
Jbham12141: oh ok
Teen2hot4u: cause my dog was barkin
Jbham12141: is your mom asleep
Teen2hot4u: yeah i think so
Jbham12141: I like to watch sometimes
Teen2hot4u: how come
Jbham12141: remember you are going to make me very happy sexually

Jbham12141: how come what love

Teen2hot4u: how come u wanna watch an not jus do it

Jbham12141: sometimes it is more fun and exciting to watch and sometimes it is more fun to do

Jbham12141: that way it won't get old

Teen2hot4u: oh cause like i dont know how to do so much yet an all

Teen2hot4u: so u might not like jus watchin

Jbham12141: it is part of my training though

Jbham12141: and then sometimes i want to do it

Teen2hot4u: like alot or mostly watchin

Jbham12141: you are here to please me

Teen2hot4u: ok

Jbham12141: well there will be times when i watch then other times when i just do it

Jbham12141: what ever i need you will give

Teen2hot4u: yes did u ever see someone my age naked b4

Jbham12141: and you will do it willingly

Jbham12141: yes

Teen2hot4u: so its ok that im so young cause i don want u to be disapointed

Jbham12141: i would like to see your whole body but i will soon

Jbham12141: yes it is great

Jbham12141: just when i want something you just give it to me

Jbham12141: I will tell you how to do it

Teen2hot4u: ok

Jbham12141: and even if it hurts a little you will make sure i am satisfied

Jbham12141: always no matter ok?

Teen2hot4u: i will but what is gonna hurt

Jbham12141: i don't know but if it does I am saying Lorie

Jbham12141: I do not want to be disappointed sexually

Jbham12141: you can do it easy

Jbham12141: just might have to grit your teeth sometimes

Jbham12141: is that ok?

Jbham12141: do you love me that much Lorie

Teen2hot4u: i know its jus important that i make u feel good no matter what

Jbham12141: thank you love

Jbham12141: my love

Jbham12141: that is the attitude Lorie

Jbham12141: for real

Jbham12141: if i wanted to do something sexually and it hurt i would expect you to make it feel so good no matter how much it hurt you.

Jbham12141: that is real love

Hamilton's idea of "real love" was Lorie being in pain while he was enjoying himself. His idea of sex was sadistic, one-sided, and extremely self-serving. If you are sensitive to sexual descriptiveness, please skip the next chat and move on to the rest of the story.

Teen2hot4u: ok but like what kind a things could hurt

Jbham12141: if you were tight one time or dry

Teen2hot4u: ok

Jbham12141: and i had to heave it then

Jbham12141: I would expect you to make it good no matter if crying or not as long as you make it feel good to me and I cum

Teen2hot4u: ok

Jbham12141: i am sure you understand that

Teen2hot4u: yes

Jbham12141: that is a basic female thing

Jbham12141: or if i squeeze your breasts too tight you would put your hands over mine on your breasts and help me make it hurt or squeeze harder

Teen2hot4u: ok

Jbham12141: that is in your soul as a woman

Teen2hot4u: so if u wanna hurt me im gonna help u cause its my job to please u?

Jbham12141: if i do yes

Jbham12141: and i am betting right now you want that more than anything

Teen2hot4u: is it something that is exciting to hurt in sex

Jbham12141: yes

Teen2hot4u: ok

Jbham12141: and it is the womans place to hurt

Teen2hot4u: is it jus me whos gonna hurt then

Jbham12141: most females will try to deny they have that feeling but most want it

Teen2hot4u: ok i understand an r u gonna hit me or something

Jbham12141: no no

Jbham12141: I might later on spank you

Jbham12141: but doubt it

Teen2hot4u: if im bad?

Jbham12141: how excited are you now Lorie

Jbham12141: or maybe in fun

Teen2hot4u: I am

Jbham12141: are you

Teen2hot4u: will i spank u to

Jbham12141: sometimes yes

Teen2hot4u: but i thought im not suposed to hurt u

Jbham12141: your not

Jbham12141: it will be light

Teen2hot4u: wont it hurt if i spank u

Jbham12141: lightly

Teen2hot4u: r u gonna do stuff like i saw in a magazine like with things like whips or chainin me up or anythin

Jbham12141: we will discuss it

Jbham12141: do you want it

Teen2hot4u: well im just curious bout what yur gonna do an all

Jbham12141: i know

Teen2hot4u: will it jus be me an u

Jbham12141: we will do it all i suspect but in due time

Jbham12141: yes

Teen2hot4u : ok

Jbham12141: Lorie how much are you really really in love are you now with me

Teen2hot4u: so much

Jbham12141: you know you are going to be mine don't you

Teen2hot4u: yes

Jbham12141: anything i need you will give me

Teen2hot4u: yes

Jbham12141: without question right there

Teen2hot4u: yes

Jbham12141: no matter how much it hurts or how much you don't want to do it

Teen2hot4u: yes

Jbham12141: thank you love

Teen2hot4u: what if like its that time of the month or somethin

Jbham12141: i have no problem with that you will be even more wild then and you can always clean up any mess we make

Jbham12141: right?

Jbham12141: Lorie are you lazy?

Jbham12141: or industrious

Teen2hot4u: im not lazy

Jbham12141: good

Teen2hot4u: am I gonna have to go to school there

Jbham12141: I don't know

Jbham12141: you are going to make me very happy

Teen2hot4u: yes i am

Jbham12141: I would let you do what you wanted to make me happy

Teen2hot4u: ok

Jbham12141: I would like it done good also

Teen2hot4u: ill try my best

Jbham12141: you will do it good believe me

Jbham12141: you will learn to like everything

Teen2hot4u: i hope so

Jbham12141:   the first time is the hardest then it is a piece of cake

Teen2hot4u: ok

Jbham12141:   are you thinking this is exciting now

Teen2hot4u: yes

Jbham12141:   excellent

Jbham12141:   you deserve to be here

Teen2hot4u: ty

Teen2hot4u: oh my moms up i gotta go will u be here later

Jbham12141:   you are my fantastic girl

Teen2hot4u: ty

Jbham12141:   thank you so much love

Teen2hot4u: yw [yw: "you're welcome"]

Jbham12141:   you will make me happy no matter

Teen2hot4u: yes i will

Jbham12141:   have you seen sex done in pictures

Teen2hot4u: no i havent will i jus wait for u to want sex or will i be askin
              for it to

Jbham12141:   you will ask

Teen2hot4u: ok

Jbham12141:   and if we can do it we will i want you to be pleased too

Teen2hot4u: ok

Jbham12141:   you want all this don't you Lorie

Teen2hot4u: yes

Jbham12141:   You don't care what i do to you do you honey?

Teen2hot4u: no but like what do u mean

Jbham12141:   you will take care of me won't you

Jbham12141:   if i wanted you to put your tongue anywhere

Jbham12141:   your truly mine Lorie

Teen2hot4u: i better go my moms callin

Teen2hot4u: i better go

Jbham12141:   ok later love

Jbham12141:   just remember all things for making me happy are ok

Teen2hot4u: ok
Jbham12141:   no matter what i ask of you
Teen2hot4u: ok
Jbham12141:   do you understand what that covers
Teen2hot4u: i think so unless u didnt tell me somethin
Jbham12141:   everything
Teen2hot4u: ok
Jbham12141:   bye for now love
Teen2hot4u: bye

That was not the entire chat. Unfortunately, due to the extremely graphic nature of the communication and gross descriptions of what Hamilton wanted to do with young Lorie once he had her to himself, I had to edit it in order to make it fit for readers. I wanted you to see the truth, to read what your children read when they are cornered by one of these perverted predators. I realize that I am desensitized to many of the things that I have been exposed to during the past few years of communicating with child molesters on the Internet. I have seen and heard things that no longer shock me; however, I have also seen the reactions of others when I share with them what the predators say to children. I've learned that there is only so much that they really want to hear, so some of the chats will be explicit, to a point, while, at other times, I will summarize what they say so you can still understand what they expect from the child without having to read every word of the chat.

In between many of Hamilton's distorted comments were some of the most repugnant suggestions that I have ever encountered. Without being too graphic, I will try to explain what he said. He not only wanted his young sex slave to perform every type of sexual act imaginable, he also insisted that the following demands be met: that Lorie allow him to attach a milking machine to her breasts so he could drink milk from her; that she perform oral sex to every orifice of his body, and that if anything should happen to come out of that orifice, no matter what it was or where it came from, she would have to swallow it. If he defecated or urinated, she was expected to consume it. As if that was not disgusting enough, he also told her that she should begin practicing it all prior to leaving for his home. Apparently, he had already indulged in the disgusting habits that he hoped she would join him in—eating and drinking those things that were part of his own bodily functions. That is about all I want to mention, but I think you can imagine the rest. Not surprisingly, he confided that he had a fifteen-year-old daughter that he was not allowed to see.

Hamilton was so deviant, so suggestive, and so immoral, that it is clear why even I, a grown woman, had difficulty dealing with his communications. That he insisted that Lorie chat with him for several hours at a time several times a day made it impossible for me to take time to clear my head and go back to him refreshed and strong. Since I was playing the role of a submissive child, I either had to go along with his demands or he would have moved on to a real child. I couldn't let that happen.

Even though it was clear that Hamilton's idea of sexuality and love was so intense and so gross that not many children would have given in to his outlandish demands, it is important to note that he moved in very carefully. I have left out much of his early chats. He only continued with the graphic descriptions of what he expected from his young sex slave because Lorie allowed him to. Had she shown the slightest bit of resistance, it was clear that he would have probably stopped telling her of his plans. Instead, he would have waited until she arrived at his house and was alone with him to instruct her about the terrible things he expected from the young girl with whom he thought he had been chatting. He wanted complete control of a vulnerable child.

During their chats, Hamilton explained to Lorie that he expected her to always walk around the house naked unless company came over. He also told her that pain is a good thing and that Lorie's pain was her gift to him. He apparently had absolutely no boundaries whatsoever, which, to me, was the most frightening aspect about him. I couldn't help but wonder how far he would actually go with a young girl. I was also nervous about what he would really do to her once he had her in his grasp. I pictured a basement full of young girls chained to the walls. Of course, that was only in my imagination. Early on, I had all kinds of thoughts about how far some of the more deviant predators would go, but I never came close to even considering the acts that Hamilton expected his young victim to perform.

While the things that Lorie promised to do for Hamilton were basically unspeakable, there is something about this story that makes it even more revolting. Hamilton was a baker who apparently prepared his goods at home and sold them to local restaurants, cafes, and bakeries. He told Lorie that she would help him in his kitchen, baking with him and then delivering his goods all around the area of Louisville, Kentucky. When he told me that, I couldn't help but gag. After all of the things that Hamilton had described doing with Lorie, many that I could not include in this book, the thought that people might be eating food that came out of his kitchen—food that he prepared with his own hands—just sickened me.

Hamilton was going to own Lorie. He told her that he planned to keep her hidden away until her eighteenth birthday. She would be completely dependent upon him and, once she turned eighteen, he would marry her. In his own words, he told her the most frightening part of his plans, "Lorie, you will disappear off the face of the Earth as far as your mother would be concerned. Nobody you know will ever see or hear from you again."

You may be thinking that if Lorie were a real girl, she wouldn't have continued chatting with Hamilton. At first glance, it appears that his words might frighten a young girl looking for a cool guy to meet. Yet, through my experience, I have learned that there are numerous young teens that want to disappear from their families. Some would run away and live on the streets to get out of a bad home life. Others are adventurous and think they can take care of themselves, to a point. Someone like Hamilton, who offered a free bus trip, a home, and a "loving" relationship, as distorted as it might sound to a mentally healthy individual, might just be some young child's ticket to what they see as freedom. There are many kids who come from the kind of homes where they haven't been taught about boundaries, human sexuality, privacy, and self-respect. Some may have been abused or neglected, and when an individual like Hamilton comes along and convinces them that he will free them from their family and take good care of them, even though he throws in some strange conditions, a child might think it still sounds better than what they already have, especially since they will be making the decision to go with him.

There is also the possibility that the child will believe that they don't really have to comply with all of his demands. They may be somewhat rebellious and think they can continue with their behavior wherever they are. Perhaps they hope they can just coast along and the man who sends for them will not be so demanding after awhile. So, there is every reason to believe that there are young girls and boys out there who would travel far away to be with someone like Hamilton, as long as it gets them away from where they are and they don't have to stay in their own bad situation or opt for living on the street.

You may be looking at your own children right about now and are unable to imagine that they would fall prey to the likes of Hamilton. You have taught them well. You have strongly warned them. Think about how manipulative Elizabeth Smart's captors were. (If you remember hearing or reading about this case, Elizabeth Smart was the fourteen-year-old girl who was kidnapped from the bedroom of her family's Salt Lake City, Utah, home in June 2002. She was found nine months later while walking down the street with her abductors a few miles from her home.) They initially kidnapped her, but they kept her for several months, traveling around, and in the end, walking out in public with her. She was wearing a disguise, but she never felt safe enough to call out for help. It boggles the mind to think about how something like that is possible. We consider that if we were being held captive and we had the slightest chance to ask for help, we would. But the vulnerable mind of a person, any person, who has been under the influence of someone who overpowers them, brainwashes them, and puts them in fear for their own or their family members' lives, is susceptible to believing anything they are told. Consider the mind of an innocent, trusting child. Think of how serious peer pressure is, how the look on someone's face can make teens doubt themselves, how affected they are by break-ups, acne, not having the right clothes, and not feeling as though they fit in with their peers. Enter Hamilton. He offers them a way out of all of the pressure. They might just want to go.

After only a few weeks of chatting, Hamilton arranged for a Greyhound bus ticket to be waiting at a New York City bus terminal for Lorie. He experienced a few minor complications on his end, but he was finally able to purchase the ticket. He instructed Lorie to travel alone and get off the bus in Cincinnati, Ohio, where he would be waiting to drive her to his home in Kentucky. He did not want her to take the bus all the way to Louisville where he lived, because he was concerned that someone he knew might see him taking her off the bus and putting her in his truck. He clearly recognized that his actions could get him into trouble. He told Lorie to pack only her knapsack, so as not to alert anyone that she might be leaving home. He instructed her to wear clothing that made her look older, and he also told her to wear a baseball cap to keep her face hidden from plain sight. He didn't want her to do anything that would draw attention to herself and raise anyone's suspicions.

Lorie was to board the bus in New York and travel for two days before arriving at her destination, the meeting place in Cincinnati where Hamilton was to pick her up. During that time, I had to stay off the Internet under the screen name that I used with him so he wouldn't see me on and realize that Lorie was not on her way to meet him. Those two days were very trying for me. I was anxious for the whole ordeal to finally be over.

Hamilton had gotten inside my head. I needed time to shake him off, to clear my mind of the sickness with which he had infiltrated my thoughts. To this day, my experience with Hamilton was the only time that any of the sexual predators was able to interfere with my everyday life. It was beyond disturbing. His demands were so unsettling and his chatting so deviant that I had a hard time going about my daily routine until our communications finally ended. I followed his lead because it was the only way to make sure that he didn't move on to a real child, but I didn't openly agree with everything he said. There were times when I questioned some of his demands, but I was careful not to make him angry. He was controlling, so much so that I knew I had to limit any concerns that I thought a young girl might want to express. I also knew that if I was too eager, it might raise his suspicions.

On June 24, 2003, John Hamilton was arrested at a Cincinnati Greyhound station while waiting for young Lorie to get off the bus. He confessed everything, including that he had also been communicating with a teenage girl from California. That other "girl" turned out to be an undercover FBI agent. Hamilton had also been chatting with agents from a Kentucky FBI office. His arrest was publicized. One newspaper headline read "Baker Nabbed in Sex-Slave Sting." His actions allowed authorities to bring him up on charges in more than one state. Due to the extreme level of deviance that he had displayed, he was held without bail. He pleaded guilty in February 2004 and received a sentence of three years in a federal prison and five years probation.

Hamilton was the second arrest that resulted from my online chats, but his was the first conviction born out of those communications, because Corso did not plead as quickly. It was a strange feeling knowing that I was directly responsible for sending someone to prison; however, nothing struck me more than realizing that there are men like Hamilton preying on young girls. I had a lot of different thoughts about what I was doing. One of them was a sense of relief that this particular man was out of circulation. For the time being, at least.

SIX

The Restless 'Groom'er

IMAGINE THAT YOU HAVE MET THE MAN OF YOUR DREAMS. He is the one you have been waiting for your entire life. You fall in love, become engaged, and plan the most beautiful wedding that you can envision. The invitations are out, the plane tickets are purchased, and the dress is hanging in your closet. Your honeymoon to a tropical island is going to be perfect. It is getting so close that you are counting the days. But something happens that forces you to change all of your plans—something that will devastate you and your entire family.

After I was finished with Hamilton's case, another somewhat strange predator caught my attention. He wasn't anything like Hamilton. I would like to think that he was one of a kind. This other predator wasn't a slave master, but he worked so quickly to get Lorie to meet him that it made me wonder what he really wanted from her. He came on very strong and insisted on meeting immediately. I don't mean after a few weeks, or even a few days. He wanted her to come out that very same night. I had never experienced anyone who worked so fast and so hard to be with a young girl. Most of the guys do not try to get a girl to meet that quickly, especially those who live as far away from them as he did.

It was during their very first chat that Vishal Patel, a twenty-eight-year-old New Jersey man, asked if he could come and pick up the young fifteen-year-old girl that he had found on the Internet. His instant message appeared on my screen very late at night. I was just about to shut down my computer for the evening, so I tried to put him off by telling him that my mom wanted me to sign off, and she would never allow me to go out that late. But the next time I stayed up late surfing the Internet, he immediately sent me another message.

In our second chat, which took place in the middle of the night between 1:00 a.m. and 2:00 a.m., he begged me again to let him come right over to pick me up. At first, I really thought he was just fooling around. In spite of his insistence, I didn't believe that he had any real intentions of coming to get me. After all, if I had agreed, he would have had to drive at least an hour and a half in the middle of the night to where he thought I lived. And, yet, he insisted that he would just head out in his car right away with barely a few sentences between us. I couldn't help but wonder what the hurry was. But, again, I put him off.

I had no choice. I had to wait until I really knew what he wanted, until I knew he was an older man looking to have sex with a minor. I had to let him continue with the chatting until he made it clear that he was really going to break the law by enticing this young girl to meet him for sex. Even if I had turned his name over to the FBI at that point, what would I have told them? He was just chatting about meeting. If I gave Agent Berglas the name of every man who had instant messaged me and started talking about a meeting, he wouldn't have had time for his own investigations. I had to be sure. I had to know for certain that I wasn't going to bring a whole world of hurt down on an innocent man and that I wasn't going to waste Agent Berglas' time.

Each night that Patel chatted with Lorie, he became increasingly insistent that she let him come right over to get her. He seemed so desperate. It was somewhat unsettling because it didn't make sense that he would go so far out of his way for a few hours with a little girl in the middle of the night. Surely, he could find someone closer. I wondered if he was more than just a garden-variety pervert. My mind ran wild with the types of things I had envisioned he might be capable of doing to a child if she did agree to such a hasty rendezvous. He didn't let up.

He caught Lorie online constantly during the first twenty-four hours and continued to beg her to meet him.

Patel laid out his plan this way: He was going to drive to New York, pick up his young victim at a mall in Queens, and take her back to a motel in New Jersey where he would drop her off. Then he was going to go to work from 4:00 p.m. until 9:00 p.m. and return to the motel for a night of drinking and sex with her. The following is part of a chat that Patel, known by his AOL screen name TheDuece6975, had with Lorie.

TheDuece6975: like what if i come get you at around 12 noon tomm . . .
and then we drive to nj..get a room and i leave for work at
3:30ish and come to the motel at 9:15ish pm? [tomm: "tomorrow"]

TheDuece6975: u dont like the idea of u staying at a room?

Teen2hot4u: well maybe thatd be ok i think

TheDuece6975: u sure?

TheDuece6975: u gotta hang out at the motel room for like 5 hours alone

TheDuece6975: is that ok?

Teen2hot4u: well i also gotta see where u could get me so early an all

TheDuece6975: 12 pm is early? i need to know tonite so i know what time
to leave tomm

Teen2hot4u: yeah im not sure right this minute cause my mom is
working the nite shift an i woulda wanted 2 leave when
shes out

TheDuece6975: are u sure shes working the nightshift. . . ?

Teen2hot4u: tomorrow im almost positive cause she told me she probly
wont be round 4 dinner but i think shes working all day on
tues . . . i think

TheDuece6975: um

TheDuece6975: what time does she leave

Teen2hot4u: oh mostly round 5 or 6

TheDuece6975: ok so she wont be home until like after midnight right???

Teen2hot4u: i think so
TheDuece6975:   ok so i could meet u around 11-11:30 pm
Teen2hot4u: u mean tomorow again
TheDuece6975:   yea
TheDuece6975:   im talking about tomm no matter we met at night, or
                        afternoon
Teen2hot4u: well can i call u tomorrow 2 tell u wut shes doin
TheDuece6975:   what time u thinking about callin?
Teen2hot4u: im not sure . . . after i find out wut shes doin
TheDuece6975:   u see this sucks cause we wont know anything
Teen2hot4u: but dont worry cause if it doesnt work 4 tomorow ill make
                        sure bout tuesday or somethin
TheDuece6975:   i dont wanna make it a week and stuff
TheDuece6975:   i dont wanna prolong it too much
Teen2hot4u: i don wanna promise about tomorow an disapoint u
TheDuece6975:   it would be nice to meet soon
Teen2hot4u: i know
Teen2hot4u: i jus met u yesterday its not so long
TheDuece6975:   lol
TheDuece6975:   i know . . . im saying like 2 weeks and stuff from now

He was in a hurry. He was too concerned that the chats would drag on
for a mere two weeks before Lorie would finally agree to meet him.
Two weeks was not a long time to be online grooming a child. Most of
the predators move more slowly than that. They're usually pretty careful about who they are meeting. I continued to wonder why he was so
desperate to meet immediately.

The communications continued. In other chats, Patel talked in
more depth about what he wanted Lorie to wear and what they would
do together once she agreed to meet him.

TheDuece6975:   what kinda clothes do u usually wear
Teen2hot4u: well i wear shorts an tanks

TheDuece6975: that sounds nice

TheDuece6975: tight?

Teen2hot4u: yeah

TheDuece6975: u wear underwear?

Teen2hot4u: sometimes

TheDuece6975: thongs?

Teen2hot4u: sometimes

TheDuece6975: if u wear some nice tight jeans a tiny top and a thong, no bra would be nice

Teen2hot4u: ok

TheDuece6975: u serious u will?

Teen2hot4u: yeah

TheDuece6975: so u have piercings?

Teen2hot4u: no jus my ears

Teen2hot4u: u?

TheDuece6975: nope nothing

TheDuece6975: what about down there are u . . .

Teen2hot4u: am i wut

TheDuece6975: what are u down there?

Teen2hot4u: wut dya mean wut m i? a girl . . .

TheDuece6975: do u shave down there

Teen2hot4u: o no not really

TheDuece6975: your natural?

Teen2hot4u: well If my pants or bathin suit is so low i shave 4 that an all

TheDuece6975: do u have alot of pubic hair down there?

Teen2hot4u: no not a real lot

Teen2hot4u: why

TheDuece6975: how low u gonna wear them jeans tomm?

Teen2hot4u: well i got a few pairs how low dya want em

TheDuece6975: cause i dont prefer girls with like a bush down there. completely shaved is nice, and trimmed, like in a line is nice

TheDuece6975: what ya mean how low
TheDuece6975: how low can they go
Teen2hot4u: i got em real low jus by the hair line
Teen2hot4u: my mom hates em
TheDuece6975: wear them real low.
Teen2hot4u: k
TheDuece6975: u got a nice flat stomach?
Teen2hot4u: yeah i do
TheDuece6975: damn, im gonna wanna lick it
Teen2hot4u: k
TheDuece6975: ud let me? [ud: "you'd"]
Teen2hot4u: i guess i would.. u wanna
TheDuece6975: yea prob [prob: "probably"]
Teen2hot4u: prob?
TheDuece6975: yes i do
Teen2hot4u: k if u wanna
TheDuece6975: even though i have no idea what u really look like

I was chatting with a sexual predator who had absolutely no idea what the person he was communicating with looked like, yet he planned to drive the long distance to meet her for a night of sex. More than anything else, my curiosity was what kept me interested in him. I still didn't believe he would really go that far out of his way to meet someone he hadn't seen. I couldn't help but wonder what was really going on with him. Did he want the physical pleasure of sex in the true sense of the word? What if Lorie turned out to be 250 pounds with stringy hair, bad teeth, and bad hygiene? Would he have just walked away or would he have still wanted to lure her out of the house to have sex with him?

I thought about some research I had done on issues of rape and how having power over someone was an intricate aspect of the act. I knew that sexual gratification was not the justifiable cause for rape. It was all about taking advantage of someone through manipulation and control. I wanted to understand what would make a person in this situation go after a young child in the first place. Then, I tried to imagine why he would pursue someone who he had never even seen. Finally, I was puzzled by his urgency.

The rest of the previous chat was pretty standard. Patel asked Lorie to bring along a bottle of baby oil for their night of sex. He described all of the sexual acts that they would perform. He also told her that they did not need to use protection. I suppose that was something these guys feel comfortable with considering that they think they are chatting with an untouched virgin. But on the other hand, they have absolutely no concern whatsoever for the young girl's health. Many of the men I chat with tell me that they don't need or want to use condoms and that they won't get the girl pregnant. Some describe what they will do to prevent that from happening. Others say they can't get a girl pregnant because they had surgery to prevent it. Yet there are those who say they actually want to get the girl pregnant, and then they claim they want to spend the rest of their lives with her and even hope to marry her. But that was not the case here.

The chats with Patel continued for only a couple more days until a meeting was scheduled, but an unexpected occurrence happened one night while I was chatting on the Internet with him. He instant messaged me what appeared to be an IP address. At the time I thought it was a link to a picture or some other fun-type thing that people send to each other, so I clicked on it. We continued chatting, but by the next day my computer crashed. There was nothing I could do. I was locked out and everything was frozen. Thankfully, the meeting with Patel had already been scheduled. More importantly, Agent Berglas was able to bring my computer to someone in his office who was able to extract my saved chats with Patel to use for evidence.

On July 8, 2003, Patel got into his car and drove from New Jersey to the Queens Center Mall in Queens, New York, to pick up the young girl he thought he had been chatting with online. When he arrived at the meeting place, he was greeted instead by a squad of FBI agents led by Agent Berglas, and arrested. In his possession, he had a bottle of

Bacardi, an email from Lorie, and a Holiday Inn pass. He claimed that he had no intention of having sex with the young girl he had traveled so far to meet.

During questioning, Patel's reason for insisting on such a swift encounter was finally revealed. He had some very important plans coming up. His wedding day was a mere one week away. I was told that it was to be an elaborate affair with all the trimmings. Patel's first words after the agents cuffed him were, "This can't happen. I'm going on my honeymoon next week." Apparently, he had planned to take his new bride on an exotic Hawaiian honeymoon. But instead of walking down the aisle to meet his beautiful fiancée, he found himself sitting in a jail cell. After his arraignment, Patel was released on a $300,000 bond. He pleaded guilty and was sentenced to three years in prison and five years probation. He was lucky. Shortly after his conviction, the minimum mandatory sentence for his type of offense was increased to five years.

Patel was among the first three predators that I was responsible for bringing to the FBI and ultimately to justice. I was still fairly new at this and often gave the situations too much thought for my own good. After his arrest, I spent weeks agonizing over Patel's fiancée and how she was dealing with this terrible breach of trust, the humiliation she must have felt having to cancel her dream wedding and her exciting, romantic honeymoon, and the thousands of dollars her family had probably lost at that late date, not to mention the money her guests must have laid out for clothing, plane tickets, and possibly, hotel accommodations.

However, I also had to remind myself of the reality of the situation. This young woman's life was not destroyed. It was saved from a lifetime of pain that she would have endured by marrying a sexual predator who chased after children. He was not just looking for that one last fling that some men sneak off to indulge in before tying the knot. He was planning to molest a child. There is a big difference between cheating on your partner and having sex with a minor. Neither of them is moral or acceptable, but having consensual sex with an adult and committing a sexual crime against a child fall into two completely different categories. And there is no way of knowing what Patel would eventually do to his own children or to their friends, or what he may have already been doing to other children.

With any luck, Patel's fiancée was able to move on with her life, meet a nice, decent man, and have the happiness that she most likely deserved. It is my wish for her that she not judge every man by the misdeeds of Patel. Hopefully, she did not waste time pining for him, believing in his innocence, and waiting for him to be released. These guys are very manipulative, not just with kids, but with everyone around them.

Corso, Hamilton, and Patel were my true initiation into the dark world of sexual predators and pedophilia. While I had already had that wrenching experience with Mark Gunning, these encounters were quite different. They weren't my acquaintances. I didn't know any of them, and they were not going after my own children. But, the biggest difference was that I was on the receiving end of their communications. With every word they typed, with every sexual comment they made, with every meeting they planned and showed up for, I stood in the shoes of the young, innocent girl who would sleep peacefully one more night because those men did not have the opportunity to go after her. So, in a way, it *was* personal. I could not portray a young girl on the Internet and talk like a young girl on the telephone without putting myself into the role that I was trying to play. I act the part when I talk to sexual predators and pedophiles. I become coy and cute and vulnerable. However, when they come on to me, when they tell me the sexual things that they want to do with me, instead of feeling special and pretty, I feel disgusted and angry. I lose my patience at times.

On a bad day, one where I have no tolerance at all for these perverts, I actually allow myself to let off some steam. One guy had a habit of sending his picture to every little girl he found in certain chatrooms. I had been using a few different screen names at one time and the same guy sent his picture to three of my names during the same week. After the third email, I finally told him exactly what I thought of him and his picture, but I never revealed that I wasn't a little girl. I did get some satisfaction out of brushing the old guy off and telling him what a pig I thought he was. I knew he was being watched and he did eventually get arrested, but it was by the local police.

Sometimes, I simply become annoyed enough to act as though I don't care either way if a guy is interested. I've made some pretty sharp comments to some individuals, and they still come back for more. Some don't like it, but they always try to figure out a way to make it up to me. One way or another, their main interest is in manipulating and conquering a young child to do with as they wish. So, they continue to move in even when they are being brushed off. I suppose that's all part of the game—to conquer the vulnerable prey. I simply turn the tables on them!

SEVEN

Bringing in the FBI

THE FIRST SEXUAL PREDATOR THAT I HAD THE UNPLEASANT experience to testify against was Matt Brand, a man who went onto the Internet using the AOL screen name Tempoteech. Early on, I occasionally switched over to a different screen name temporarily if an investigation of one of Teen2hot4u's contacts was moving toward an arrest and Agent Berglas wanted me to stay away from the suspect for a little while. So, I had been using the AOL screen name Xxxxpartygurlooo and the name Sara when Tempoteech found me.

Brand was a teacher, of sorts, and he found Sara in one of the usual places, the "I Love Older Men" chatroom, where sexual predators seem to regularly congregate or peruse in search of their next prey. His chat with Sara began in the familiar way, by him working his way into the young girl's life with the lure of something that a vulnerable teenager would definitely be excited about. In fact, he made so many promises that it would have been hard for any child to resist his tempting offers. The following chat is how my long and complicated involvement with Tempoteech began.

> Tempoteech: hi sara i'm matt whats up
> Xxxxpartygurlooo: hi

The fact that Brand immediately called Sara by name let me know that he had read her profile. Thus, he was very well aware that he was communicating with a child. By this time, I had lowered my "age" from fifteen to thirteen.

Tempoteech:	i'm matt from jersey
Xxxxpartygurlooo:	im in ny
Tempoteech:	nice we are neighbors
Tempoteech:	are you single
Xxxxpartygurlooo:	yeah
Tempoteech:	me too
Tempoteech:	would you like to trade a pic
Xxxxpartygurlooo:	well im to young to get married
Tempoteech:	thats ok you can date right
Xxxxpartygurlooo:	yeah
Tempoteech:	well maybe you will like how i look and we can get to know each other
Xxxxpartygurlooo:	k

It doesn't sound very much like the way a teacher would be chatting with a prospective student, so he has gotten my attention.

Tempoteech:	so trade
Xxxxpartygurlooo:	i dont have one
Tempoteech:	oh what do you look like
Xxxxpartygurlooo:	5'3 blond blue eyes 105
Tempoteech:	very nice
Xxxxpartygurlooo:	ty
Tempoteech:	so are you in manhattan
Xxxxpartygurlooo:	cool pic
Tempoteech:	thanks
Tempoteech:	i'm old
Xxxxpartygurlooo:	how old
Tempoteech:	36
Xxxxpartygurlooo:	thats cool

Tempoteech:	you like old how old are you
Xxxxpartygurlooo:	13
Tempoteech:	and you like older guys
Xxxxpartygurlooo:	yeah
Tempoteech:	cool so where are you from
Xxxxpartygurlooo:	long island

Brand has now made it clear that he is happy that Sara likes older men. Again, there is nothing very specific yet, but it is pretty obvious that he has an interest in her that appears to go beyond the student/teacher relationship.

Tempoteech:	ah yes i know it i'm by great adventure
Xxxxpartygurlooo:	thats cool
Tempoteech:	ever been there
Xxxxpartygurlooo:	yeah a couple a years ago
Tempoteech:	its ok you were here and didn't say hi
Xxxxpartygurlooo:	sorry
Tempoteech:	well you could now lol
Xxxxpartygurlooo:	yeah if it wasnt so far
Tempoteech:	well you can do anything you set your mind too

It may not seem obvious, but Brand was planting the idea in Sara's mind that she can make the decision to be with him if she wants to. Of course, looking back, it seems clear. But, at the time, it was barely anything Sara would have been concerned about, and it certainly did not give me any indication that it was time to report him to the FBI.

Xxxxpartygurlooo:	yeah well its to far to go by myself
Tempoteech:	well we could meet in manhattan
Xxxxpartygurlooo:	thatd be cool

Brand has suggested that he and Sara meet. That was something that pulled me in a little further. He knew how old Sara was, and he still talked to her about meeting. People who are not sexual predators usually stop chatting at the point when they find out that a girl is thirteen. But, Tempoteech commented that if Sara liked how he looked, they could get to know each other. Then, he suggested a meeting. At this point, I had to wonder what he wanted to meet her for because, due to the age difference, it did not seem it could be for platonic reasons. I had to be patient and wait to see where he would take the communication next.

Tempoteech: do you ever talk on the phone
Xxxxpartygurlooo: not really

When he asked if Sara talks on the phone, I thought he was interested in phone sex. When someone asks that, I usually let him or her know right up front that I don't because what this generally means is that they want to talk sexually over the phone while masturbating. Once my answer is "No," if they continue chatting, it lets me know that they are probably interested in more than phone sex. There is still the possibility that they are only looking for cybersex, which means they will chat about sex on the computer, also generally while masturbating. Once I told Brand that I wouldn't talk on the phone, he continued to chat with me:

Tempoteech: oh well we can talk here then
Xxxxpartygurlooo: k
Tempoteech: k so what do you do for fun
Xxxxpartygurlooo: hang out with friends play music an sports an stuff
Tempoteech: very cool
Tempoteech: do you like to sing
Xxxxpartygurlooo: yeah why
Tempoteech: cause i am a singer
Xxxxpartygurlooo: cool
Tempoteech: yes i was in a few shows

```
Xxxxpartygurlooo:  what kind
Tempoteech:        broadway
Xxxxpartygurlooo:  really thats so cool, like what ones
Tempoteech:        cats
Xxxxpartygurlooo:  cool
Tempoteech:        yes i liked it alot
Xxxxpartygurlooo:  yeah
Tempoteech:        maybe i can sing for you sometime
Xxxxpartygurlooo:  very cool
Tempoteech:        cool anytime
Xxxxpartygurlooo:  hey my moms home i gotta go
```

The chat seemed fairly innocent. It was just enough to know that Brand, a much older man, was interested in chatting with a thirteen-year-old girl, while making a few cute comments along the way. He tried to catch Sara's attention by telling her that he had been in *Cats*, a Broadway show that he probably assumed all kids have heard about.

At that point, the chat was still only enough to peak my curiosity. He sparked my interest because he was a thirty-six-year-old man talking to a thirteen-year-old girl and he wanted to sing for her. But more importantly, he also wanted to meet. However, there was no solid reason to turn him over to the FBI just yet, so I put him on my buddy list and waited to see if he instant messaged me again. One week later, he did.

```
Tempoteech:        hi sara its matt again
Tempoteech:        remember me 36 single from jersey
Xxxxpartygurlooo:  oh hi
Tempoteech:        hi whats going on miss
Xxxxpartygurlooo:  not so much jus hangin out an doin some home work
Tempoteech:        thats sounds fun
Xxxxpartygurlooo:  no way
Tempoteech:        want some help
```

Xxxxpartygurlooo: well yeah i wish
Tempoteech: well i will help you if you want i'm free
Tempoteech: i am a teacher
Xxxxpartygurlooo: what dya teach
Tempoteech: theater
Xxxxpartygurlooo: thats so cool
Tempoteech: do you act or sing
Tempoteech: where are you from
Xxxxpartygurlooo: well i do like to sing
Xxxxpartygurlooo: ny
Tempoteech: i am in jersey
Tempoteech: see we could hang

What happened in this chat was something I have seen many times. Brand seemed to be starting over with me. As with some of the other sexual predators, he probably hadn't been keeping track of all of his communications with girls, so he chatted as though he needed to refresh his memory or get information he didn't think he had already asked for in a prior chat.

Tempoteech: we could sing and do your homework
Xxxxpartygurlooo: well i cant really come all the way there
Tempoteech: i could come to the city
Xxxxpartygurlooo: really
Tempoteech: yes
Tempoteech: did we trade pix
Xxxxpartygurlooo: no cause i dont have one
Tempoteech: oh want to see mine
Xxxxpartygurlooo: ok
Tempoteech: mail
Xxxxpartygurlooo: u r real good lookin
Tempoteech: well thank you

Tempoteech:	i bet you look better than me
Xxxxpartygurlooo:	ty
Tempoteech:	so you live near manhattan
Xxxxpartygurlooo:	im on long island but i go to nyc sometimes cause i have a friend who lives there
Xxxxpartygurlooo:	could u teach me to sing
Tempoteech:	well see we could meet there
Xxxxpartygurlooo:	cool
Tempoteech:	yes I could teach you to sing thats what i do
Xxxxpartygurlooo:	wow u must be real good
Tempoteech:	yes i have been singing for 23 yrs
Xxxxpartygurlooo:	wow
Tempoteech:	so you want lessons
Xxxxpartygurlooo:	yeah
Tempoteech:	ok
Xxxxpartygurlooo:	but i dont realy have any money
Tempoteech:	thats ok you could do my shows as pay
Xxxxpartygurlooo:	what dya mean
Tempoteech:	i do theater you act in my shows and i'll train you
Xxxxpartygurlooo:	wow for real
Tempoteech:	i'll teach you to sing and act yes for real
Xxxxpartygurlooo:	omg i cant believe it [omg: "Oh my God"]
Tempoteech:	well its true

This time, he told Sara that he was a singing and acting teacher, and he was going to give her free lessons and put her in his shows. Once again, he said he was going to travel into Manhattan to meet her.

After that last chat, my interest progressed a bit more. It was highly unlikely that he was truly interested in driving all the way to Manhattan to give a young girl free singing and dancing lessons. He had never even seen a picture of her, so he had no idea what Sara really looked like. On the off chance that he was just fooling around, I continued to respond to his instant messages.

Tempoteech:	so when would you like to start
Xxxxpartygurlooo:	well i have to figure out when i can come to nyc an stuff cause i got school
Tempoteech:	well there is the weekends
Xxxxpartygurlooo:	like where would we meet
Tempoteech:	well we could meet by port authority
Xxxxpartygurlooo:	well i guess so
Xxxxpartygurlooo:	but where would we go for u to teach me stuff
Tempoteech:	i have nowhere to teach in the city
Xxxxpartygurlooo:	oh no
Tempoteech:	i teach at peoples houses or my house
Xxxxpartygurlooo:	ok i guess thatd be ok
Xxxxpartygurlooo:	cause u r a teacher an stuff
Tempoteech:	i could get you home whenever you needed to be
Xxxxpartygurlooo:	well i guess but how would i get to your house
Tempoteech:	well i would meet you in the city and take you there then bring you back to the city
Xxxxpartygurlooo:	ok like u would pick me up or somethin
Tempoteech:	yes in the city at the port authority
Xxxxpartygurlooo:	how come at there
Tempoteech:	cause its a central place i guess
Xxxxpartygurlooo:	k

The picture was becoming clearer. Brand conveniently overlooked the opportunity to come to Sara's house to teach her. That told me a little more. If lessons were truly on his agenda, it would make much more sense for him to come to Sara's house, give her the lesson, and take the ride back home to New Jersey. Instead, he would rather drive to Manhattan, pick her up, drive all the way back to New Jersey, then back to Manhattan and back to New Jersey again. This really grabbed my attention. But, I was still not ready to turn him over to the FBI, because it wasn't clear that he intended to have sex.

Xxxxpartygurlooo: do u teach lots of girls my age
Tempoteech: yes
Tempoteech: you want to meet them
Xxxxpartygurlooo: yeah i guess so if you want
Xxxxpartygurlooo: whatever u think is ok
Tempoteech: ok
Tempoteech: did you ever model
Xxxxpartygurlooo: no but i want to
Tempoteech: well i shot calanders fun ones
Xxxxpartygurlooo: really thats so cool
Tempoteech: what do you look like again
Xxxxpartygurlooo: 5'3 blue eyes blonde hair 105
Tempoteech: wow very nice
Xxxxpartygurlooo: ty
Xxxxpartygurlooo: do u think i could model
Tempoteech: well i would have to see you but you could
Xxxxpartygurlooo: oh yeah
Xxxxpartygurlooo: do the other girls model
Tempoteech: to bad no pic i could tell right away
Tempoteech: yes and some do beauty pageants
Xxxxpartygurlooo: for real
Xxxxpartygurlooo: wow i bet there pretty
Tempoteech: yes and one is on broadway
Xxxxpartygurlooo: wow what is she in
Tempoteech: whistle down the wind
Xxxxpartygurlooo: oh i didn't hear of that one
Xxxxpartygurlooo: u must be real good at teaching
Tempoteech: well i think so lol
Tempoteech: well when your ready we can start
Xxxxpartygurlooo: ok r the lessons hard
Tempoteech: they can be
Tempoteech: depends on how you work

Xxxxpartygurlooo: i would work real hard
Tempoteech: and then you would be good
Xxxxpartygurlooo: i hope so
Tempoteech: you will be fine

Brand had now enticed Sara with the idea of being a model and partic-ipating in beauty pageants. Just putting the idea out there is enough to convince a young girl that he could make it all happen for her. What teenager would not want to be a model? Brand was grooming her, in the true sense of the word, giving Sara all the reasons to be comfortable enough to meet him. He complimented her on the description that she gave him, and he told her that all of her dreams would come true with him. But, there was more:

Xxxxpartygurlooo: will there be other girls being taught when i am
Tempoteech: no most classes are private do you want to be in a class
                with other girls
Xxxxpartygurlooo: well id want to do whatever u think is best
Tempoteech: ok well alone first is good

It was now clear that Brand had every intention of getting Sara alone with him since he had used the ruse that he gave private lessons at his house, and he thought that "alone first is good." A young teen would feel like the luckiest girl alive to have someone so talented training her privately. Every kid knows that private acting or singing lessons would be more special than learning in a group.

Tempoteech: we will have fun
Xxxxpartygurlooo: i hope so
Tempoteech: we will
Xxxxpartygurlooo: cool
Xxxxpartygurlooo: im real good at doin what im told an stuff so i would
                learn fast

Tempoteech:	good and the faster you learn the sooner you can be in shows
Xxxxpartygurlooo:	cool i will be real good
Tempoteech:	ok
Tempoteech:	and you may even like me lol
Xxxxpartygurlooo:	i already do
Tempoteech:	thats great we will get along good

This is where Brand began to take a step over the line. He wanted Sara to like him. This is not the kind of talk that a teacher has with a student. It did not appear as though he meant that Sara would like him as just her teacher. He had moved in a little closer to her—past the student/teacher relationship—but there were still some questions about his intentions that needed answers. I did not think I had enough to be sure, so I did what any teenager in that position would have done. I continued chatting with him to learn more about what his intentions were.

Xxxxpartygurlooo :	i hope u will like me to
Tempoteech:	i do now
Xxxxpartygurlooo:	really
Tempoteech:	yes
Xxxxpartygurlooo:	im so happy
Tempoteech:	good i am glad
Tempoteech:	do you dance
Xxxxpartygurlooo:	well i like to
Tempoteech:	well i will teach you
Xxxxpartygurlooo:	really u know everything
Tempoteech:	yes i have been doing this along time

Brand added another incentive. He was going to teach Sara to dance. This was just one more way to pull her into his web. He continued chatting, telling Sara that he had a huge theater at a summer camp, that they would have fun on the car ride there, that he would do impressions for her, that they would be good friends, and, most importantly, that Sara would trust him.

> Tempoteech: you will trust me
> Xxxxpartygurlooo: yes i will

Brand had moved into another area that has a very fine line. Let's face it, when someone wants to teach things to a child, legitimate lessons, they do not start talking about being their friend and telling the child that she will trust him. But, on the off chance that he is just a little strange or has no clue about how to act appropriately, I still did not report him. However, it was not long before Brand stepped across the line.

> Tempoteech: would you want to hang out with me even though i'm 36
> Xxxxpartygurlooo: yeah i would
> Xxxxpartygurlooo: is that ok
> Tempoteech: very cool
> Tempoteech: and i am single no one wants me
> Xxxxpartygurlooo: no way
> Tempoteech: yup can't find a girlfriend
> Xxxxpartygurlooo: how come
> Tempoteech: cause girls here don't like nice guys they want bad boys
> Xxxxpartygurlooo: i hate bad boys
> Tempoteech: well then we are a perfect match
> Xxxxpartygurlooo: yeah
> Xxxxpartygurlooo: cool
> Tempoteech: why you want an older boyfriend
> Xxxxpartygurlooo: well i never realy thought bout it cause i jus figured a older guy would think i was just a kid or somethin
> Tempoteech: well i don't i think your a nice girl

Xxxxpartygurlooo: ty

Tempoteech: your welcome you never know we might like each other alot

Xxxxpartygurlooo: that would be so cool

Tempoteech: why would go out with a guy like me?

Xxxxpartygurlooo: well yeah if u would realy want to but like i never been with a guy your age

Tempoteech: well would you like to go places and do things with me and hold hands and have fun

Xxxxpartygurlooo: i sure would

Tempoteech: well then wanna be my girlfriend

Xxxxpartygurlooo: for real

Tempoteech: for real

Xxxxpartygurlooo: omg i cant beleive it

Tempoteech: is that a yes

Xxxxpartygurlooo: yeah it sure is

Tempoteech: so you are my girlfriend

Xxxxpartygurlooo: yeah ok

Tempoteech: well i can't wait to see you

Xxxxpartygurlooo: me to

Tempoteech: can i say your my baby now

Xxxxpartygurlooo: yeah i like that

Tempoteech: can i hug you when i see you

Xxxxpartygurlooo: yeah

Tempoteech: maybe a kiss

Xxxxpartygurlooo: well yeah but i might not be such a good kisser like girls your age

Tempoteech: i only want to kiss you

Tempoteech: then we will kiss till you are

Tempoteech: i am yours now

Xxxxpartygurlooo: cool an u wont mind

Tempoteech: not at all

Xxxxpartygurlooo: wow i realy like u

```
Tempoteech:        maybe one day you'll love me
Xxxxpartygurlooo: i know i will cause ur the best
Tempoteech:        well thank you baby
```

This is where Brand passed the point of no return. He told Sara he had no girlfriend. He was thirty-six. She was thirteen. He made her feel sorry for him because "girls don't like nice guys." He complimented her by letting her know that he didn't view her as a kid. He called her his girlfriend, told her he would hug her, hold hands with her, kiss her until she was a good kisser, and maybe someday, she would love him. There was no mention of lessons anymore. He was expecting a thirteen-year-old girl to get into his car, travel with him to his house in another state, and be physical with him. And, if that was not compelling enough, read on:

```
Tempoteech:        but what if another boy wants you
Xxxxpartygurlooo: well its to bad for him
Tempoteech:        wil you be mine always
Xxxxpartygurlooo: if u realy want me to
Tempoteech:        i do
Xxxxpartygurlooo: ok
Tempoteech:        say your my girlfriend
Xxxxpartygurlooo: i am im your girlfriend
Tempoteech:        matt and sara always
```

It is clear that this man was grooming his prey. He is a sexual predator. After this chat, I recognized the need to let the FBI know about him. While their investigation commenced, I continued chatting with Brand a little longer. I had held off on agreeing to a meeting by telling him that my mother was sick and that she had been home in bed for a while. He thought it would be easier for Sara to go with him while her mother was at work, so he was willing to wait until her mother was better. He had already reached the point where he felt confident that

Sara would keep his secret, so he dared to take the relationship one step further.

Tempoteech:	so when does your mom go back to work
Xxxxpartygurlooo:	im not sure but i hope soon
Tempoteech:	me to will you come then
Xxxxpartygurlooo:	yes
Tempoteech:	i hope its soon then
Xxxxpartygurlooo:	me to i realy do
Tempoteech:	she works nights
Xxxxpartygurlooo:	yeah most of the time
Tempoteech:	then we can spend some time at night together
Xxxxpartygurlooo:	yeah
Tempoteech:	how long can you stay with me
Xxxxpartygurlooo:	well it depends cause she works real late an sometimes i even stay at a friends or my cousins
Tempoteech:	so what will you tell her when you come see me
Xxxxpartygurlooo:	well i dont know if i should tell her the truth cause i dont think shed realy let me go what do u think
Tempoteech:	what would you say
Xxxxpartygurlooo:	im not sure but sometimes i even go to a friends after she leaves an stay over an she doesnt check cause she gets home so late she just goes to bed an sleeps all day an stuff. we been doin it that way forever
Tempoteech:	did you tell her about taking classes with me
Xxxxpartygurlooo:	well no i didnt tell her yet cause i was scared u were only foolin around
Tempoteech:	so then tell her your going there
Xxxxpartygurlooo:	do u think i should
Tempoteech:	how bad do you want to see me
Xxxxpartygurlooo:	so bad
Tempoteech:	then do what you have to

Xxxxpartygurlooo: ok i will
Tempoteech: ok

If there had been any doubt at all about what Matt Brand was looking for, it was erased with that chat. He confirmed that he wanted to be with Sara when her mother was at work, so she wouldn't know that her daughter was with him. He specifically told Sara to lie about where she was going. He had progressed from saying, "you can do anything you set your mind to," to "do what you have to do" to be with him, even if it means lying to her mother. But, he was not finished:

Tempoteech: i need to see you
Xxxxpartygurlooo: do u realy
Tempoteech: yes baby so bad
Xxxxpartygurlooo: im so happy
Tempoteech: i love you sara is that ok
Xxxxpartygurlooo: omg yes it is
Tempoteech: do you love me
Xxxxpartygurlooo: yes i do
Tempoteech: say it
Xxxxpartygurlooo: i love u
Tempoteech: i want to be with you sara
Xxxxpartygurlooo: i want to be with u to
Tempoteech: i hope you can get here soon my baby
Xxxxpartygurlooo: me to it will be so cool
Tempoteech: yes it will
Xxxxpartygurlooo: i realy hope u still love me when u meet me
Tempoteech: i will with all my heart
Xxxxpartygurlooo: i mean im just a kid an all
Tempoteech: your my baby
Xxxxpartygurlooo: did u ever have a girlfriend my age yet
Tempoteech: no is that bad
Xxxxpartygurlooo: no im just hoping u arent disapointed

Tempoteech:	i won't be
Xxxxpartygurlooo:	i never had a real serious boyfriend yet
Tempoteech:	well now you do
Xxxxpartygurlooo:	very cool
Tempoteech:	very wonderful
Xxxxpartygurlooo:	im so glad
Tempoteech:	i am too
Tempoteech:	if you still love me when your 18 we could get married
Xxxxpartygurlooo:	for real
Tempoteech:	yes
Xxxxpartygurlooo:	wow thats so great
Tempoteech:	would you marry me then
Xxxxpartygurlooo:	yes i will
Tempoteech:	i love you very much
Xxxxpartygurlooo:	i love u very much to
Tempoteech:	always and forever

So, there you have it: Matt Brand, a thirty-six-year-old man had just made a lifetime commitment to thirteen-year-old Sara, a girl whose picture he hadn't even seen. He told her how much he needed her, wanted her, loved her, and that he wanted to marry her when she turned eighteen, if she still loved him. This was to convince Sara that he would always love her and it would be up to her if they were to be married. It made her feel secure about him, knowing that he would never change his mind. It also allowed her to feel that she had some control in the relationship, so she didn't think that he was taking advantage of her.

Looking back on how the chats between Matt Brand and Sara had progressed, it is clear that there were never any lessons to teach—at least not the kind that a grown man should be teaching to a thirteen-year-old girl. It was all about what Brand wanted: power, control, and sexual gratification. That last chat was part of only the third communication between Matt and Sara. Three chats and he was already in love with her, a girl he had never even seen or heard; no picture, no phone calls yet, just a stranger he thought and hoped was a child. He groomed her in every sense of the word. He made her feel good about herself and also about him. He deliberately offered Sara special things that he assumed were out of her reach, thinking that she would be drawn to him because he could give them to her. He showered her with compliments and he said everything he could to convince her that he really wanted her. If Sara had been a real child, living with a single mother who worked long hours and rarely had the money for things like acting, singing, and dancing lessons, she might have jumped at the chance to meet Matt Brand, someone who claimed to be in *Cats* on Broadway. If Sara was lonely and inexperienced, she may have fallen into his trap. Brand wanted to spend a lot of time with her, have fun singing and dancing with her, do impressions for her, and finally, love and marry her. Is there any doubt that their relationship was way out of line?

Sara and Matt had only two more chats. It had been during his second chat with Sara that Brand offered and gave her his phone number. She didn't call right away. But on February 11, 2004, Brand heard her voice for the first time. However, I was not calling as Sara. I was calling as his next victim, Julie, Agent Berglas' Internet persona who Sara had introduced Brand to and with whom Brand had already begun chatting. As Sara, I told him in one last, brief chat that I had been in a car accident and was injured badly enough that I would not be able to meet him for several weeks or longer. As expected, Sara never heard from Matt again. No more promises of lessons and talks of all of the fun they would have together. No more discussions of the love that they seemingly shared. No more plans to get married. Matt dumped Sara because she had been injured and couldn't meet him right away. How much clearer could he have been about his real motives and intentions toward the thirteen-year-old girl to whom he had been professing his love? She couldn't come out and play, so he was finished with her.

Brand quickly moved on and began chatting with thirteen-year-old Julie. She had a lot in common with Sara. They both became excited at the thought of taking lessons with Brand, and they both seemed anxious to meet him. Brand treated them both alike. He groomed Julie the same way that he had groomed Sara, but with Julie, the chats quickly became sexual in nature. After the usual attempt to build up her self-esteem, and after making her the same promises that he had made to Sara, he told Julie that he would use a condom so she would not get pregnant. He also asked her if she would like him to lick her crotch and her breasts. When he saw that she was receptive to his advances, he finally arranged to travel into Manhattan to meet her.

On February 12, 2004, Matt Brand arrived at a taxi stand at Port Authority in Manhattan for a 1:30 p.m. meeting with Julie. He appeared at the arranged place at the agreed upon time, wearing the exact outfit that he had described to her in their last telephone conversation. As he walked up and down scanning taxicabs for his young, new girlfriend, FBI agents moved in and arrested him. In his possession was a small sign with Julie's name on it.

While being questioned, Brand admitted that he had chatted with other young girls on the Internet, some as young as ten years old. He also stated that he knew that what he was doing was wrong and illegal. Brand further admitted to having received pornographic images of children as young as eight years old. However, forensics experts examining Brand's computer were later able to recover nude images of children as young as three or four, one in particular where the child was known to be six and was depicted being penetrated by an adult male.

Brand's indictment contained two counts: Under Count One, he was charged with "unlawfully, willingly, and knowingly, traveling in interstate commerce for the purpose of engaging in sexual acts with an individual he believed was 13 years old"; Under Count Two he was charged with "unlawfully, willingly, and knowingly, using the facility and means of interstate commerce, a computer, the Internet, and a telephone, to attempt to persuade, induce, and entice an individual he believed to be a 13-year-old girl to engage in sexual activity." He pleaded not guilty.

Brand was the first sexual predator that I had dealt with who decided to take his case to trial. In spite of the overwhelming evidence against him, he must have thought he could convince a jury that the government had entrapped him. Entrapment would have come into play if the agents gave Brand the idea to commit the crime, if they then convinced him to commit the crime, and if he was not ready and willing to commit the crime prior to the agent's interaction with him.

It was strange to think that someone would try to fight the charges considering all of the evidence against him, including several documented Internet chats, as well as recorded telephone calls. However, Brand was not merely denying his actions. He was claiming that he was not at all responsible for them. His lawyer's apparent strategy was to present the case in a way that would make the jury view Brand as a man who was duped and manipulated by a bunch of corrupt government officials. The attorney was aware that pornography had been discovered on Brand's computer and that there was more than one federal agent willing to testify against Brand. Brand had been told the truth about Sara, that she was an older woman who sits in chatrooms looking for child predators the same way Brand searches for children, except that I do not contact the predators first. They come to me, and they take control of the entire situation from beginning to end. I do not encourage them, except to let them think that I am willing to go along with their games. I do not initiate anything: the chats, the sex talk, the emotional stroking, the psychological manipulation, the phone calls, or the meetings.

Brand had become aware that Julie was Agent Berglas, the person behind the computer screen impersonating the young teenage girl who Brand had chatted sexually with online. He had also been informed that he had not been conversing sexually on the telephone with a thirteen-year-old girl. But, he didn't know that it was me! He was also well aware that the prosecution team would be presenting more than a *he said, she said* case. The evidence was solid with the chats and monitored phone calls. Yet, he apparently thought he could beat the rap. He must have known that there would be others testifying against him, other law enforcement officials who posed as young girls. He knew that his parents would be coming to court, that if they watched the trial they would hear what he had said to the "teens," and they would find out the *truth* about him. But *his* truth may have been the same one that many child predators delude themselves with, that they are giving love to children and that they should not be frowned upon for wanting to treat them so warmly.

No matter what Brand said to justify his behavior, he had still broken the law. He committed a premeditated, calculated, illegal act against a minor child. He searched for one, set her up, groomed her, arranged a meeting, and followed through by traveling to New York City's Port Authority, as planned, to meet her. Now, he had to face the consequences, and I was going to be right there on the front lines making sure that he did!

EIGHT

Taking the Witness Stand

MATT BRAND DID NOT TAKE A PLEA AS THE OTHERS HAD. He was going to trial, and I was an important and necessary witness since the case had been initiated by me.

When I envisioned coming face to face with a man who I had turned over to the FBI, it was quite unsettling. Even when the possibility of having to testify was raised after the first arrest that I was involved with, I never imagined that my participation with catching Internet predators would really take me to that point. So, when Agent Berglas called me to tell me that the trial was scheduled and I was expected to appear in court, I was stunned. My mind raced with so many fears that I didn't know how I would ever be able to get through what I perceived as an ordeal. Brand was going to see my face, hear my name, find out where I live, and learn about my life and my family. If the jury convicted him, how safe would I ever feel again? Even if Brand was acquitted, I would be afraid that he or someone he knew would want revenge. After all, his entire family, and possibly his friends, would all have that same information about me. What if they came looking for me? Could I really deal with this? Could I sit on the witness stand and look this man in the eye and testify against him?

Prior to the trial, in order to prepare for my testimony, I had a couple of meetings (prepping sessions) with the United States Attorneys in Manhattan. Prepping is a normal procedure by which the prosecutors try to get an idea of what my demeanor will be like on the stand and what type of testimony I will give. I was very uneasy. I suppose I shouldn't have been so nervous considering that I am an attorney, but this was putting me on the other side of the fence, so to speak. As an attorney, I never really expected to be a witness, especially in a case like this one. I usually defended people, but in truth, I could never stand this breed of slime, let alone come to their defense. This entire experience was way out of my comfort zone.

As the trial drew near, I became even more unsettled. I had thoughts of failing, ruining everything, making a fool out of myself, all the normal concerns which would run through most any witness' mind. But, I think this was a little different in that I viewed it as a game of dominos, where one witness' poor testimony might infringe on everyone else's. And, my testimony would be the focal point. It was not just a bolster to someone else's proof. Brand was getting away with his actions until he met Sara. She chatted with him. She talked on the telephone with him. She was the reason that he was turned over to the FBI and I was the one who determined that it was time to turn him over. Of course, the FBI made the ultimate determination as to whether there was enough evidence to arrest Brand. But, if I had never gotten involved, his prosecution would not have been happening, not at that time, anyway. He was there because of me, and I had to face him and tell the jury what he had said to me. I had to repeat every word of it.

My growing concerns made me question everything I had been doing. I began to wonder what the jury would think of me. For one thing, a lot of people hate lawyers. Would they see me as one of those snakes who chases ambulances? What would they think of a woman who spends several hours every day talking to sexual predators on the Internet? Maybe they would wonder what was wrong with me for being able to do that. What if they thought that I was some kind of pervert, too? And, how about my law degree? Would they wonder why I wasn't busy in a law office somewhere rather than talking to predators all day long?

The more I questioned myself, the clearer the answers became—to me. But, the jurors did not know me. They were not aware of my past, the terrible car accident that I had been in six days after graduating from law school that sent my life into a tailspin for a couple of years. They would not be told that I had spent a few years in excruciating pain while I worked with a physical therapist to walk without assistance, and that I finally came out of the darkness and went to work as an attorney. They had no way of knowing that I had once again returned to law school to obtain another law degree, a masters of International Law, just to prove to myself that I could do it, just to show that I was back. The jurors would not find out that right after that last graduation another car plowed into the back of mine, throwing it into and under the car ahead and sending me back into physical therapy and recuperation. They might only see a woman who chats with perverted slugs, who talks to the lowest forms of humanity on the telephone, and who receives disgusting pornography from pathetic, desperate souls who are so lost that they have to victimize defenseless children. Really—what *would* they think of me?

The trial was scheduled to begin on Wednesday, January 19, 2005, and a jury of twelve men and women, plus four alternates was impaneled. I was summoned into Manhattan on that day, and I registered at a hotel not far from the Federal Courthouse. The plan was that Special Agent Berglas would testify first, and then I would be called to take the stand immediately thereafter.

The jurors were sworn in and the attorneys made their opening statements. I was prohibited from entering the courtroom until it was my turn to testify because, as a witness, I was not allowed to hear anyone else's testimony so as not to taint my own.

I appeared at the Assistant United States Attorney's (AUSA) Office around 4:00 p.m. to go over some things about the trial. I was not instructed as to what to say on the witness stand. I was merely prepped, meaning that I was told what to expect and how the process worked so I would not become overwhelmed by anything. I was informed as to what the specific charges against the defendant were and that he was claiming the defense of entrapment. That enabled me to know what the focus of the trial would be, and it allowed me to think clearly about the importance of answering the questions as carefully and accurately as possible. That is not to imply that I would not have done that had it not been for this meeting. However, walking into a situation knowing what to expect makes it much easier to adapt to it and to think with a clear head and a defined focus.

The meeting was also important for me to inform the AUSA of any issues that I was not comfortable discussing in open court. I had some reservations about giving out my home address, considering the situation. I also did not want to delve too deeply into my personal life, not that it had any bearing whatsoever on my credibility or the case, but I did not feel comfortable exposing too much in front of someone I was going to testify against. It was not as though I was one of his real victims who had to talk about the harm that he had inflicted upon me. I was more closely aligned with the FBI agents, and in their capacity as law enforcement officers, they do not have to sit on the stand and talk about their personal lives. I realized that I was not in the same arena with them, so I understood the need for the jury to know my motives for doing what I do on the Internet and to become somewhat familiar with the kind of person that I am. I suppose that was the part that worried me the most.

On Thursday, January 20, 2005, Agent Berglas took the stand and began his testimony. I was told to appear at the AUSA's Office at noon when they were expected back there on a break from court. I arrived on time but was informed that Agent Berglas' testimony was running long and I would not begin that day, so I was sent back to the hotel and at the AUSA's request, returned to their office at 5:00 p.m. to prep again. The session took the rest of the evening. The next day, Friday, January 21, 2005, I was expected to testify. Agent Berglas was still on the stand, but he was due to finish shortly. I was brought into the witness room where I was to wait my turn. A few other witnesses in the case were also in there. They were all members of law enforcement. Apparently, Brand had been chatting on the Internet with other law enforcement personnel from different parts of the country thinking they were all teenage girls. They were going to testify at his trial about their own experiences with him. We all sat huddled in the small witness room that was so close to the courtroom that we could hear the murmured voice of Agent Berglas testifying through the wall. We could not make out what he was saying and we wouldn't have recognized his voice, but we were told that I was next and I knew that I was going on the stand after him. As I sat there wondering what his testimony was, I knew that at any moment I would hear nothing—just a long period of silence that meant Agent Berglas was finished and I would be called to testify. So I kept an ear open amid the chatter in the witness room, waiting for the pause in Agent Berglas' testimony.

There I sat, amid talks of other cases and suspects, news of older cases that I had been involved in, and discussions of life in the child predator arena, all to make the time pass. My nerves were getting pretty shaky with all of the "what if's" still going through my mind. Every now and then, I took a walk out into the main hallway just to calm my nerves. Brand's parents were sitting out there, and as much as I did not want to see them, or have them see me, I really needed to move around. I don't think they knew who I was at that point, but I could only imagine what they would have been thinking if they did. Their son was on trial for a hideous crime, one that they probably could not even fathom that he had committed. I assume that I'd feel the same way if my own sons had been accused of such a crime. But the evidence in the case against Brand was compelling. There was no doubt that he was guilty. I understood that his parents did not know that and most likely did not want to know it. They probably didn't even see the evidence.

Brand's father was planning to testify. He was not allowed into the courtroom to watch the proceedings, and his wife sat in the hallway with him while he waited his turn. I thought that it might have been easier for them to deal with what was happening to their son if they knew the truth, if they had seen the transcripts of the chats and heard the tape recordings of the conversations between Brand and the young girl he was clearly meeting for sex. It might have made them understand that he was dangerous, and at the very least, needed to be as far away from children as possible.

I walked around the hallway briefly and, after stretching my legs, headed back towards the witness room. As I passed Brand's parents, our eyes met. I quickly looked away and walked through the double doors to the hallway leading back to where I was to wait. They may not have known who I was yet, but I knew that I was about to put the key into their son's prison cell door and turn it tight.

I joined the others and waited. Suddenly, the witness room became silent, as did the courtroom. I heard footsteps coming towards the door, and my heart began to pound. The door opened and everything I was thinking and feeling felt as though it had been drained out of my body through my feet. I stood up and leaned on the table for a moment to steady myself. The AUSA's paralegal peaked in and let me know it was time. She led me into the courtroom and down the long aisle to the witness stand. I passed by the jury box to the left and briefly glanced over at the faces that followed me as I passed by. There was a mix of men and women, all concerned-looking individuals. To my right, I passed the defense table with Matt Brand and his legal team. In front of them was the prosecutor's table with the AUSAs, their paralegal, and Agent Berglas. I felt more comfortable seeing him sitting there.

I climbed into the witness box and was sworn in. A couple of deep breaths helped me relax a bit as I sat down and scanned the room. I had been at trials many times as an attorney, but this was different. I was going to be testifying against someone and the results could be devastating, but I had a responsibility to tell the truth and finish what I had started.

I was asked my name and where I lived. I had been previously informed that I did not have to reveal my actual address, just the general location of my residence. I was asked about my marital status and the details about my family, my children, my grandchildren, my education, and my work history.

The ice was broken. The more I talked, the more relaxed I became. There were even a few laughs in the courtroom when the judge commented that I shouldn't go back to school again because of my history with car accidents right after graduation.

The questions continued. I was asked how I began doing Internet work with the FBI. I described to the court how a sexual predator had gone after my son and other neighborhood boys and how I went onto the Internet looking for him. I talked about how I invented a screen name and profile and found the chatrooms where sexual predators hang out. I discussed what the chats with them were like and the types of pictures they send to me thinking that I am a young girl. I described the nude pictures of men with their genitalia displayed and the ones showing people having various forms of sex and sometimes, just showing the man masturbating.

I was asked about my involvement with the FBI and how and why I came to calling them the first time. I recounted how the first man had instant messaged me, and I discussed the nude pictures of him that he had emailed me within the first few minutes of our chat. I told the jury about the phone calls that I have been asked to make to sexual predators and how they are arranged. I described the types of phone conversations I have, some that they had already heard on the courtroom tape recorder.

Then, the questioning became more specific regarding why I was there that particular day. I was asked about my contact with Brand while he was using the screen name Tempoteech. After discussing the screen name that I had created and the young girl's name that I used, I talked about the chatroom that I frequent in search of a place where child predators might congregate. Then, the questioning became even more focused. Brand's photograph was shown to me, and I was asked if I could identify it. It was one that I recognized from an email that he had sent to Sara. I stated that it was, in fact, the picture that I received from him. Next, my chats with Tempoteech were introduced into evidence. The transcript of my first chat with him was displayed on a large screen opposite the jury box where everyone in the courtroom could see it. I was given a laptop-sized screen and a pointer and I was instructed to use the pointer to identify the participants in the chat. The original chats were time-stamped, so it was clear what time of day or night we were communicating. I explained who Tempoteech was and who Sara was and anything else that appeared on that particular screen. I then proceeded to discuss how the chat had progressed. I was asked to read from it and sometimes to summarize what we had said to each other.

By this time, I felt pretty comfortable. The judge had put me at ease with his comments, and the jury looked engrossed in everything I was describing. I did not get the impression that they questioned my credibility. I felt that my answers were coherent and that the evidence that I was discussing was clearly helping the jury to see the whole scenario between Brand and Sara as it had unfolded. One after the other, the chats were put up on the screen, and I went over them, pointing out all of the important details that the jury needed to see.

I rarely looked at Brand, but, when I did, I noticed that he never seemed to change his expression. I suppose he knew that he was finished with his quest for children as well as his freedom. He had participated in all of the chats with me and, to be honest, from what I subsequently heard, he pretty much said the same things to all of the "girls" with whom he thought he had been chatting, both before and after me. He knew that other witnesses would be providing similar testimony after I was finished, so it would be hard for him to explain all of that away.

The transcripts of the chats were explicit. There was really no way to give the impression that there was anything innocent about them. And, as with the others, this was not a "he said, she said" situation. It was all in black and white.

Brand had chatted with Sara before he chatted with Julie, but Agent

Berglas went on the stand first to lay the groundwork about my work with him, how the communications on the phone take place, and what Brand said to him during their chats. The jury was seeing some of my information as repetition of what Brand said to another girl, but that was good because it was easier for them to remember it that way, and it also made clear the fact that Brand was going after different girls saying the same things. There was no mistake and no misinterpretation.

During Agent Berglas' testimony, the jury had also heard the recordings of the phone calls that I made to Brand. So, they were able to listen to the actual voices of Brand and one of his potential, young victims. That was extremely damaging for him. The first phone call that I made to Brand was on February 11, 2004. He had requested it from Julie, a.k.a. Agent Berglas. They were planning to meet the next day at Port Authority and Brand probably wanted the call so he could reassure himself that he was truly communicating with a young girl rather than the police. We talked mainly about where the meeting was supposed to take place. He instructed thirteen-year-old Julie to take a cab to Port Authority where he said that he would be waiting with a sign that had her name on it. That way she wouldn't have any trouble recognizing him. During that first call, Brand told Julie he was on his way to teach and asked her to call him back later, so I did. The second call was more specific. It turned to sex. The following is part of that phone conversation. It has been edited to delete any non-relevant parts of the communication. Nothing has been done to change the context or meaning of the conversation.

Brand: Now don't going learnin' all this stuff that you want me
        to teach you and go finding some other man.
Julie: I wouldn't do something like that.
Brand: Okay.
Julie: Like, tell me like what kind of stuff you're gonna
        teach me.
Brand: Well, you tell me what you wanna learn.

Julie: Well, like you said.

Brand: I wanna hear you say it, what do you wanna learn?

Julie: I don't know, everything, I guess.

Brand: Like? What do you wanna do with me?

Julie: Well, you said like you were gonna show me how to be a woman and everything. So, what do you mean by that?

Brand: Tell me what you want me to do to you, come on. Don't be embarrassed. Tell me.

Julie: Well, cause, like I don't know so much, you know like, sex stuff and everything.

Brand: What do you wanna learn sexually?

Julie: Like, whatever you meant when you said you were gonna teach me stuff.

Brand: You want me to touch you?

Julie: Yeah.

Brand: Where do you want me to touch you?

Julie: Well, where do you wanna touch me?

Brand: I know where I wanna touch you. Where do you want me to touch you?

Julie: So, where? I feel funny sayin' it.

Brand: Don't be, don't feel funny, just tell me. I would love to touch you.

Brand: Do you want me to touch your breasts?

Julie: Yeah.

Brand: Do you want me to touch your crotch?

Julie: Yeah.

Brand: And, where do you wanna touch me?

Julie: Wherever you want me to.

Brand: Do you have nice breasts?

Julie: I think so.

Brand: You gonna let me touch them.

Julie: Yeah, I want to.

Brand: Do you want me to put my mouth on them?

Julie: Yeah.

Brand: Okay.

Brand: Do you have a nice ass?

Julie: Yeah.

Brand: Do you want me to touch that?

Julie: Yeah.

Brand: Yeah? What about your crotch? Do you want me to touch that?

Julie: Yeah.

Brand: What do you want me to touch it with?

Julie: Well, whatever you want would be good.

Brand: I just wanna make you feel good.

Julie: Will it hurt?

Brand: I won't hurt ya.

Julie: Okay.

Brand: Be very gentle.

Julie: 'Cause my friend says some sex hurts.

Brand: Well then, you have to tell me if it hurts.

Julie: Like, what would hurt?

Brand: Well, maybe using my penis would hurt.

Julie: But, your not gonna like, make it hurt like that?

Brand: I'm not gonna hurt you. I wouldn't do anything that you don't want me to do and I won't hurt you.

Julie: Why does it hurt?

Brand: Because maybe it's too big and because you're a virgin.

Julie: How could it not hurt?

Brand: 'Cause I don't have to use my penis.

Julie: Oh, you don't want to?

Brand: I do, but I don't have to use it right away.

Julie: Like, what else could you do?

Brand: Use my fingers.

Julie: Okay.

Brand: Use my tongue.

Julie: Okay. You really want to?

Brand: Do you want me to?

Julie: Yeah.

Brand: You want me to put my tongue on you?

Julie: Yeah.

Brand: Tell me.

Julie: I feel funny.

Brand: Tell me where you want me to put my tongue.

Julie: Well, all the stuff you said.

Brand: It's okay. It gets me excited if you say it.

Brand: Do you wanna kiss me?

Julie: Yeah.

Brand: Do you wanna hold me?

Julie: Yeah.

Brand: Do you wanna be with me?

Julie: Yeah.

Brand: Okay. You might even wanna be my girlfriend.

Julie: That'd be so cool. Do you really want me to?

Brand: Would I have said it if I didn't?

Julie: No.

Brand: What do you want?

Julie: All the stuff you said it's what I want.

Brand: Do you want me?

Julie: Yeah.

Brand: Do you wanna be with me?

Julie: Yeah.

Brand: Do you wanna be my girlfriend?

Julie: Yeah.

Brand: Then tell me.

Julie: I wanna be your girlfriend.

Brand: Okay, then. I'm not gonna hurt you. I'm not gonna do anything you don't wanna do. I'm gonna take care of you and make you feel good.

Julie: Am I gonna like, get pregnant or anything?

Brand: No.

Julie: How come?

Brand: 'Cause I'll use protection . . . I'll use a condom.

The jury heard that tape along with two others, the last of which was to confirm the meeting. The evidence was compelling. Brand knew that Julie was thirteen, and he made clear his intentions to have sexual relations with her. He never hesitated. He could have stopped at any time. He could have answered that last question by telling her, "You won't get pregnant because we are not going to have sex." But, he didn't say that because it would have defeated his entire purpose for meeting her.

By the end of my first day of testimony, the defense attorney began his cross-examination and it became obvious that I would have to travel back into Manhattan on Monday, January 24, 2005, for another day on the witness stand. We adjourned for the weekend. I was due back at the hotel on Sunday night, but a major snowstorm hit New York from Saturday night through Sunday, leaving at least two feet of snow. We were buried in it, so I had to wait for it to end and dig out in order to drive back to the hotel on the treacherous, icy roads. I was hoping that my trip wouldn't be for nothing. The possibility existed that someone else who was crucial to the trial might be snowed in and unable to appear. Thankfully, that did not happen.

On Monday, I took the stand feeling pretty confident. I had already spent a lot of time testifying, and I believed that I had made a good impression on the jury. I did not have any of the reservations that had plagued me during the previous week. I walked across the courtroom, climbed up into the witness chair, and waited for the defense attorney to begin his cross.

It became clear that his questions were meant to confuse and intimidate me. He was trying to convey to the jury that I had latched onto his client and encouraged him to talk to me about sex. He portrayed me as a liar, since I use a fake name and profile and tell sexual predators that

I am thirteen years old. He was grasping at straws. All of the evidence against his client was damning. He ignored the notion that the jury might recognize the need for people to go undercover in order to catch certain types of criminals. It is common practice. That is what undercover stings are all about. Yet, the defense attorney must have thought that by making me confess that I had lied to men on the Internet, the jurors would view me as lacking credibility.

Another futile attempt that the defense attorney made to discredit me was the suggestion that when I respond to men with nice comments after they had made one to me, it meant that I was encouraging them, instigating more chats, and leading them into sex talk. For example, after Brand said he wanted to meet me, by asking him what we were going to do when we met, the attorney implied that I was encouraging sex talk. He dramatized everything I had said to make it look as though it was me who kept the conversation with Brand going. And, he apparently tried to convince the jury that I was deceitful because I hid my true identity. Of course I did! Imagine if I had revealed who I really am to one of the sexual predators. "Hi, I'm married, a mother, and a grandmother. Are you a child predator? Because if you are, you should know right up front that I'm going to turn you over to the FBI if you talk about sex with me." Better yet, consider an undercover officer telling a suspect, "I'm an agent with the FBI. Are you a sexual predator?"

The other issue that the defense attorney appeared to be trying to use to his advantage was the fact that I responded to Brand that I liked him after he told me he liked me. The attorney must have thought it significant to get me to confess that I didn't really like Brand so he could prove I had lied about that, too. I had to laugh at that one. What if a predator told me he liked me and I responded, "I don't like you"? Did the defense attorney expect me to answer that way? Did he think the jury would fault me for allowing a predator to believe that I wanted to be his girlfriend so he would come on to me rather than a real child? His suppositions were quite ridiculous considering how many undercover operations are used to catch criminals every day, but he pressed on with other seemingly irrelevant questions.

He asked me if I had any training in psychology, or dealing with people who suffer from depression, or communicating with people with low self-esteem. It was clear where he was heading with that. He was going to claim that his client was depressed, had low self-esteem, and was vulnerable enough to fall prey to someone posing as a thirteen-year-old girl. I suppose he could have gotten the jurors' attention with that, had I gone after Brand and hounded him into discussing sex and meeting me, but all of the evidence painted quite a different picture. I did not make first contact. I did not talk about dating him first. I never brought up sex first. I never told him "I like you" or "I love you" first. I did not ask for a meeting or for his phone number, and I only called when he requested me to. There were no firsts for me. The final proof that this man was nothing more than a calculating and manipulative child predator was the fact that he had never even seen my picture, yet he had already discussed how much he loved me and wanted to marry me. I gave him every chance to walk away, and he finally did, but only after I told him that I had been in a car accident and had broken some bones, so I couldn't meet him for a long time. He did not hesitate to move on to Julie.

He didn't seem very vulnerable when I was talking to him on the phone as Julie and he was telling me all of the sexual things that he wanted to do to me, insisting that I tell him the things that I wanted him to do. He had complete control of the conversation. Most of my responses consisted of the word "Yeah."

Something else to consider were the other witnesses who were called to the stand after my testimony ended. One was a special agent who performed a forensics examination on Brand's computer to see what was on the hard drive. It was filled with child pornography. Also testifying was the special agent who aided in Brand's arrest and the search of his car. He testified as to the contents of the vehicle. Among the items found were three individually wrapped condoms in Brand's glove compartment. Also in the car were Polaroid pictures, one of a young girl wearing a t-shirt and lying on a bed. She was seen holding a giant toy Game-Boy; another picture was of the same girl, but her image was taken in the mirror while she was wearing yellow pajamas, smiling, and holding a very large toothbrush and a tube of toothpaste; the third depicted the same girl with her image taken in a mirror, wearing the same pajamas and holding the same toothpaste and toothbrush. Several other pictures of young girls were also found in the car.

The next person to testify was an FBI agent from out-of-state who also posed as a thirteen-year-old girl on the Internet and was contacted by Brand. Posing as Tempoteech, he offered to sing with her, dance with her, hold hands, and kiss.

Then, the special agent who had initiated the pat-down search of Brand after his arrest was called to the stand. He testified that he found in Brand's pocket an 8 x 11 piece of white paper with the name "Julie" on it. That agent also participated in Brand's questioning. He stated that Brand had admitted that he was at the Port Authority Bus Terminal to meet the girl that he had been communicating with for about a month through chats, emails, and phone calls. He said that his conversations with Julie began with voice lessons and progressed to discussing the sexual acts in which they would engage. He admitted to having told her he would lick her breasts and her crotch, and that she would not get pregnant because he would use a condom. He also acknowledged receiving and viewing child pornography on the Internet, saying that some were images of children as young as eight years old. Brand also admitted having chatted with Sara.

The final government witness was a detective with the sex offense squad of an upstate New York Police Department who was assigned to the FBI's Innocent Images Task Force. She had also posed as a thirteen-year-old girl on the Internet and had a chat with Brand while he was using the screen name Tempoteech and she was sitting in one of the chatrooms generally frequented by sexual predators. Their chat was a typical Tempoteech chat. He invited her to come to New Jersey by bus and offered to pay her back for the fare. When it became clear that the "girl" was not getting on a bus to meet him, he cut the chat off and ended communications with her. The situation was just one more piece of evidence that Brand was scoping out chatrooms looking for young girls to meet.

When the defense put on their case, they painted a picture of Brand as a "vulnerable and depressed man" who was so desperate for someone to tell him "that he mattered" and that he was "okay," that he fell into some kind of government trap. The defense attorney used the fact that Brand had stopped contact with a few of the law enforcement people as proof that he did not plan to go any further than chat. They also relied on a claim he had made after he was arrested that he thought about canceling with Julie on his way to the meeting place but felt "guilty about leaving her standing at Port Authority" alone.

The idea that those who chatted with Brand would have needed "training in psychology" and "depression" was used to show that we did not know how to handle someone with emotional problems and that we "didn't care" what would happen to someone who had those problems. The defense attorney said we used "guilt" to get Brand to meet Julie because we made phone calls to him on the day of the meeting, even though those calls were made at his insistence. The attorney claimed that, "The FBI, through its tactics, can manipulate, seduce, and entrap a vulnerable and susceptible, and depressed man."

The defense also stated that Brand was not predisposed to committing this type of crime. You may wonder what that claim was based on. I sure did! They based it on the fact that Brand had never before been accused of this type of crime. Translated into my language, this was simply the first time Brand got caught.

Another claim that was made was that Brand's possession on his computer of several images of child pornography, child erotica, and various pictures of young girls depicted in different stages of undress had no bearing on what he would have done in person with a child. Okay, but what about predisposition? Possessing child pornography does put Brand into the category of someone who has sexual thoughts about children. That's a pretty significant place to start, but also consider the things Brand said in the phone calls, and the chats, and the actions that he took to meet a thirteen-year-old girl.

So, let's connect the dots. Matt Brand, using the screen name Tempoteech, signed onto his computer and searched through chatrooms where older men hang out trolling for young girls. On a number of occasions he came across thirteen-year-olds with whom he made first contact. When he saw that some of them lived too far away to meet, he quickly cut them off and moved on to find another child. His chats were pretty consistent, mentioning singing, dancing, kissing, etc. Then he found Sara, a young, teenage virgin from New York. Finally, he had found someone close enough to meet. He immediately began grooming her, talking about dating, asking for a description, telling her about all of the things he could teach her, offering her free lessons, trying to convince her that she could be a model and an actress, talking about being in love with her and getting married, then, asking her to take a cab to Port Authority where he'd meet her and pay for it. Just the fact that he called her his girlfriend and said that they would get married is pretty clear. It was also obvious that Brand was not looking for a real relationship, a mature one that might fulfill the needs of a lonely, depressed adult male. He just wanted to have sex with a young girl, and he had made several attempts to do that until he finally found the perfect target. Then, he offered her the world, thereby convincing her to meet him.

In short, Brand was not entrapped. After all, who was the vulnerable one in the relationship? Was it the thirty-six-year-old man who consistently went after young girls on the Internet, or was it the person who did everything she could to portray a young, inexperienced thirteen-year-old teen? She never brought up sex. She never even sent him her picture. She rarely responded beyond, "Yeah." The few chats they had progressed quickly. Then, she told him that she was in a car accident, so the vulnerable, depressed Brand, the man who was so desperate for someone to simply tell him that he matters, went ahead and dumped the little girl who was sitting home suffering with broken bones. It was that easy. He never communicated with her again. Instead, he moved right on to groom Julie, who also lived in New York and happened to be Sara's best friend. He did the same thing with her that he did with Sara. He offered her free lessons. He sent her his picture and asked for hers. Imagine what the jurors thought when they heard that her picture was found in Brand's computer in a folder entitled "Possibles." Wasn't that a bit telling? Possible what?

Brand complimented Julie. He talked to her about having fun. He told her that he was single. He asked if she liked older guys. He told her he was free. He commented that she was gorgeous. He offered himself to her as a boyfriend. He said he wanted to take her out, and he told her that she was not too young for him. Then, he asked her to be his Valentine.

But the vulnerable, depressed Brand also said that he knew what he was doing was wrong and that he could get into trouble for it. His intentions were clear. He was not talking about getting into trouble for telling her she's gorgeous. He had moved in quickly. It did not take any time at all for things to get hot and heavy between him and Julie. He gave her his number and asked for phone calls. He wanted to hear her voice. He wanted to set up the meeting. When she called, he discussed all of the different sexual things he wanted to do to her even though she told him that she was nervous. She responded in a way that made him say, "Don't be shy, what do you wanna do with me?" He planned to take her back to his house. "We'll have privacy," he said. He told her all of the things he wanted to do to her. He wanted to kiss her breasts and her crotch. He was going to use his fingers and his tongue. He would use a condom to keep her from getting pregnant. Julie's responses can only be described as coy and shy, just like an innocent, teenage virgin. He encouraged her to say more, to say things that excited him. He had complete control of the conversation as well as the entire situation. He arranged everything: the meeting place, the taxi fare, the sign he would hold when she arrived so she would know who he was. He did everything he could to make it enticing to her. He never hesitated, never told her he had second thoughts, never even implied that this was nothing more than a fantasy of his. He had a calculated plan from the moment he began hunting through chatrooms for little girls. He would find one vulnerable enough to let him move in on her, groom her, talk to her on the phone, and ultimately meet her for sex.

So when it came to Brand's defense of entrapment, it was hard to see how it would hold up in the face of such compelling evidence. The government would have had to induce Brand to commit the crime, to go after him, and push him to do something he would have never done under ordinary circumstances. But they didn't, and that's why they claimed as part of their case that Brand had the propensity to commit the crime, that he was ready, willing, and able to do it.

It was clear that there was no inducement on the part of the agents. Brand initiated all of the communications with the people he thought were young girls, and he admitted communicating with many more of them. Further, all of the evidence clearly demonstrated that Brand had a definite propensity for committing this crime. Add to that his collection of child pornography, which, in and of itself, did not warrant a verdict of guilty in this case, but it did show what his state of mind was, how he thought about young children, and what his interests in them were. The fact that he acted on those interests is what brought him to where he was on that day, sitting in a courtroom on trial.

The prosecutor, in his closing argument, referred to the investigation and arrest of Matt Brand as one of the FBI's finer moments. He had laid out all of Brand's actions during the trial and finally ended by explaining to the jury he had proven Brand's guilt beyond a reasonable doubt, a finding necessary in a criminal trial to obtain a conviction. The prosecutor had made a compelling case against Brand, one that was hard to beat. Then, the case was turned over to the jury.

On January 27, 2005, three days after my testimony, the jurors filed back into the courtroom. They had deliberated carefully, calling for much of the evidence for review. They had reached a unanimous verdict, finding Brand guilty on both counts of the indictment. He was immediately remanded to federal prison. After the jury announced its verdict, I received the news from Agent Berglas that we had won. I breathed a long, deep sigh of relief.

Subsequently, Brand was sentenced to serve a term of five years in federal prison.

Matthew Brand appealed his conviction, and on October 19, 2006, in a forty-eight page decision in the case of *United States v. Brand*, 05-4155-cr., the U.S. Court of Appeals for the Second Circuit upheld the ruling of the district court by affirming Brand's conviction.

NINE

Confessions of a Sexual Predator

IT ISN'T OFTEN THAT WE HAVE THE OPPORTUNITY TO SEE A sexual predator in action, as he or she explains away their reasons for showing up to meet a thirteen-year-old girl. Yes, we have seen some of them on television news programs, shows specifically set up to demonstrate to us how easy it is for predators to communicate with our children and how very eager they are to meet with them in person. Those deviants are often seen fleeing from the cameras or using the typical excuse that they never had anything to do with a child before and that they would not have had sex with the one they showed up to meet. Sounds like the same old story from people who don't want to be arrested and prosecuted for breaking the law in such a disgusting and immoral way.

My story takes the sexual predator's explanation one step further. I bring you right into the courtroom where you will see what a sexual predator actually claimed as he sat on the witness stand and spun his tale for the jury.

Dennis Joseph, also known on AOL as Dsax25, first instant messaged thirteen-year-old Lorie, Teen2hot4u, in July 2005. In describing who he was, he used his real first name (Dennis) and his real location (72nd St. by Central Park). He discussed his real profession (musician) and even told the young girl that he was married. It was obvious that he wanted to impress her and make her like him. So he bragged

143

about his accomplishments, probably thinking that this young teen would be so enamored by him that she would allow him to lure her out of her house to meet him. He even attempted to entice her by revealing the more impressive locations where he played his music, Broadway, Carnegie Hall, and various other places where he traveled to with his band. And, in fact, Dennis Joseph really did play at impressive locations. His band's website, www.MartyStevens.com, lists him under what appears to be his stage name, Dennis Stevens. Next to his picture, there is a biography that says he is a "world class musician" and that he "has played at Carnegie Hall" and "conducted at Avery Fischer Hall." It continues that he has "performed with such celebrities as Ashford and Simpson, Stevie Wonder, Bill Cosby, Sting, and the Billy Strayhorn Orchestra." Even more impressive, the site states that he "was featured on stage in the Broadway show *Fosse,* and plays on the soundtrack for Martin Scorcese's film, *The Aviator.*" Dennis Joseph let the young girls he chatted with know all about his "impressive" credentials in an apparent attempt to groom them into being with him.

But, Dsax25 didn't stop there. He chatted a great deal about sex, graphically describing each and every sexual act he wanted to perform with Lorie, "69, oral sex, bondage, doggie style, tantric sex, [and] mutual masturbation." Yet, when it came time for him to testify in a court of law and explain how and why he would talk to a young girl the way he did, he claimed it was all part of a fantasy world where people make up everything they say in order to role-play or have cybersex on the Internet.

Dsax25 first approached Teen2hot4u in her usual Internet chat-room hangout, "I Love Older Men." He moved in on her the same way that many others had: complimenting her, talking about her interests, and letting her know how much more understanding men are than boys. It was his grooming method, and he continued to instant message Lorie and email her at least fifty times over the course of less than two months. His chats quickly became sexually explicit, leaving little to the imagination. After communicating with the young girl for several weeks, he then moved on to one of her friends, a thirteen-year-old gymnast named Julie, also known as Agent Berglas. Dsax25 had suggested meeting Lorie, but she never agreed. However, when he asked Julie to meet him, she complied.

On August 31, 2005, Dennis Joseph ventured out to attend two meetings in Manhattan. The first was about business. Then, he headed for his second meeting, one that would forever change his life.

He boarded the *C* train, which stopped near Franklin Street. He exited the train and asked someone for directions to his destination, the place where he was to meet the young thirteen-year-old girl he knew as Julie. He headed south until he arrived at a place called the Franklin Street Café. There, he stood looking around for Julie, when he suddenly felt a tap on the shoulder. That was when his nightmare began.

Instead of seeing the little girl he had planned to meet, he came face to face with an FBI agent. Other agents soon arrived and Dennis Joseph found himself face down on the ground in handcuffs. He was arrested, searched, and brought in to FBI headquarters in Manhattan for questioning and processing where he acknowledged that he thought Julie was thirteen.

Due to his background in music, his specialty apparently being saxophone, a *New York Post* newspaper article detailing his arrest was entitled "Sax Pervert."

Dennis Joseph was charged with using the Internet to attempt to entice a minor to engage in sexual activity. In order to prove their case, the government had to show three things: that Dennis Joseph used a means of interstate commerce, i.e. the Internet; that he attempted to entice a minor to engage in a sexual act; and that had he succeeded in engaging in the sexual act with the minor, it would have been a violation of New York law. Two prongs of the government's case were not in dispute: one, there was no question that Dennis Joseph used the Internet to chat with the young girl; and two, sexual contact with a person under the age of fourteen is a crime under New York law. The only thing left to prove was the intent of the defendant.

Dennis Joseph retained the same defense counsel as Jason Corso, also known as "Profphoto j," the first man I had turned over to the FBI. Corso pleaded guilty. Dennis Joseph took the other option of going to trial. His claim was that everything he said to Julie and Lorie was merely role-play. In other words, he was apparently going to try to convince the jury that he had made up a persona and playacted the entire time, claiming that his only interest was in cybersex, or, in his words, "tantalizing conversation."

His trial was somewhat more interesting than others I have taken part in, because this defendant took the bold step of testifying on his own behalf. He wanted to lay his cards right out on the table for the whole world to see, as embarrassing as that must have been. But, I suppose he felt that a little humiliation was better than going to prison.

Apparently, Dennis Joseph's attorney, Robert Altchiler's, strategy was to discredit me, as well as the other witnesses. I understood his need to do that, but there was just no way he was going to succeed, mainly because he had one big problem—his client was guilty and the evidence was in black and white!

Altchiler had given a forceful opening statement, probably planting some very arduous seeds into the jurors' minds. He told them about a woman named Stephanie Good, a "very nice lady." But, he also made sure to explain that I am "not trained the way that FBI agents are trained to do investigations like this." While he put the suggestion before the jury that I am "not trained," he also let them know in no uncertain terms that his client, Dennis Joseph, "is an expert" on the Internet, because "he has actually seen profile, after profile, after profile." His comment was most likely meant to open the door for a discussion about what he referred to as my "sexually-charged profile," Teen2hot4u.

Then, Altchiler took his description of my actions one step further; "Stephanie Good has a plan," he explained, "because . . . she needs to now create a crime. And that is what she is intent on doing." In essence, he was saying that I needed to find material for this book. So, he presented to the jury a picture of the events that had transpired between Lorie, Julie, and Dsax25 to make it appear as though I had gone after his client and pressured him into the arms of FBI Agent Berglas, disguised as Julie. Altchiler insisted that I had done everything I could to "lure" his client to contact Julie when, in fact, Dennis Joseph jumped at the chance to move on to another thirteen-year-old girl after Lorie continuously said that she couldn't meet him. And, Altchiler claimed that his client suspected very early on that Julie and Lorie were really adults. He said that one reason his client believed this was because Julie's picture was of a girl with long nails, and his "client, who spends a tremendous amount of time studying women's bodies, noticed immediately" that "this is no gymnast." Here's why that theory was problematic. Agent Berglas used the childhood picture of a close friend of mine, Dorothy Welch. And Dorothy, in fact, *was* a gymnast as a teenager. But, she was also involved with something else. She loved having long nails. So, she had them as long as she could. And, when Dorothy did gymnastics as a teenager, she did it with long nails.

There was also something else that this "expert" suddenly claimed, one year after chatting with Julie. He said that the two pictures that she had sent him of herself were of two different girls. However, they were not. One was taken of Dorothy at a theme park and the other was taken the same year during a holiday when she was dressed up. Dorothy was called to testify and I would imagine that it was a big surprise to Dennis Joseph when he had to face the truth in front of the jury; he was no expert!

Altchiler also said that at some point in time, Dsax25 stopped communicating with Teen2hot4u. He used that as proof that Dennis Joseph was only fantasizing and would never have met Lorie. The truth is, there had been many gaps in our communications besides the six days between our last chat and the day Dennis Joseph showed up to meet Julie and was arrested. As a matter of fact, one gap was three weeks long!

My theory is that had Julie put off meeting Dennis Joseph, he would have bounced back to Lorie. However, because Lorie had never agreed to Dsax25's suggestions of meetings, and because she began telling him things like how she wasn't feeling well, she had to go to the dentist, and that it hurt to have a cavity fixed, he got bored and moved on to Lorie's good friend Julie, Agent Berglas in disguise.

But, Altchiler posed a different theory. He accused me of "pushing" Julie on his client. I assume that his intention was to influence the jury to believe that I was trying to convince, or induce, his client, a man who claimed that he had no interest in having sex with a thirteen-year-old girl, to have sex with Julie. In truth, I did mention my friend Julie to Dsax25 throughout some of our communications. It's that simple. I didn't ask him to have sex with her. I merely mentioned her. I didn't have her contact him, and just like any other sexual predator who is hunting for young girls to have sex with, Dsax25 jumped at the chance to chat with her. He emailed her first. He instant messaged her first. Nobody forced him to communicate with her. He did it because he wanted to. When Altchiler kept pounding at me on the witness stand about "pushing" his client to talk to Julie, my response was honest. Here is how the dialogue went:

> Altchiler: And again, at this point you are powerfully trying to influence him towards Julie?
>
> Me: He had just said to me, "My God the things I could do to you, make your whole body tingle. So, I mention Julie again, because I don't want him to make my body tingle. I want him to make Agent Berglas' body tingle."

As you can imagine, there were quite a few chuckles in the courtroom. We volleyed back and forth, with me often deflecting the ball back into Altchiler's court. He seemed to mischaracterize chats in an apparent attempt to convince the jury that I had been breaking the rules that the FBI had laid before me. The judge often stopped him in his tracks, as did the prosecutor. In the end, I left the witness stand feeling that I had accomplished what I had set out to do; I had told the truth and it came across loud and clear. I doubt that Altchiler was very pleased with me.

Altchiler's other apparent trial strategy was to try to convince the jury that his client had some sexual limitations that not only prevented him from having sex with a minor, but that it would also prove he would have never even tried. It appeared as though he wanted the jurors to get the message that in the event that Dennis Joseph might have actually ventured out to meet a child for sex, well, that was nothing more than a set-up, because according to Altchiler, Agent Berglas and I enticed and lured his client into breaking the law. In other words, we had entrapped him.

On July 11, 2006, Dennis Joseph took an oath to tell the truth. Then, he sat in front of the jury in a federal courthouse and spun his web of deceit.

Dennis Joseph discussed his main interests, muscles and body-building, and said that he spent a lot of time searching the Internet for bodybuilders and pictures of muscular women. It must have been difficult for jurors to believe his claims since neither Julie nor Lorie's profile contained anything to indicate that they were either muscular or interested in bodybuilding. In fact, when Dsax25 mentioned to Lorie that she "might have some muscle" on her, she responded that she wasn't "so muscular." However, Dennis Joseph spent days testifying about his obsession with muscle flexing, even going as far as to confess that whenever he chatted, he had a picture of a female bodybuilder in the center of his screen to focus on. The following is some of his testimony. I often comment throughout the following pages in order to clarify inconsistencies or sometimes just give my opinion. Certain parts may be edited for purposes of space, however nothing that changes the context of testimony has been deleted.

ALTCHILER: Who is Dsax25?

DENNIS J.:   Dsax is really a version of myself. My personal fantasy online has developed to be a version of myself that does things I can't really do. I can't have tantalizing conversations in real life, but I can do them as Dsax25. I can't have any kind of casual sex or any kind of really kinky off-the-wall kind of sex in real life, but I can do that online as Dsax25 online. My age as Dsax25, although it implies 25, I can be any age that's appropriate to whatever situation I'm chatting about. My marital status can be any situation that I want that's appropriate to what I'm chatting about.

The things such as bodybuilding, music, movies, those muscles, and I would pretend that my arms were 18 or 19 inches; that my chest was 50 inches; that, you know, I could bench three or four hundred pounds. And I would give a description of things that I had read in bodybuilding magazines or, you know, use my imagination to come up with something that would sound realistic.

But, he didn't seem to be using his imagination when he was telling Lorie all about himself and his life, did he?

ALTCHILER: Did anyone teach you nuances or did anyone give you an education about how it worked?
DENNIS J.: No. There is no education. You get the software. You install it. And you just go and do, and you learn from experience.
ALTCHILER: . . . what led you to seeing [Lorie's] profile?
DENNIS J.: I searched the database for female bodybuilders that were online, female weightlifters that were online, female power lifters that were online,

ran through my hierarchy of muscle-related topics. Whatever profile popped up that I sent a "hello" to, probably didn't respond.

Anyone who frequents AOL would know that it is highly unlikely that Dsax25 could wade through all of those databases and not be able to find one single person with whom to chat at any given time of day.

DENNIS J.: So, I would look in the next step for me was looking in the adult sex theme chat rooms on the part of America Online that's with all the chat rooms. And, under "Special Interests," there's several chat rooms that I would look through, titles such as "Dominant women," "Older women."

He has now claimed to have searched through at least two chatrooms without any luck!

DENNIS J.: Eventually, I got to "I love older men." I got to the chat room. I'm not actually going into the chat rooms. I'm clicking on a button that allows you to see the names of all the screen names that are in each chat room.
In this particular chat room, there were two names, Gary something or other. I don't remember what it was, and Teen2hot4u.

I have been going into the chatroom "I Love Older Men" for four years and there has never been one time when only two people were in there. In fact, I don't think I've ever been in that particular chatroom when there weren't at least twenty or more people in there. I can't say with one hundred percent certainty that it has never happened. But, I am certain that Teen2hot4u has absolutely never been in "I Love Older Men" with only one other person.

ALTCHILER: When you saw [Lorie's] profile, what was your reaction to it?

DENNIS J.:   Well the screen name Teen2hot4u is a very sexually suggestive screen name. It's a sexual come-on for anybody who knows anything about cybersex, that's an I-want-to-role-play, I-want-to-cybersex profile.

So, from this profile where almost everything —every single criteria that you can fill out has something sexual about it, combined with a really suggestive and sexual screen name. In an adult theme chat room, make it absolutely clear to me that this person was interested in cybersex.

The way that the profile is constructed is crafted as a complete tease from top to bottom. Everything is sexually suggestive. Everything is—has—seems to have a purpose to it. And my conclusion from that is that this is an adult.

I created the following profile for Teen2hot4u. It has evolved over a period of time. There were many things happening on the Internet that led me to add various items, but it has remained this way for a few years now (some Web-specific formatting like colors and fonts have been eliminated for inclusion here):

Name	LORIE
Location	NYC an anywhere as long as its with u
Gender	Female
Marital Status	IM 13 SO ITS JUS ME
Hobbies & Interests	BOYZ

Favorite Gadgets	BOY TOYZ / BOY TOYZ / BOY TOYZ
Occupation	SCHOOLLLLLLLLLLLLLLLLLL AN I HOPE I GET FIRED!!
Personal Quote	Lifes like this . . . uh huh . . . its all been done b4
	Say it aint so
	DONT BOTHER ME WITH ASL
	CAUSE ITS BORIN
	IM 5'3 GREEN EYES BROWN HAIR
	AN YEAH I GOT BOOBS BUT
	THATS ALL U NEED 2 KNOW . . .
	oh, an if u dont wanna send a pic . . .
	dont ask for mine!
	an if ALL u wanna do is cyber. . . ur a
	looza. . . yugh!

There is one glaring clue in the profile that lets readers know right up front the most important detail about the person who created it. If you scroll down to the fourth line next to "Marital Status," you will see that it says, "IM 13 SO ITS JUS ME."

Dsax25 claimed that he saw Lorie's profile as that of an adult woman who wanted to role-play on the computer. What he meant by that was that Lorie was an adult who wanted to make believe that she was thirteen, and that her fantasy was to talk about sex to an older man who would agree to treat her as a thirteen-year-old girl. In my opinion, that explanation was a well-thought-out defense, one that he came up with after the fact to find a way out of the mess he had gotten himself into by talking the way he did to a young girl. Let's continue looking at the profile, because this was a big part of Dsax25's defense. Most people who are familiar with Internet chatrooms, especially ones where people are trolling for sexual partners, know that there are standard questions that are asked almost ritualistically. The first is "a/s/l." As I mentioned earlier, this means that the person wants to know the age, sex, and location of whomever they are trying to contact. After hundreds of guys ask those same questions, it gets old. I have lost my patience for the redundant requests that come so often that I wonder if there is a script these guys follow, so I put specific comments into the profile in the hopes that people will read them and be discouraged from asking about those things. For a/s/l, I add the comment, "DON'T BOTHER ME WITH ASL CAUSE ITS BORIN."

Another seemingly important question that men in search of young girls almost always ask Lorie is "What size are your [and this word comes in many variations from breasts to . . . please excuse the terminology . . . tits]?" I realize that Lorie is supposed to be a young teen girl, but there is only so much daily degradation that I can put up with from those degenerate misfits. So, I added a comment into the profile that I believe sends the message to most people with an ounce of human intelligence that I really don't want to answer that question. This should be a deterrent, "AN YEAH I GOT BOOBS BUT THAT'S ALL U NEED TO KNOW." I think that makes it pretty clear that that's as far as the breast conversation is going to go; however, Dsax25 claimed that the statement was an open invitation to talk about the young girl's breasts.

The most common request Lorie gets is for her picture. It is also common for a girl to send one and not get one in return, thus the reason for "OH, AN IF U DONT WANNA SEND A PIC . . . DONT ASK FOR MINE!"

The one comment that Dennis Joseph's attorney specifically focused on during the trial was this one: "an if ALL u wanna do is cyber, ur a looza . . . yugh!" I created that one to keep away the guys who think it's fun to masturbate while chatting online about sex. As I mentioned earlier, it's easy to spot those deviants, because they almost always ask the same questions in the beginning of a chat. For example, "What are you wearing right now?" "Are you home alone?" "Can anyone see what you're typing?" "What color panties do you have on?" They get crude really quickly and it only goes downhill from there. I realize that anything written online is up for interpretation, but I did create that statement to drive those people away. I thought it would send a strong message that the young girl was not going to sit there and type sexual comments to them while they do whatever it is they want to do to themselves.

Dennis Joseph's attorney saw it as a clear message that Lorie *did* want to cyber, but that she also wanted more. That was a point of contention for him. Altchiler tried to push the issue that I was really into cybersex, that my profile as a teenager reeked of sex, and that his client had no choice but to go after me because I was so enticing. In other words, and this is my own translation after seeing transcripts of the testimony, his client has a compulsion to instant message people who he perceives as having sent out a sexual mating call by posting a profile, and it doesn't matter that the profile belongs to an apparent minor; Dennis Joseph still had no choice but to respond. If my interpretation is correct, he apparently thought that the inability to control himself was a defense that would keep him from getting into trouble. It's an interesting point of view, if you're into fantasy, role-playing, and baloney!

The rest of the profile apparently wasn't an issue, at least from the defense's point of view. When you step back and look at it objectively, as the jurors apparently did, and you hear the explanations for the comments in it, it is fairly easy to interpret it the way I meant it to be understood. For one thing, it looks like a lot of the teenagers' profiles on AOL. And, in spite of Altchiler's insinuations that it was "sexually suggestive," I have had many conversations with Agent Berglas about Lorie's profile. I recently interviewed him for purposes of this book and he reiterated his feelings that my profile is fine for the work that we do, and that he "never thought it was oozing with sex." He said it was "more like a thirteen-year-old girl's profile would be." He "never had a problem with it" and "he never thought it was jeopardizing any investigation," and the proof of that is that "not one defendant [of ours] has ever been acquitted."

The way the profile is written, coupled with the different colors and the language used, has obviously led all of the other people I have turned over to the FBI, as well as many others, to believe that they are chatting with a child. I'm not going to dispute the fact that there are those people who question whether or not I am a cop or working with the FBI, but that usually happens right before we are about to meet and the predator begins to think twice about with whom he has been communicating. However, not one time in the entire four years plus since I began identifying sexual predators, has anyone ever even remotely suggested to Lorie that she is an adult who merely wants to role-play as a child. That has only come out at trial—after a sexual predator was arrested.

I can only suggest from my vast experience on the Internet that Teen2hot4u's profile screams young girl. And, to those people who are so bold that they risk going after the person who created it on the off chance that it really belongs to an adult who wants to role-play, I say, you deserve what you get when you get caught! To put it plainly, if you are not a sexual predator and you are not looking to get arrested, don't take a chance on role-playing with a person who clearly identifies herself as a thirteen-year-old girl. You should say to yourself, "I had better stay as far away from her as possible!" Many people do stay away. Rarely, someone instant messages Lorie prior to seeing her profile, but when they do, and they find out that she is thirteen, if they are not a sexual predator, they say good-bye. That's the end of the chat. I do not have to cut them off. I do not have to end the chat or sign off. They do it.

Dsax25 didn't end the chats. He continued chasing after Lorie for several weeks, and he never once suggested that he was role-playing; not a hint, not a clue, and not any indication that he didn't truly believe that he was chatting with a young girl. I never wavered in my claim to be thirteen, even injecting comments about my "mom" and "gramma" into the chats. In fact, every single thing he said indicated to me that he not only believed that he was communicating with a young girl, but that it turned him on to chat with one. Then, one year later, Dennis Joseph had to come up with a defense. I believe he had finally found the opportunity to role-play and fantasize, and it was so unbelievable that the jury didn't believe him. The following pages contain more of Dennis Joseph's testimony and questions from his defense attorney, Robert Altchiler. Mixed in are more of my comments or clarifications, as well as comments from the trial judge. The testimony is edited for space, but the context remains the same.

> DENNIS J.: I wasn't thrilled with the idea of doing role-play, this whole thing with someone pretending they're 13. I was definitely uncomfortable with that. You know, I wish I would have stopped it, but I didn't, and I just—you know, it was just a pretend thing and I just kept it going, just trying to—I don't even know.

I find it odd that he was so uncomfortable role-playing with a young girl, yet he kept it going for several weeks.

> DENNIS J.: Two minutes into the first conversation, I'm already making suggestive comments and we are now nine minutes into this conversation, and I have made a whole bunch of suggestive—"long beautiful legs, extremely attractive." The world in the chat room moves really fast, talks about sex very quickly.

Dsax25 never chatted with Lorie in a chatroom. It was all done in private instant messaging sessions initiated by him.

> DENNIS J.: And, you know, I really think this is an adult—I can't be one hundred percent sure. And, you

know, I didn't expect her to say anything other than, "yeah, I'm 13," because that is who she wants to be . . . And, so, I have to stay with the 13, and I said, "Oh God—and I wouldn't be able to touch you, what painful torture." She says, "How come?" And I, again, I say, "Because I bet you look so beautiful and delicious, my eyes would be caressing every inch of you, longing to touch your beautiful skin, your gorgeous legs and stomach. But, I couldn't." And she says, "How come?"

ALTCHILER: Why are you writing these things at this point?

DENNIS J.: I—I am—same thing. It is the conversation that I'm after. It is not real. This is the way I chat. I—I do it with everybody. I have never been in this situation before, but this—this is what I do on the Internet, on the role-play on American Online. And it is just conversation. It is just chatting. I didn't think it meant anything.

ALTCHILER: Go on.

DENNIS J.: So, I say "I could get arrested." She says "ooo, well, my mom would kill me so I wouldn't tell her." Which was an interesting answer. I mean she didn't, like, recognize that there was any kind of danger for me in it at all; you know, the whole notion of police or anything. Her only concern was her mom, which is fine.

That should have been a signal that he was talking to a child! A thirteen-year-old would be more afraid of her mother finding out what she was doing than of the police arresting some guy she's chatting with on the Internet. He seemed to be trying to convince the jury that a real child would have been deeply concerned about his potential legal problems. At the same time, I would imagine that the jurors were concerned that Dennis Joseph never appeared to give a thought about the danger he might have been putting a thirteen-year-old girl in by talking to her the way he did.

> DENNIS J.: So, you know, I went ahead. "Oh my lord, I can tell you would tease the shit out of me, make me dying to touch you." She said, "Well, if you wanted me to," which was a good answer for me for role-plays, because teasing, you know, tantalizing is teasing, that kind of thing. And I like that. So I said "Tease me, I love to be teased." And she said, "If I met you, I would." And that is, you know, that is a role-play answer, absolutely, "if I met you I would." . . . It is generally never phrased as "if I met you, I would."

First he claimed that Lorie's response to his comment "Tease me, I love to be teased" or "If I met you, I would," was a role-play answer. Then, he seemed to contradict himself by suggesting that "it is generally never phrased like that." What was the jury to think? Was Lorie's response a role-play answer or not?

> DENNIS J.: I would have expected something like, you know, "well, I would love to tease you, how could I tease you?" Or, "Would it tease you— what would you think if I did this or what would you think if I did that?" But, you know, it is still a role-play answer. So I question, "Well, what would you do?" She says, "Whatever you want." And I say, with a smile, "Well that's a dangerous statement." And she says "Why?" And I say "Well I would definitely

like to see your legs, maybe some of your abs," because, to me, that is like reminiscent of the bodybuilder that I am currently looking at in the middle of the screen while this is going on.

ALTCHILER: How do you know that while you're having this Instant Messaging session chat there are muscle women on your screen?

DENNIS J.: Because that's first and foremost of what I do when I go to the computer for this kind of purpose, is look at those pictures. And I'm always looking at those pictures. And I'm always channeling as much as I can, all of the instant messages into the woman that I'm looking at in the middle of the screen, and I use that as imagery for whatever I'm doing.

When he "channeled" thirteen-year-old Lorie's chats into the muscular woman on the screen, was he actually envisioning an adult or a child? You might have your own opinion on that later on after finding out about some of the pictures that Dennis Joseph was actually looking at online.

ALTCHILER: In any of these chats that you are going to testify about—and you have seen, you know, so far in the case—have you had any of these chats without having those muscle pictures on the screen?

DENNIS J.: No. Never would be.

ALTCHILER: Please continue.

DENNIS J.: "I would definitely like to see some of your legs, some of your abs." And then "Teen2hot4u" gives a response that is the complete opposite of the responses she gives when she is really excited about something. When she is really excited

about something, there was a giant open mouth
[an emoticon which is a tiny picture with a face
on it] smile, there was a kissie face [emoticon],
there was an extended everything [meaning
"everythinnnnnn"] which are clearly, you know,
that is what I like, talk like that. Those are the
responses I like. This is not even "okay," this is
just "k," which, is interpreted by people who do
a lot of cybersex

PROSECUTOR: Objection.

The objection is due to Dsax25's comment about how a lot of people
interpret "k." He can only speak for himself.

DENNIS J.: My interpretation is that is not what I wanted
to hear. So I come back with what I think would
be a better answer for her. "Saying whatever
you want to an older, experienced man, there
are so many things I have done that I would
think of doing to you, but shouldn't." . . . Now
she is more excited, she says, "Cool, like what?"
And then I decided to sort of kind of just lay it
on the line and, you know, see what is going on
here, and send a barrage of, you know, different
topics that you could talk about; "sixty-nine,
oral sex, bondage, doggie style, tantric sex,
mutual masturbation," et cetera. And, in the same
minute, she gives me a response, immediately,
"What is tantric?" And, that response told me a
lot of what was going on here.

In essence, as Altchiler discussed in his opening remarks, what Dennis
Joseph appeared to be saying was that because Lorie only asked him

what tantric was, he was "thinking that she was definitely not a thirteen-year-old." Dennis Joseph said he was talking to a number of other people at the same time, and he was focusing on a picture of a muscular woman during the chats, yet he expected the jury to believe that he was also in deep thought about every word the teen said to him while analyzing who she must have been in real life. From my years of experience on the Internet, when people are role-playing and doing cybersex, they have a goal and they achieve it any way they can without worrying about who the other person is in real life. Someone who is not a child predator would not be doing it with Lorie, a person who clearly identified herself as a thirteen-year-old girl. Dennis Joseph's actions were not indicative of role-playing. As mentioned earlier, he sent Lorie his real picture and told her details about himself that were all true. And, that is why this next exchange is so significant.

ALTCHILER:	Why do you use your picture?
DENNIS J.:	Well, like I said before—I think it was yesterday—"Dsax25" is just basically a version of me. I am not, you know, my picture is fine, where I live is fine. You know, I'm quite proud of the fact that I'm a musician; people find it pretty impressive. I play at Carnegie Hall. I live on the upper west side of Manhattan. Most people are really impressed by that. There is no reason for me to, you know, have to make something up. It is easier to remember who I am and what I do. And, it is just, you know, it is just conversation.

Just conversation? Remember when he said, "My age as Dsax25, although it implies 25, I can be any age that's appropriate to whatever situation I'm chatting about. My marital status can be any situation that I want that's appropriate to what I'm chatting about." He talked about pretending that he had huge arms and could bench hundreds of pounds and how he would use his imagination to come up with something that would sound realistic. He was claiming on one hand to be into role-play, cybersex, and fantasy, while at the same time the jury was seeing that he told Lorie all about his real life.

The following is his comment about receiving Lorie's picture.

> DENNIS J.: Well, the picture itself, definitely could be a 13, 14 year old girl. But, all of the other clues that I have had in the conversations from her screen name and profile, her reactions to different various things that she said, and her reaction to my picture, over balanced to the side that she is not a kid.

He acknowledged that the picture could be that of a young teen and he had not heard anything from the "girl" to indicate that she was an adult who was role-playing. Judging from the way his testimony was going, the other clues he was referring to included his interpretation that her answer "k" meant that she was disappointed about one of his comments to her, and that a smiley face was an indication that she wanted to talk about sex. He eventually brought up his comments about meeting.

> DENNIS J.: I say, "And then let's talk about meeting," which is her fantasy.

He claimed that having a meeting was Lorie's fantasy. To prove that, he kept referring back to a previous chat when he said to her, "tease me, I love to be teased," and she responded, "If I met you, I would." He used her comment to say that she was the first one to bring up a meeting, something I've been instructed by Agent Berglas not to do. However, Dennis Joseph didn't mention the fact that, earlier in the same conversation, he commented about "not being able to touch you" and "I bet you look so beautiful and delicious, my eyes would be caressing every inch of you, longing to touch your beautiful skin, your gorgeous legs and stomach." None of the evidence presented at trial demonstrated that Lorie had ever suggested having a meeting with Dennis Joseph. I merely said the word "met" before he did, and it was in the proper context, because he had given me every indication that what he planned to do, he would do face-to-face and not online in some fantasy scenario that he had apparently created to impress the jury. On the other hand, there was solid proof to dispute his claims that Teen2hot4u was the one pushing for a meeting. While he continued to claim that everything he said to Lorie was all part of "role-playing," the fact is, on a number of occasions he mentioned to her that he planned to be in her neighborhood. For example:

DENNIS J.:   "I'll be in [your area] on Monday."

And, in fact, he really did have a meeting scheduled for that Monday right near where Lorie lived, but he explained it away to the jury like this:

DENNIS J.:   Although I've been doing this role-play now for like a month-and-a-half, I've never been comfortable with the thought of the fact that she wants to be 13 and—but I've been doing it anyway. And now, she's talking about meeting, and meeting, and meeting, and I kind of just called her bluff, you know. I'm going to be [in your area Monday].

ALTCHILER: All of these chats, these role-playing chats that you've had over the years, have you ever actually had a meeting?

DENNIS J.:   Not with anyone I've ever chatted with, no.

Of course, there was no way for the prosecutor to verify many of the claims he made regarding what he had or hadn't done before in connection with his Internet relationships.

ALTCHILER:	Please continue.
THE COURT:	I'm not clear on what you've been saying here. You're the one who says, I'll be in [your area] Monday, and that's, I gather, you tell us that's to suggest that you have a meeting? That's what you're telling, giving that possibility that's where you could have a meeting, right? I'm just taking that answer that I'm not quite clear about, right?
DENNIS J.:	Yeah, it's suggested in there, yes.
THE COURT:	That's the suggestion, that there could be a meeting on Monday?
DENNIS J.:	Yes.
THE COURT:	Now, she hasn't said anything about a meeting before that?
DENNIS J.:	Yes, she has.
THE COURT:	Where?
DENNIS J.:	On August 9.
THE COURT:	No. No. No. I'm talking about the chitter chat that you have in the minutes preceding the statement on 8-17 on Exhibit 77. She doesn't say anything there.
DENNIS J.:	Well, not on that particular day.
THE COURT:	That's my question.
DENNIS J.:	But it's in the scenario that she set up.
ALTCHILER:	Right. And how many times before that point did she bring up meetings?
THE COURT:	No. That's not what we're talking about.
ALTCHILER:	That's what we're talking about, Your Honor, because his answer before was in response to

her repeatedly bringing up meetings. He put
that out there. If we're going to be accurate, that
was his testimony.

THE COURT: She hadn't brought up the meeting that day
which is what I was trying to clarify.

Here is what was happening. Dsax25 brought up meeting Lorie when it
was clear that he was the only one in that chat talking about a meeting,
but Altchiler apparently thought that by throwing out the idea that
Lorie had previously pushed the idea of meeting his client over and over,
the judge and jurors would forget that she hadn't and think that Dsax25
had only brought it up because she had been twisting his arm to meet
her all along. Thankfully, the chats spoke for themselves and the jurors
had heard and read every word of them.

The testimony continued:

DENNIS J.: "So, if we met, tell me what you would envision,
what would happen?"
Because again, she likes to tell me that she
likes when I talk about all these scenarios but
she hasn't said anything herself. And cybersex is
best when it's things coming from both sides, so
I wanted to hear something from her.

He has just commented that he hadn't actually engaged in cybersex
with Lorie, but he insisted that she had somehow communicated to him
that she liked when he talked about sex.

DENNIS J.: So, she says, "Well, like the stuff you said is
cool," which is the same comment about all the
kinds of sexual things I've said.

I use words like "stuff" for a reason. I leave my comments vague, and
in that way, the door is left open for him to take it where he wants the

conversation to go. He could have interpreted "stuff" to be about his music or sports, but because he wanted the chat to go in a specific direction, he now, one year later, claimed that "stuff" opened the door for sex talk and showed him that this was what the girl wanted from him.

DENNIS J.:   So, I comment, "That would get extremely hot quickly." She says, "I guess." And then she asks me, "What would you do? So, she puts it back in my lap once again, so I have to do the work."

He has to "do the work." I think this is where he probably lost the jury, because he had claimed that all he wanted was cybersex, yet he spent several weeks pulling words out of Lorie in an effort to get her to engage in it with him, to no avail.

DENNIS J.:   So, I say, "Well, I want to go at your pace. There's quite an age and experience difference between us." Again, now, she sends me a very clear message that's the opposite of the emoticons, that's a disappointed, that's-not-the-answer-I-want-to-hear "k."

In that moment of deep thought, the one where he was having a few other conversations, the one where he was fixated on a "muscle-builder" in the middle of his screen, at that moment where he was so entrenched in Lorie's every word, he decided that a thirteen-year-old girl's response of "k," which is short for "okay," was a sign of disappointment, rather than a simple sign showing that she was in agreement with him.

DENNIS J.:   She doesn't want to hear that. She wants to hear something more graphic, more exciting. So, I can do that, too.

ALTCHILER: Please continue.

DENNIS J.:   So, I do something kind of over-the-top, "I'd love to rip your clothes off and take you over and over and over in all sorts of ways," and she smiles. [sends an emoticon] Again, that to me was a response of an adult, you know, pretending, role-playing, trying to act like someone who's inexperienced, who understands what rip your clothes off and take you over and over is all about.

Apparently, his explanation wasn't very convincing:

THE COURT: The smile, that's what that said?

DENNIS J.:   The smile. That's what that said.

THE COURT: That's what that's saying. Okay.

I wasn't in the courtroom when Dennis Joseph testified, so reading the transcripts was the first time I saw his testimony. In my view, he was simply making up stories to justify his behavior. Every one of his claims appeared to be manufactured out of the most innocent of comments or emoticons that Lorie had sent to him. The fact that she had held his interest for so long when she wasn't engaging in the kind of talk that he claimed to have wanted must have spoken volumes to the jury, but, the defendant wasn't finished testifying yet. He had a lot more time to put his foot in his mouth and he didn't disappoint anyone.

ALTCHILER: Now, I'm going to ask you to take us through both of these chats that took place on August 22, so if you have to, pull one of them out to lay them side by side, because I'm going to ask you to take us through the things that were happening simultaneously that day.

DENNIS J.: Okay. At about 10:04, about eight minutes after I had emailed Teen2hot4u . . . [she] sends me an instant message that says she got my email. And I say, smiley, and I say, "Well, I hope you liked the last email."

ALTCHILER: Now, just for clarification purposes, is that 10:04 message from Teen2hot4u.

DENNIS J.: Yes.

ALTCHILER: To you?

DENNIS J.: Yes.

ALTCHILER: Is that the first time that she has instant messaged you at the beginning of an instant messaging session?

PROSECUTOR: Objection.

THE COURT: Come to the sidebar.
(At the sidebar)
Seems to me that something was brought to all of our attention the other day that this Teen2hot4u at 10:04 was in response to something from him about five or six minutes earlier.

ALTCHILER: Which it says—

THE COURT: What?

ALTCHILER: —Judge—

THE COURT: But your question was, is that the first time she initiated with you. And the answer is, it isn't.

ALTCHILER: It is.

THE COURT: It is not.

ALTCHILER: It is an instant messaging chat.

THE COURT: No, I know, but your question is, as in this context of who starts these off, this was not started off with that. And, we know that from something that happened the other day and, therefore, your question is without foundation.

ALTCHILER: It is entirely, 100 percent accurate.

THE COURT: No, it is not accurate.

ALTCHILER: Of course, it is.

THE COURT: It is not accurate. You're leaving out background in order to indicate an impression that is unsure. I'm not going to permit it, period.

ALTCHILER: That is entirely untrue.

THE COURT: Counsel, is there any question about that?

PROSECUTOR: No. In fact, the witness just testified that it was in response to the email, and he didn't like the answer, so he started doing, "is this the first time?"

ALTCHILER: No, I didn't.

PROSECUTOR: Just for clarification, you led and created a different impression.

THE COURT: You put that as a leading question, and it isn't so, and I'm not going to permit it.

ALTCHILER: That's fine. The evidence—first of all, it is self-evident that it is in response to an email and I think I'm clarifying that point.

THE COURT: No, you—look, please read back the question. (read back) [Is that the first time that she has instant messaged you at the beginning of an instant messaging session?]

THE COURT: And that is creating an impression that she started the sequence off which was, in fact, started by his email, [eight] minutes earlier.

THE COURT: I'm not going to permit that. I'm going to tell the jury that it is based on something that came [eight] minutes earlier.

ALTCHILER: Why are you going to tell them that?

THE COURT: Why? Because your question is erroneous, wrong, creating a false impression, and you know it.

ALTCHILER: I'm going to ask for a mistrial then based on the Court's intervention before in trying to lead the jurors to believe—

THE COURT: No.

ALTCHILER: —that my client was not accurately testifying.

PROSECUTOR: That is completely, that is completely inaccurate.

THE COURT: You are not accurately putting the question.

ALTCHILER: It is right there in the email.

THE COURT: Do you want to correct yourself?

ALTCHILER: I'll correct it myself.

THE COURT: Fine. There is an email six or eight minutes before, the other way.

ALTCHILER: Look at the instant message.

THE COURT: Sir, all I'm—

ALTCHILER: No, I—

THE COURT: Sir, just you be quiet, or I'm going to find you in contempt for talking while I'm talking. Now, just be quiet. You created the impression, with that question, that this is one where she began the thing. She did not begin it, and you know she did not begin it, and yet, you're trying to keep it in there that way. And, I'm not going to let it happen. Now, do you want to correct it?

ALTCHILER: Yeah, sure.

THE COURT: All right.

ALTCHILER: What I said was 100 percent accurate.

THE COURT: No, it wasn't.

ALTCHILER: Of course it was.

Do I really need to comment?

The jury listened and watched as Dennis Joseph continued to trip over his own words trying to explain why he had said things like "I would love to touch and kiss you all over, lick you between your thighs, on your clitoris, and make you orgasm"; "I bet you will make a lot of noise when you come"; "I thought about us both naked, sitting, you playing, stroking my cock while we kiss and I caress your breasts, your nipples. And then, when I'm fully hard, turn you around and sit on me, facing away, hold you tight and lift you up and down on me while you have your legs spread wide and straight. . . ." Those words were actually said to his next intended victim, thirteen-year-old Julie, Lorie's friend. In fact, at trial, Dennis Joseph had to explain his actions towards not just two teen girls, but other people with whom he chatted who also identified themselves as young girls, including a man who said he was a ten-year-old female.

But this was just Dennis Joseph's direct examination. This is where the defense attorney is supposed to put his client's best foot forward, allowing him to come up with what he had hoped would appear to be rational reasons for his criminal behavior. This is the defendant's only hope, because when cross-exam begins, no holds are barred.

TEN

Putting the Final Nail in His Coffin

DENNIS JOSEPH SAT ON THE WITNESS STAND FOR APPROXIMATELY three days spinning a tale that he probably thought would win him an acquittal. The direct exam had been pretty straightforward, but, judging from what I read in the transcripts, as well as the events that followed, it appears to have hurt the defendant more than it helped him. However, in my opinion, it was the prosecutor's cross-exam that sealed his fate. While talking about Teen2hot4u's profile, Dennis Joseph was pretty much caught with his pants down, no pun intended. Here's why:

PROSECUTOR: You said that this profile was, quote, "one of the most sexually charged profiles that I have seen online?"

DENNIS J.: Yeah.

PROSECUTOR: Right?

DENNIS J.: Mm-hmm.

PROSECUTOR: Now, you have been role-playing for ten years, correct?

DENNIS J.: Approximately, yeah.

PROSECUTOR: You have role-played with other men?

DENNIS J.: Yes.

PROSECUTOR: And you've role-played, I believe you said this morning, with a 6-foot woman who has male genitalia, correct?

DENNIS J.: Yes.

PROSECUTOR: Who likes to dominate men, right?

DENNIS J.: Yes.

PROSECUTOR: Who likes to sodomize men, right?

DENNIS J.: Yes.

PROSECUTOR: And this, sir, your testimony, is one of the most sexually charged profiles you've seen in your ten years of role-playing?

DENNIS J.: Without a doubt. Absolutely.

PROSECUTOR: Without a doubt, right?

DENNIS J.: Absolutely.

PROSECUTOR: And, let's look at it. Because what you forgot to testify was where it says "marital status."

PROSECUTOR: Under "marital status," it says, "I'm 13 so it's just me," right?

DENNIS J.: Mm-hmm.

PROSECUTOR: And you saw that on July 6, 2005, right?

DENNIS J.: Yes.

PROSECUTOR: You saw that she wrote that she was just 13?

DENNIS J.: Yeah.

PROSECUTOR: You didn't think anything of it?

DENNIS J.: No. I thought that it bothered me, but . . .

PROSECUTOR: Bothered you, but it didn't prevent you from instant messaging her, did it?

DENNIS J.: No.

PROSECUTOR: You didn't think anything from the "School and I hope I get fired?"

DENNIS J.: No, nothing.

PROSECUTOR: Nothing from the "Life's like this, uh-huh, it's all been done before?" Nothing?

DENNIS J.: Nothing.

PROSECUTOR: You did take, however, when she said "Yeah, I got boobs but that's all you need to know" that—a woman says, I got boobs but that's all you need to know, that meant she wanted to talk about her breasts?

DENNIS J.: Absolutely.

PROSECUTOR: Absolutely?

DENNIS J.: Never saw that before in a profile.

PROSECUTOR: So, at 6:27, after seeing someone named Teen2hot4u and with a profile that lists her age as 13, you send an instant message, right?

DENNIS J.: Yes.

PROSECUTOR: Now, we'll go a little out of order here, sir. You testified that on August 17, 2005, in one of those many instant messages, you raise the issue of a meeting with Lorie, correct?

DENNIS J.: Yes.

PROSECUTOR: And you do that because you want to call her bluff. That was your testimony?

DENNIS J.: Yes.

PROSECUTOR: And that's because, to use your own words, she's the one who's talking about "meeting, and meeting, and meeting," right?

DENNIS J.: Yes.

PROSECUTOR: So, let's go back to Government Exhibit 57. At 6:53 p.m., you write, I would be in severe trouble around you, helpless LOL, correct?

DENNIS J.: Yes.

PROSECUTOR: And your testimony is when you wrote, "I would be in severe trouble around you," you were role-playing?

DENNIS J.: Yes.

PROSECUTOR: You didn't actually mean when you were around her in person?

DENNIS J.: No.

PROSECUTOR: And, that when you wrote, at 6:56 p.m. "Oh God, and I wouldn't be able to touch you," you were role-playing?

DENNIS J.: Yes.

PROSECUTOR: You didn't mean that b[y] touching her in person, right?

DENNIS J.: No.

PROSECUTOR: You weren't suggesting being there in person, correct?

DENNIS J.: No.

PROSECUTOR: And then, at 6:57, when you say "My eyes would be caressing every inch of you," once again, you're talking about role-play?

DENNIS J.: Yeah.

PROSECUTOR: And then when she says later on, "Well, if I met you, I would," you also testified you didn't understand her to mean an actual meeting there, correct?

DENNIS J.: No. I didn't think so.

PROSECUTOR: You thought she was role-playing there?

DENNIS J.: Yeah.

PROSECUTOR: You didn't think she meant meeting in person, right?

DENNIS J.: No, not there. No.

PROSECUTOR: And just so we're all clear, you weren't saving these instant message chats, were you sir?

DENNIS J.: No.

PROSECUTOR: So, this chat is on July 15, 2005. By the time August 9 comes around, you don't have them to refer back to, do you?

DENNIS J.:   No.
PROSECUTOR: And during this time period, you're speaking to hundreds of people?
DENNIS J.:   No.
PROSECUTOR: Dozens of people?
DENNIS J.:   Between the 15th and August 9th?
PROSECUTOR: Correct, Sir.
DENNIS J.:   Okay, a couple dozen.
PROSECUTOR: The next time we have is Government Exhibit 68. This is August 9th, 2005, right?
DENNIS J.:   Yes.
PROSECUTOR: And, at 1:35 p.m., when you write, "I fear what would happen if I actually saw you," you're not actually talking about in person, right?
DENNIS J.:   No.
PROSECUTOR: You mean a role-play, correct yep.
PROSECUTOR: And when you say at 1:39, "If I knew it was you, I would definitely introduce myself," you're not talking about in person there either?
DENNIS J.:   No.
PROSECUTOR: Talking about a role-play?
DENNIS J.:   Yes.
PROSECUTOR: And when you turn the page, the first time, sir, that you understand her to mean an actual meeting, you testify, was at 1:57 p.m. when she says "guys on here are older so you figure they're going to be nicer, but some even say they're going to meet and never do," right?
DENNIS J.:   Yeah.
PROSECUTOR: So, let's look at your responses. At 2:07 p.m., you write . . . "I think it's time for me to go before I talk you into meeting me, LOL." You wrote that, right?

DENNIS J.:   Yes.

PROSECUTOR: Two minutes later, you write "I am very, very, veryYYY" which you put with the emphasis with the y's, "interested in meeting you," correct?

DENNIS J.:   Yes.

PROSECUTOR: Two minutes after that, sir, you write "Let's just say hypothetically, where would you want to [meet]." That's you, right?

DENNIS J.:   Yeah.

PROSECUTOR: And, when you turn the page, you ask, "Around where [do] you live?" Correct?

DENNIS J.:   Yes.

PROSECUTOR: And you give your real address . . . right?

DENNIS J.:   Yes.

PROSECUTOR: That's you?

DENNIS J.:   Mm-hmm.

PROSECUTOR: When you turn to Government Exhibit 70 . . . next day, you're the one who writes, "If we did meet, what would you wear?" That's you writing it, correct?

DENNIS J.:   Yes.

I think you can see where this is going. In my opinion, Dennis Joseph was being pushed into a corner and there was no way for him to come out of the questioning looking innocent. It had become crystal clear that the claims he had made that the young girl hammered away at him about a meeting were completely untrue. The prosecutor took apart each and every comment in the chat until the very last words were spoken, and at no time did it ever look as though Dsax25 was anything other than a sexual predator who hunted for young girls on the Internet.

The testimony was in, and it was time for the attorneys to have their final say to the judge and jurors.

Altchiler began his summation by discussing Tantalus, a figure in Greek mythology. He talked about how Tantalus was punished by the gods for wrongdoing. He was placed into a pool of water and whenever he was thirsty, he would lean down to get a drink, but the gods would move the water further and further away from him. Altchiler added that when Tantalus was hungry and tried to pick fruit from the vines, the gods would move the vines away from him, too. This introduction was apparently given in an effort to suggest to the jury that Dennis Joseph's only interest on the Internet was tantalizing conversation. He said, "Just like Tantalus, it's going to seem real. It's going to seem like you can reach out and grab it. Seems like you . . . can actually touch it, but you never are."

It appears that Altchiler was trying to compare the "tantalizing conversation" that Dennis Joseph claimed to be looking for on the Internet to the torture that Tantalus endured. The only comparison that I see in Altchiler's explanation is that, not unlike Dennis Joseph, Tantalus had committed crimes; one being that he had killed his own son, boiled him, and served him to the gods. As punishment, he was sent to the Underworld where food and drink were always just beyond his reach. His fate was not about sexually stimulating conversation and being teased. It was about suffering for committing a heinous crime. How Altchiler could equate Tantalus to Dennis Joseph is beyond me!

Altchiler also stated that "the government's entire case is based on the notion that if you say something like you mean it, then you mean it. And it must be true. And if you type something as if you really mean it, then it must be true." And, he went on to suggest that the evidence contradicted the government's case.

So, let's take a look at how he may have come to those conclusions.

Altchiler proposed that the defendant's main objective was to find people on the Internet and engage in cybersex, and that he was willing to go along with someone else's fantasy in order to do that. Thus, when Dsax25 met the young teenage girls that he made first contact with, he,

Altchiler claimed, suspected that they were adult women who were role-playing, but since Dsax25 wanted to keep the role-playing going, he never questioned their ages. This claim was made in the face of clear evidence that the girls' profiles stated that they were thirteen, that in their chats with Dsax25 they stated that they were thirteen, and that they never wavered from that claim. Yet, Dennis Joseph went ahead and took a chance by showing up to meet Julie, and Altchiler repeated Dennis Joseph's excuse for that by maintaining in his summation that if the girl was really thirteen, his client was only going to warn her. Mixed in with all of the defenses and justifications that Altchiler put before the jury were comments that, in my opinion, were meant to discredit an entire group of people, including government agents with impeccable reputations. This was apparently done in the hopes that his client, a man who made explicit sexual comments to people identifying themselves as children and then showed up for a meeting with one of them, would look honest in a court of law.

The fact is that Dennis Joseph never mentioned to the FBI agents who arrested him that he was merely role-playing. Altchiler tried to convince the jury that it was because the defendant used the words "role-play" and "chatting" in the same context, because "they mean the same thing." The jurors had been listening to days of testimony that made clear that there was, in fact, a huge difference between role-play and chat. And when the jurors saw and heard the transcripts of chats between Dsax25 and the "girls" in this case, it was clear that he had represented himself as exactly who he was. People who indulge in sexual role-play do not tell you all about their real lives. They make things up and get right into sex talk. If they don't get what they want, they quickly move on to someone else. But Dsax25 didn't move on. He told Lorie and Julie the truth about his age, his location, even his name and occupation. He talked about business meetings and stated their real locations and described places where he had played his music, and they were all real. And, when he scheduled a meeting with one of the girls, he showed up—on time—at the agreed upon location. But, Altchiler apparently thought he could still convince the jury that everyone involved in this case was role-playing, even Dennis Joseph. His comparison between role-play and chatting was made in almost the same breath with the statement "everything that Stephanie Good said to my client was a lie," "that was all roleplay," and "everything that Agent Berglas was saying [to] my client, those were all lies, that was all roleplay." Then he told the jurors that Dennis Joseph was doing the same thing: that he was only making believe that he wanted to meet young girls, that he knew they were adults, and that he went along with their fantasy because he was seeking "tantalizing conversation." But his claim didn't wash because Dsax25 never got "tantalizing conversation" from the two teens. Instead, he heard vague answers to his sexual suggestions, so Altchiler, probably in an attempt to do damage control, insisted that even the slightest thing, such as an emoticon with a smiley face or answering with a simple "k," was meant to instigate a sexual conversation.

And, in justifying all of the "truths" that his client had told the "girls," Altchiler talked about an old expression, "The blackest of lies is the half truth." He explained it this way: "if you are going to tell a good lie, or you're going to be in a good role . . . incorporate certain things that are true, and . . . that makes it more believable." He immediately went on to quote Mark Twain: "Telling the truth is easier, because you never have to remember anything."

Mark Twain was not talking about half-truths and role-play and neither was Dennis Joseph! This excuse was not going to fly in a court of law. But, Altchiler continued. He claimed that even though Dsax25 did tell the truth about himself, when he talked about what he wanted to do to the young girls, that was all made up; Dsax25 didn't mean any of it. But, Stephanie Good was a role-player and a liar. And, Agent Berglas was a role-player and a liar, too.

I'm not sure it was a wise strategy for a defense attorney to face a jury and accuse someone like Agent Berglas of lying to catch a child predator. Agent Berglas' government career has shown him to be an exemplary human being. He was never drafted into government service. He chose it. In 1993, upon graduation from Dickinson College in Carlisle, Pennsylvania, he joined the Army and was commissioned as a second lieutenant. He spent the next six years as a Light Cavalry Officer serving in various roles, spending the majority of his time with the 3d Squadron, 2d Armored Cavalry Regiment in Fort Polk, Louisiana. In 1995, he was deployed to Haiti as part of "Operation Uphold Democracy," where he spent six months. In 1997, he earned the rank of captain. In 1999, he left the army and reported to Quantico to be trained for a position with the Federal Bureau of Investigation.

He told me his reason for joining the FBI. He said he wanted to continue working in a capacity where he could serve his country. Once he was given the opportunity to decide where to be placed within the FBI, Agent Berglas chose Squad C-20, the Crimes Against Children Squad, and he has been recognized many times over the years for his commitment to children, both within the FBI as well as outside of it. For instance, as recently as April 2006, he received the Voice For All Children Award from the Coalition Against Child Abuse and Neglect.

And, after spending over six years doing everything he could to keep children safe, this defense attorney stood before a jury and challenged Agent Berglas' credibility. The chats spoke for themselves. The words were all in black and white. Altchiler seemed to be trying to convince the jury that Agent Berglas would put his entire career on the line to trap this one man. Even if Altchiler could have somehow made it appear as though Agent Berglas and I had crossed a line, he still had to explain away something else—the testimony showed that there was another person with whom the defendant had communicated online that claimed to be a ten-year-old girl, "Tinaballerina10F." Yet, strangely enough, Dsax25 instant messaged all of us, even though we were all portraying children.

Altchiler also claimed that Dennis Joseph was an "expert" on the Internet. But, Stephanie Good "is not trained. It is a hobby." He said it was "going to be a pretty lucrative hobby for her, because she has a book deal." In other words, Altchiler accused me of having a "financial motive," in that my work on the Internet was for the purpose of having material to write a book. Here is where I believe an explanation is in order.

I had no plans to use Dennis Joseph's case in this book. In fact, at the time that my book deal was made, this particular sexual predator meant nothing more to me than just another deviant trying to go after a young girl on the Internet. Our chats began in July 2005 and the projected date for me to turn in my manuscript was January 2006. I saw no problem with completing the work by that date, as I had more than enough sexual predators to fill a chapter or more about each one. My plan was to write only about those predators who had been convicted, because there is always the chance that a jury would acquit one of them, and although it wouldn't make the person innocent in my eyes, I would not put myself or my publisher in jeopardy by naming someone who had been set free. Additionally, there was no reasonable expectation that anyone I was chatting with in July 2005 would have been arrested and convicted prior to my January 2006 manuscript completion date, so it never even occurred to me that Dennis Joseph would be included in here.

However, in August 2005, I was asked to put this book aside to work on another one, *Aruba: The Tragic Untold Story of Natalee Holloway and Corruption in Paradise* with Dave Holloway and Larry Garrison, and I agreed. By that time, the investigation of Dsax25 was winding down and moving towards an arrest. Then, several months passed as did my original January 2006 manuscript completion date, and I was given until September 2006 to turn this work in to my publisher.

In the meantime, Dennis Joseph's case went to trial and the events that took place were so unsettling that I decided to include them in this book. But, Altchiler implied that I had gone out of my way to trap his innocent client for the purpose of having convicted sex offenders to write about. He appeared to be saying that there were more important things to consider than the evidence. He even called me a "paid confidential witness doorman." One reason that I believe he said that was because I testified that I open the door for the men, and they can choose to walk through it or they can turn around and leave. And, that's exactly what I do. I offer vague comments that can be interpreted by them any way they want. I don't invite them to have sex with me. I say things like "stuff," "k," and "cool." The other reason that I believe Altchiler called me a "paid confidential witness doorman" was because there were times during the first two years of my work with the FBI when I received reward money from them for the many hours of hard work that I had performed. There was no rhyme or reason for the money. None of the payments ever depended upon any specific arrest or conviction. It was a gesture on the government's part to thank me for working with them on a full-time basis without pay, because, in fact, I was chatting with sexual predators several hours a day, several days a week at times, especially during an ongoing investigation. But I haven't received any money for almost two years at this writing, and I have never expected to receive any. That was never a motive for me to do this work and I have continued to do it, identifying sexual predators, chatting with them, talking to them on the phone, and testifying against them at trial, all with no payment and with no expectation of payment. But Altchiler seemed to want it to look as though I am paid by the arrest or conviction. It was an apparent attempt to divert attention away from his client's actions. It's that simple!

The following is another comment Altchiler made about me to the jury: "Because [Stephanie Good] is a lawyer that has a book deal, that has a book contract, but she is not willing to tell you how much money she is going to make on it." Altchiler was referring to the future sales of my then-unfinished manuscript. He cross-examined me about it and then seemed to twist what I said to make it look as though I had lied.

Here is how the questioning went:

ALTCHILER: How much money—what are the percentages that you will get on the book deal, depending on how much the sales are?

ME: Honestly, I don't recall all the terms of that contract. It's been a long time since I reviewed it.

ALTCHILER: I ask that you look at what's been deemed or marked as Defense CCC for identification. Is that your contract, your book contract?

ME: Yes.

ALTCHILER: We offer that, Your Honor.

PROSECUTOR: Objection.

THE COURT: Let me see it. Come to sidebar.
(At the sidebar)

THE COURT: What's the purpose of CCC?

ALTCHILER: This goes to her financial motive in creating material for her book.

THE COURT: She's already told you what she's getting as an advance and this, that, and the other.

ALTCHILER: She's already said that she doesn't know how much money she's going to be making depending on how many books she sells.

PROSECUTOR: She said she didn't remember. You can use it to refresh her recollection. You know perfectly well that her contract is neither relevant to this case besides saying that she had the motive, which she already testified to.

THE COURT: I sustain that objection.

ALTCHILER: You're sustaining it as to it can't help refresh—

THE COURT: No.

PROSECUTOR: Of course you can help her refresh her recollection. It's not coming in evidence.

THE COURT: You're not offering it for that.

ALTCHILER:	So, I'll just have it refresh her recollection. (In open court)
THE COURT:	Objection sustained.
ALTCHILER:	I ask that you look at Defense CCC because I want to ask you a question about what your percentages are going to be on the books, depending upon how many books sell.
THE COURT:	Can you figure out what that is?
ME:	There's several different ways to look at it. Depending upon how many are sold in each category, the percentage changes. And then it depends on if it's hard cover, trade, paper, export, mass market, book club, direct sales, free copy . . .
THE COURT:	These things have not come to pass?
ME:	Oh, no, there is no book yet.
ALTCHILER:	So how much money do you stand to make?
THE COURT:	That's sustained.
ALTCHILER:	If your book based on your work with the FBI sells a hundred thousand copies, how much money will you make?
THE COURT:	Sustained. Big "if" in there.
ALTCHILER:	Are you saying that you have no idea how much money you're going to make from your book?
PROSECUTOR:	Objection, your Honor.
THE COURT:	I'll permit that.
ME:	I haven't written the book yet. I don't even know if they'll accept my manuscript.

Now, remember the comment Altchiler made to the jury during his summation? "Because [Stephanie Good] is a lawyer that has a book deal, that has a book contract, but she is not willing to tell you how much money she is going to make on it."

How did Altchiler expect me to know how much money I was going to make when the manuscript wasn't finished? I had no idea how much money the book would even sell for in any of the various markets. But, Altchiler apparently waited until his summation to make my words fit another purpose. He was either lying about what I had said, or he couldn't keep the testimony straight. Either way, he mischaracterized many of my answers in an apparent attempt to fit his client's excuses for his criminal behavior. That statement about me not being willing to tell the jury how much money I was going to make on this book was ludicrous. Altchiler wanted a number. He insisted on having a number that I would receive from book sales and he implied that I was holding it back from the jury. There had been no meetings on projected sales that I had been part of and there was no way of knowing if I would actually finish this book or if it would make it onto the bookstore shelves. But, Altchiler didn't stop there: "She is a lawyer that has a book proposal that she submitted and, under oath, she swore to you that she didn't. And then, we put it into evidence." Again, Altchiler offered his own version of the truth.

ALTCHILER: Is it fair to say that before you actually got your book deal, that you had submitted a book proposal for prospective publishers?
ME: No.
ALTCHILER: I ask that this be deemed, Defendant's F for identification. Please look at that.
ME: Uh-huh. Okay.
ALTCHILER: Is that your book proposal?
ME: Yes.
ALTCHILER: So you actually did submit a book proposal, is that right?

ME:	No, that wasn't the question.
THE COURT:	The question [was] of when.
ALTCHILER:	Let me ask you this question, then. Is it fair to say that you actually submitted a book proposal at some point?
ME:	Yes.
ALTCHILER:	In July of 2005?
ME:	That, I believe, was the date.

Altchiler's question was very specific. He wanted to know if "before" I got my book deal, I "submitted a book proposal for prospective publishers." The answer was "No." That is because my publisher heard about me from my brother, Larry Garrison, President of SilverCreek Entertainment. Subsequently, I met with the publisher, we discussed my work with the FBI, and I was offered a book deal. Then I wrote the proposal while negotiations were in progress. And when Altchiler tried to pass that issue by, the judge called him on the fact that the question referred to "when." And still, Altchiler went before the jury and gave his own version of the truth. "She is a lawyer that has a book proposal that she submitted and, under oath, she swore to you that she didn't. And then, we put it into evidence."

Altchiler continued:

> She is a lawyer, who, in her book proposal, was talking about a film series that she was going to get out of this. And, then she swore, under oath, and said that is not true, even though her brother runs a film production company.

I denied it because it's not true and Altchiler had no business using something that was written one year before, something he obviously hadn't researched to see what the current status was, something he threw out in front of the jury in a court of law for the sole purpose of planting a seed about whether or not it was true. The proposal had been written in July 2005, before his client was even arrested, and it was now July 2006, and the status of things that I had written in my proposal had either changed or were tabled temporarily due to my work on *Aruba*. In my opinion, Altchiler's move was risky, because the jury had obviously kept track of the testimony and if an attorney mischaracterizes the truth, it can prove fatal to his client.

But, the worst part of Altchiler's statement came next:

> Before she thought you could all learn about all of these other things that were going on, she was very willing to just deny them, stare you in the face and completely deny it. But now you know it is true.

Altchiler was fully aware that I knew my book proposal and deal would be discussed at trial. Here's why. This was a retrial. Dennis Joseph had already been tried for this crime in April 2006 and there was a hung jury, with a 10–2 verdict to convict. Prior to that trial, I had turned over my book proposal and my contract to the prosecutors who, in turn, turned them over to Altchiler. He had vehemently questioned me about them at the first trial—in front of a jury. Yet, there he stood, giving his summation barely three months later in July 2006, at Dennis Joseph's second trial, telling the jury that before I thought they "could learn about these other things that were going on," I "was very willing to just deny them, stare you in the face and completely deny it." And, Altchiler didn't let up:

> Let's talk about Stephanie Good, because she plays a big role in this case. And if you want to talk about lying, and if you want to talk about not being candid to people who come and sit on a federal jury, let's talk about Stephanie Good. She is someone who is out there, just doing this. Some people fish. Some people knit, and she figured okay, what I am going to do is I'm going to sit on the Internet and the FBI says, you're our gal.

And you heard from Agent Berglas . . . and you know this already. Okay, the stakes are remarkably high in something like this when it comes to issues like entrapment, and prison, and federal convictions. It couldn't be more serious. And, that's why the FBI, even with their agents who have already gone to Quantico, who have already gone through their first round of training, they are going to do this work, they are specially trained. And there is a reason for that. Because, it is not easy. No one can just get online and start doing things like this, this happens. But, it is almost like Agent Berglas just didn't care. His instructions, his training to her, minimal.

Now, look at those statements in contrast to what Altchiler said about his client. Dennis Joseph "is an expert," because "he has actually seen profile, after profile, after profile." Dennis Joseph is an "expert," a highly experienced chatroom role-playing, tantalizing conversationalist, profile-reading expert? He knows it all? He can see through it all? He knows when someone is lying, fantasizing, and role-playing? Against all of the hard evidence, he was able to recognize that someone was an adult when they claimed to be a child. Yet, for some reason, he apparently enjoyed chatting with people who claimed to be children, because he was talking to more than three of them. Not only did he like chatting with them, he sought them out. And, it was not just with those people who testified at trial. In fact, the evidence showed that Dennis Joseph also belonged to a very interesting Internet Yahoo group called Muscleteens. He became a member in June 2005, one month before chatting with Teen2hot4u. According to the prosecutor who researched Muscleteens, it is an "Internet group that solicits photos of muscular girls between the ages of 5 and 18." So, evidently he liked looking at pictures of muscles—muscles on children. I have to wonder if those are the pictures that he had in the center of his screen while he talked to Lorie and Julie. We don't know because unlike Agent Berglas and me, Dennis Joseph didn't save any of the chats he had or screen captures of the pictures he was "channeling" while he communicated with the young girls. So all of his testimony was based on his own word, his own credibility, or lack thereof.

And when Altchiler said that it looked like "Agent Berglas just didn't care," was he implying that his client *did* care? Was Dsax25 worried about his affect on children? Did he ever stop to think that he might just be endangering the welfare of a minor, or that his actions would be illegal if, in fact, these people *were* children? Or, did he recklessly go after them with a total disregard for anything other than his own self-gratification?

Everything Dennis Joseph did on the Internet indicated that he, in fact, did have a special interest in children. It seems like he had a predisposition. In other words, his claim that we lured him into our teen fantasy was, well, a fantasy.

But, contrast that with what Altchiler said about me. He said I wasn't trained to do what I do on the Internet with the FBI. I am a highly trained attorney with a master's in law, who has practiced criminal law, who had, at the time of Dsax25's arrest, been working on the Internet with the FBI for almost two-and-a-half years, on a daily basis, often as much as seven days a week, chatting with thousands of people, having already been responsible for turning several sexual predators over to the FBI who had admitted to their criminal behavior and had pleaded guilty or had gone to trial and been convicted. I had testified at other trials, and I had never seen one of the men I turned over to the FBI acquitted. But, Altchiler claimed that I needed more training to recognize when a forty-year-old man is trying to lure a thirteen-year-old girl off of the Internet to have sex with him, because "it is not easy." You read what Agent Berglas said about why he allowed me to work so closely with him. None of this work was taken lightly. And as I mentioned earlier, I was chatting with sexual predators on the Internet before Agent Berglas' squad began doing it. In fact, the first three cases that I was involved with, Corso, Patel, and Hamilton, were primarily from the work that I had performed, and Agent Berglas was the facilitator.

More importantly, much like Agent Berglas, I too have a past that speaks well for me. I have never been involved in anything just for money. I chaired a committee to clean up a chemically contaminated landfill. I was on the board of directors of a youth association that only *had* a board because I uncovered the theft of thousands of dollars that the president and vice president had been siphoning off of money earmarked for children's sports in a Section 8 housing project. I did not receive any compensation for those activities. They were volunteer positions that I participated in when my children were young.

When Christian was in first grade, I entered college, where I earned many honors, including the academic awards for excellence in both political science and English, the Costigan Scholarship, a Distinguished Transfer Scholarship, summa cum laude, and Phi Beta Kappa—all in four years. I continued on to law school where I was awarded a prestigious public interest fellowship and earned a Juris Doctor (law) degree. After graduating, I performed more pro bono work as an attorney in my first year of practice than many attorneys do in their entire careers and I continued to do pro bono work when needed. I returned to law school ten years later to earn an L.L.M. (master's degree) in International Law.

I am also a trained emergency room companion for victims of rape and domestic violence, and that is not something to be taken lightly. It isn't easy holding the hand of a woman who has just been brutalized and raped, trying to convince her that everything will be okay. I have also been a court-appointed special advocate for children in foster care. Again, neither of those activities were paid positions.

My family wasn't surprised that I was doing the Internet work. It didn't shock them that it wasn't a paid position with the FBI. I didn't go into it with the thought of becoming an FBI agent. I'm much too old for them to accept me. It was nice that there was a possibility that I would be given a reward. Of course, I was happy when I received it. It was a wonderful gesture for the many hours of hard work that I had performed. But, not once did I ever expect it, ask for it, or consider stopping what I was doing simply because I haven't received anything in almost two years. It has no bearing on why I identify child predators. So, no matter what Altchiler gave the jury to bring into the deliberation room with them, there had been nothing said in that courtroom from anyone but him that could have possibly made jurors believe that I would deliberately entrap an innocent man.

But, here is the key: I turn people over to the FBI. I don't go out and arrest them myself. The FBI takes the information and evidence that I provide, and then they conduct their own investigation prior to an arrest. And strangely enough, not once has Agent Berglas ever come back to me and said I had the wrong guy. Not once have I ever misinterpreted what a sexual predator's intentions were.

Apparently, Altchiler was trying to use every angle. He said I "pushed" Julie on Dsax25. The fact that I mentioned her on a number of occasions throughout the time that I chatted with his client probably made Altchiler assume that he had the ammunition to tell the jury that the mention of someone's name is called entrapment, and that by mentioning Julie, I was inducing his client to commit a crime. But, as one of the prosecutors stated during summations, "Inducement doesn't equal introduction to an undercover agent. It just does not. No matter how many times defense counsel stated it. Inducement does not equal introduction of an undercover agent. By that theory, in every undercover operation, that would be entrapment."

As I understand the law, I could have said Julie's name in every single sentence and it would not have been considered entrapment or inducement. Altchiler didn't stress the fact that Julie never communicated with Dsax25 until he contacted her first. He didn't get into the vague way that Julie and Lorie answered Dsax25, never asking for sex, never asking for a meeting, answering his suggestions for sex with emoticons and comments like "k" and "cool." He didn't remind the jury that Dennis Joseph actually complained during the trial that he "was doing all the work." Of course, I didn't expect him to do that. But, those *were* the facts.

Altchiler also said that "the other part of entrapment is predisposition," and then he proceeded to get into the definition of predisposition. He said that, "it means that if this guy is out there already committing crimes like this or already interested in committing crimes like this, then that's something you can consider with entrapment, because those are people . . . who are going to do it anyway, and it's not the case here."

But the fact that Dennis Joseph had never been caught before did not eliminate predisposition. The evidence demonstrated that he was more than "interested" in "committing crimes like this."

Altchiler added, "Because, in this case, for the first time, he was lured out of his little fake Internet world by the government who was seeing things that weren't there, by Stephanie Good who, two days after she referred him to the FBI, still questioned, still doesn't know, refers him to the FBI on August 22, and on August 24, she's still sending him instant messages saying, 'Is this real or is this cyber,' remember that?"

Yes, we all remembered that. The jury must have recalled how I explained that I give the guys an out, how I consistently question them about their intentions, even when it is clear that they are looking to meet a young girl for sex. I don't want any gray areas. I want the evidence to be clear and valid, and if one of those guys had said that this was all a fantasy or that they were never going to come face to face with a girl, and they stuck to that story, that would have been where it ended for me.

Altchiler also said this in defense of his client:

[I]t's very important to try to get somebody to make you an offer of money, or a shopping spree or an iPod or anything, and there's nothing like that here . . . if somebody's showing up with lubricants, with porn, with sex toys, with a hotel reservation, anything like that, it's somebody making offers, I'll bring you money, I'm right by a bank, I'll come down and get you a hundred dollars. It's someone saying I'm going to take you to a mall shopping, all the clothing you want, anything. That's what inducement looks like beyond a reasonable doubt. That's what enticement looks like. That's what persuasion looks like. Not like this. Not like this.

It is true that many sexual predators offer those things to children who may be reluctant to meet them. Those are the incentives that sometimes get kids out of the house and into the arms of deviants. However, there is no rule, no set program that says that in order to be convicted of the crime for which Dennis Joseph was arrested, he had to offer to buy the girl a present or give her money. In essence, what Altchiler was saying was that all of the descriptive sex talk didn't matter and showing up to meet the girl didn't matter because there was no iPod, no shopping spree, and no money involved.

Altchiler continued, but I don't know what he was thinking when he said this:

So, when you go back to the jury room and the judge, having received instructions from the judge, he's going to tell you about the burden of proof. He's going to tell you about what it means to have a presumption of innocence. Okay? And that's going to put you in a very different place than the investigators as a starting point, because if you go through Agent Berglas' testimony, he will tell you that his mindset when he's out on the street is that if someone tells him something, "I assume it's real." That's what he's, that's what he comes from. Folks, you come from a different place. Okay? And, listen to what the judge says about where you're supposed to start from. Okay? You're supposed to assume that it's not real, presume that this is innocent conduct, and then go to the evidence and say, so—

Altchiler may have gotten confused. He was giving the jury information that was clearly incorrect. It sounded as though he was telling the jury to presume that what Dennis Joseph had said and done with Lorie and Julie was all innocent conduct. So, the judge had no choice but to stop him in his tracks:

THE COURT: No, no, I am not going to charge that. You just listen to my charge.

ALTCHILER: Okay.

THE COURT: I'm going to charge a presumption of innocence, nothing to do with specific conduct, presumption of innocence.

In other words, jurors should enter a courtroom thinking that a defendant is innocent until proven guilty. That's where going over all of the evidence comes into play.

Altchiler's summation ended and the prosecution had a little more to add to the mix. During the prosecutor's rebuttal, the definition of inducement, as it related to this case, was laid before the jury:

Inducement to commit the crime starts with the defendant. He's the one who goes trolling through each of these chatrooms. He's the one who finds someone named Teen2hot4u, and seeing that she's just 13 years old on the profile, he goes there and he initiates sex conversations with her. And he initiates them for the purpose of enticing her. He's the one who does this because he has an interest in teenaged girls. And you know that not only from the chats, not only from him talking to [the people posing as young girls], you also know that because he purposely joined a group, Muscleteens.

The prosecutor also talked about me, making it clear that the chats spoke for themselves in that there was a stipulation before trial that the chats were completely accurate, that none of them were altered by anyone. That means that Dennis Joseph and Altchiler agreed that there was no question as to the validity of what Dennis Joseph said in the chats and what Agent Berglas and I said to him.

The evidence was in and the jurors deliberated.

On Friday, July 14, 2006, late in the afternoon, Dennis Joseph faced the jury one last time to hear their verdict. They found him guilty of using the Internet to attempt to entice a minor to engage in sexual activity. Nearly five months later, in December 2006, he was sentenced to ninety-seven months in a federal prison. I suppose that now that he calls a prison cell his home, he can finally identify with Tantalus after all!

I received the call about the verdict while I was at the hospital. I had just been informed that my husband Ed had to have emergency open heart surgery the following morning. Ed's life was in jeopardy and Dennis Joseph had just lost his freedom. It was a moment of mixed emotions, a moment that has been imbedded into my memory. A wonderful man was lying in a hospital room waiting to see if doctors could save his life. At the same time, a sexual predator, a deviant whose mission it was to hurt children, had just been informed that he was most likely going to spend a substantial amount of time behind bars. His conviction was a bittersweet victory for me. I had put many hours into taking this man off the streets and away from children. The FBI and the Justice Department had finished the job. And the jury had validated my decision to turn Dennis Joseph over to the federal authorities. I had a brief moment of satisfaction before going back to my husband's bedside.

I quietly shared the news with him not even knowing if he would understand what I was saying. It looked as though his mouth turned up with a smile, but I wasn't sure. It was only when I reached down to hold his hand that I noticed it—he had made a fist and his thumb was extended upwards. He had given me the thumbs up.

For that brief moment, all was right with the world.

ELEVEN

The Wall of Shame

THERE IS SOMETHING AT THE NEW YORK OFFICE OF THE Federal Bureau of Investigation that demonstrates the Crimes Against Children Squad's level of commitment and passion for the work that they do to protect children. It is called the Wall of Shame and it is located in the squad area for all to see. There, prominently displayed, are the photos of those who have been arrested by the squad for committing crimes against children. I've been up to the FBI building and I have seen the Wall, and I have to admit that I look at it with a great sense of pride. Many of the faces are familiar to me, because I was personally involved with their cases. Those pictures are symbols of what the FBI agents do every day of their lives and what I have done to assist them in their very important mission. I am so honored to be a part of their work and to have been given the trust and respect that they have so generously bestowed upon me.

Besides the sexual predators whose stories fill the pages of these chapters, there are many others whose arrests I was involved with that I haven't written about yet, and whose pictures are included on the Wall of Shame. Some of them were cases that happened so quickly that there isn't enough material to fill a chapter, while others are so typical that their stories would have been redundant. A couple were just not worthy of any more attention than they already had. However, those predators were just as deviant, just as perverted, and just as culpable as all of the others. So, I will briefly let you know who some of them are.

As Julie, I had made several phone calls for Agent Berglas to a man named Ernesto Morales. His screen name on AOL was Tito708. At the time, I was acting as thirteen-year-old Julie from Astoria who went to school in Manhattan. Morales told Julie that he was thirty-four and lived in Astoria with his mother and brother. He wanted to pick the young girl up and take her back to his house for a weekend of sex because his brother was going to be away and his mother would be asleep. During one of our phone conversations, he asked me to turn on the television to prove to him that I wasn't calling from a police station.

On March 17, 2004, Morales was arrested at his home for the numerous pictures of child pornography that he had sent to Agent Berglas while chatting with him as Julie, as well as the chats that he used to entice "Julie" to meet him for sex. On November 17, 2004, after pleading guilty, Morales was convicted on charges of using the Internet to attempt to entice a minor to engage in sexual activity. He was sentenced on February 23, 2006, to five years in a federal prison.

Another sexual predator that I spoke to as Julie was Joseph Zito, who was using the AOL screen name Jazliny. He was arrested on March 30, 2004, on the same two counts as Matt Brand, when he showed up at a Manhattan restaurant to meet the young girl he thought he had been chatting with on the Internet and talking to on the phone. He was convicted on February 16, 2005, and sentenced to five years and ten months in a federal prison.

David Camus, known on AOL as Local1DC, was a forty-three-year-old man from Orangeburg, New York. I chatted with him on the computer under the AOL screen name Angelnybaby13 and the name Jen, and I spoke to him on the telephone as Julie, who he was also chatting online with after I had made the usual introduction. Camus arranged a date with Julie and on June 2, 2004, he arrived at the agreed upon meeting place. When he realized he was about to be arrested, he tried to drive away. Agent Berglas had to physically block his car from leaving the scene. Camus was taken into custody and held without bail due to his Internet conversations with several agents from all over the country. On December 22, 2004, he pleaded guilty. He was sentenced to five years in a federal prison.

Michael Brennan, a man from Deer Park, New York, using the AOL screen name Diesel pwr, first instant messaged Angelnybaby13, also known as Jen, on March 6, 2004. She was thirteen and he was thirty-eight. He was extremely domineering, giving Jen and eventually Julie specific instructions about her daily life. For example, he told her what she was allowed to wear, or not to wear, to school each day. She was not to wear panties, a thong, or a bra under her uniform, and she had to sleep naked at night. He made an exception, allowing her to wear a thong, but only on gym days, saying that he would let her "slide" on those days. He told Jen that her "ass belongs to him" and that she was to "do what he says, no questions asked." He also wanted the young girl to call him "Daddy."

One night, he instructed her to strip down in her living room and walk into her room naked, even though her mother was home and had already seen her in her pajamas. He also told her that whenever she received email she was to send it to him right away. He actually believed that the girl was listening to his crazy demands. He eventually made a date with Julie and was arrested on April 21, 2004, when he arrived to meet her at a prearranged meeting place. He was charged with using the Internet to attempt to entice a minor to engage in sexual activity. He was not released on bail. He was convicted on July 11, 2005, after pleading guilty. On October 3, 2005, Brennan was sentenced to five years in a federal prison.

Josef Badash, also known on AOL as Motek, first instant messaged Angelnybaby13 on July 13, 2004, while he was at work. He was a forty-eight-year-old Israeli citizen, who lived in Brooklyn, New York, and he wanted to meet Jen right away. He was very clear about wanting to have sex with her, even telling her that she would feel good right after they did it. He also asked her for a naked picture of herself which, of course, he never received. At the same time that he was chatting with Jen, he was chatting online with Julie. He arranged to meet Julie and on July 15, 2004, he arrived at the meeting place and was arrested. He was charged with using the Internet to attempt to entice a minor to engage in sexual activity. He was released on $500,000 bail. After pleading guilty, he was convicted on August 27, 2004, and sentenced on May 17, 2005, to five years in a federal prison.

I spoke to Joseph Minnici on the telephone while posing as Julie. Minnici had been on AOL under the screen name Poetdom4u when he first instant messaged the young "girl." He was a fifty-one-year-old insurance salesman and a coach for ten- to fourteen-year-olds. He was also a cross-dresser. Every time Julie responded to one of his questions on the phone, he would say, "Mmmm." It was revolting! He also sent Julie a package and instructed her to put a pair of her worn panties in it and send it back to him.

On August 31, 2004, Minnici drove for three and one-half hours from Pennsylvania to New York to meet Julie for sex. Agent Berglas said that when the FBI agents asked Minnici to step out of his car, Minnici blurted out that he was only going to spank Julie. He was carrying with him directions to the meeting place, lubricant, condoms, and a planner with Julie's name in it. He was arrested and charged with enticement. He was released on a $200,000 bond and put under house arrest. His attorney argued for bail using an old law that said it was okay to have sex with a minor. He pleaded guilty on November 9, 2005. At his sentencing, he received five years in a federal prison and five years supervised release.

Robert Riley, also known on AOL as BigD4u2com, was a Jamaican resident alien who lived with his brother. He worked as a copy tech and had a criminal record consisting of seventeen convictions and five bench warrants all issued on drug-related charges. He instant messaged me while I was using the screen name Teen2hot4u. He told Lorie that he was thirty and immediately began talking sexually with very vivid descriptions about the things he wanted to do to her. After an introduction by Lorie, he also chatted with Julie and was arrested on April 15, 2005, after showing up to meet her at a fast food restaurant. He pleaded guilty and was sentenced on November 16, 2005, to seventy months in a federal prison.

A *US Weekly* reporter, Timothy McDarrah, using the AOL screen name "Ps41alum," answered an advertisement posted on June 22, 2005 on Craigslist.com offering "the freshest, youngest girls available in all ages." Not realizing that he was communicating with Agent Berglas, he offered to pay $200 to have sex with a thirteen-year-old girl. He then began communicating with Julie (Agent Berglas) and from July 2005 through September 14, 2005, McDarrah chatted with Julie on the Internet and on the telephone (me, acting as Julie) and described explicit sexual acts that he wanted to perform with her. He also offered to buy her various items, including CDs, an iPod, and clothes. On September 14, 2005, when McDarrah showed up to meet the person he thought to be the thirteen-year-old girl with whom he had been communicating, he was arrested by FBI agents and charged with using the Internet to persuade, induce, entice and coerce an individual younger than eighteen-years-old to engage in sexual activity. On December 20, 2006, after a jury trial in Manhattan Federal Court, McDarrah was found guilty. The following day a New York Post article entitled "'Kid Sex' Perv Writer Nailed" announced his conviction. He faces between five and thirty years in prison.

Frank Gagliardi, a sixty-two-year-old cement mason who lived with his wife, used two AOL screen names to chat with Lorie and Julie. One was Brooklynfrank3 and the other was Scemonito. He instructed both girls to take their ages out of their profiles so he could claim that he thought they weren't underage if he was caught with them. After chatting with both girls for several weeks and going as far as repeatedly offering one of them money in exchange for sex, he scheduled a meeting with both of them.

On the morning of October 5, 2005, he told his wife that he was leaving for work and called his boss to say that he would be late. He arrived at the arranged meeting place, a park, at 8:00 a.m. and was arrested when agents pulled him out of his car. He had one Viagra pill and two condoms with him, but he claimed that he wasn't going to have sex with the girls. His family put up his $350,000 bail and he was released under house arrest. He opted for a trial and on May 8, 2006, jury selection began. I was called to testify. The experience was everything you would expect considering the descriptions of the trials that I have already discussed. On May 12, 2006, the jury reached its verdict, declaring Gagliardi "guilty of the enticement of a minor to engage in sexual activity." On September 21, 2006, he was sentenced to five years' imprisonment.

There are other predators whose cases I have been involved with but whose convictions are still pending, thus they are not mentioned here. There are also predators whose cases I have worked on who were arrested by local police while FBI agents were in the middle of their own investigation of them. For example, during November 2004, a man using the screen name Specimen29 began chatting with me while I was on AOL under the screen name Emily13LINY. He introduced himself to Emily with the opening line, "Long Island master here . . . hi there." Then, in February 2005, he began chatting with Teen2hot4u and, at the same time, he was communicating with Julie13nyc. In July 2005, while still chatting with me under the name Specimen29, he began instant messaging me using the screen name Sniffler29, and when I told him I didn't know who he was, he quickly identified himself as Specimen29 and reminded me of the things we had chatted about. He referred to himself as "Sexy Daddy," and said he was "46, 6'4" and 220 lbs." At other times, he said he was "40" and also "50." He sent me his real picture and made it clear that he "was definitely not looking for cyber," that he was interested in meeting for sex, saying that he wanted Lorie to "do some naughty things." He was extremely explicit in telling the thirteen-year-old girl about the sexual things they would do together.

His name was Jan Kabas and he was a real estate attorney who had an office in Jericho, N.Y. On August 25, 2005, Kabas was arrested in Nassau County, New York, when he showed up to meet a person he believed to be a thirteen-year-old girl. In reality, he had come face to face with a member of the Nassau County District Attorney's Technology Crime Unit that he had met while searching in the AOL chatroom "I Love Older Men." At the time of his arrest, Kabas was out on bail pending a federal criminal trial on charges involving mortgage fraud. On September 9, 2005, he pleaded guilty in Nassau County Court to "attempted disseminating of indecent material to minors in the first degree," a Class E Felony.

There are numerous other predators still trying to arrange meetings with "girls" like Lorie and Julie, so, my work continues.

By the time this book comes out, I will no longer be using the screen name Teen2hot4u, and Julie13nyc will also be retired. In fact, Agent Berglas' excellent performance with the Crimes Against Children Squad has earned him a promotion. So, we will no longer be working on these cases together. He is currently the Supervisory Special Agent of Squad C-37 in Manhattan, also known as the "Cyber Crimes Squad," which is responsible for investigating computer hacking, intellectual property rights, Internet fraud, and Internet extortions.

I recently asked Agent Berglas what his proudest moment with Squad C-20 was and this is how he responded, "All of it. They were all victories. The work was so important and I enjoyed it so much. I never thought any of the arrests were mistakes. I truly believed that the men would have had sex with any thirteen-year-old girl."

It has been the greatest honor of my life to have worked with Agent Berglas and I wish him well in his new position.

The Wall of Shame awaits me and I will respond. It is a humbling experience to stand before it and look into the faces of the lowest species of society, the weakest of the weak, and the cruelest of the cruel. In the eyes of those deviants are the reflections of the numerous victims they have left in their wakes, and it is for those children that I continue to make new additions to the Wall in the sincere hope that I can save others from ever having to look into the eyes of sexual predators like those I have already identified for the FBI.

TWELVE

The Meeting Place

EVEN THOUGH I'VE BEEN IDENTIFYING SEXUAL PREDATORS on the Internet now for close to four years, I still find it alarming just how many people are interested in having sex with young children. I often wonder why it is so prevalent now as compared to when I was growing up. But, is it? Maybe it just seems that way because of the numerous avenues by which predators can now reach children. They were always out there, searching, lurking, looking for a way to latch on to a child. However, with the Internet at their fingertips, they not only have their choice of thousands of kids previously out of their reach, but they are also forming bonds with other sexual predators who all have the same goal—preying on innocent children.

There are chatrooms specifically frequented by and websites directly catering to people who indulge in pedophilia, child pornography, sexual slavery, child molestation, and various other fetishes, addictions, and perversions that those of us who are decent human beings find repulsive.

I am not commenting on the behavior of consenting adults. I have no qualms with what people of legal age do in the privacy of wherever they choose to do it. But I do take issue with the older adult who seeks to take advantage of the underage, minor child, whether or not they think the child has consented. In fact, a minor child does not have the legal right to consent. Under the law, the adult is culpable. This is something that never seems to be taken into consideration by groups such as the North American Man/Boy Love Association (NAMBLA), whose stated goal on their website (www.nambla.org) as of this writing is to "end oppression of men and boys who have freely chosen mutually consensual relationships." They seem to think they can explain away their perverse actions against boys by equating themselves with homosexuals and using the argument that since society is homophobic, that is why people are against NAMBLA. Using claims of discrimination and the desperate need for equality, they prey upon young boys out in the open and cry foul when they are caught. In a section of their website entitled "Entrapment Alert," there is a discussion on "taboos." Again, there is the implication that men who "love" boys are victims of an irrational society. It states the following:

> Affection for a boy not one's direct relative is at best considered strange and suspicious. Add to it the slightest erotic dimension and the consequences can be calamitous. Taboos are irrational and so are the punishments inflicted by the societies that hold them. In the United States, the manufactured fear and aversion to man/boy love has exploded to unbelievable proportions. Police agencies, no longer finding "victims," are busy entrapping boy lovers by posing themselves as "victims." The scams are conducted almost exclusively on the Internet.

I cannot help but wonder where they came up with the idea that there are no real victims. Is it their contention that children who are molested are not victims because they are just being "loved"? Moreover, they appear to be suggesting that the police go onto the Internet and make believe that they are children just to entrap these loving and well-meaning individuals who look for children to "love."

There is obviously a misconception on their part as to the definition of entrapment. Sexual predators on the Internet hunt for children and instant message several of them in the hopes of finding one who will actually go off the computer to meet them. In the process of doing what every other predator does by grooming them, they send pictures of themselves, often of their genitals, and make illegal and obscene comments to them. Then they show up for a meeting for the specific and stated purpose of having sex, and when they are caught, sometimes carrying such things as condoms, drugs, weapons, and motel room keys, and are arrested, there is nothing even remotely close to the definition of entrapment in what the authorities have done. Due to that, the predator often pleads guilty rather than go to trial. Yet, these NAMBLA supporters would like us to believe that what they do is good for children and that the laws are bad. So when they talk of entrapment, it appears as though they are saying that an adult who gets arrested under laws that make it illegal for an adult to have a sexual relationship with a child is entrapped.

Imagine what the world would be like if children could consent to anything and everything that they "wanted." There have to be limits on such things as driver's licenses, alcohol consumption, joining the armed services, getting married, and especially, and most importantly, having a sexual relationship before they are even old enough to understand the ramifications or joys of one. It is clear that there is no moral dilemma here; adults who even dream about having sexual relations with a child are truly lacking the ability to think rationally, in my opinion.

Working with the FBI has allowed me to understand how the system functions from the inside, on certain levels. I have watched and learned from Agent Berglas, and he has demonstrated nothing but honor and integrity in his work. There is never a conspiracy to go after anyone. There is never even a suggestion that we tempt or entice someone. The predators come to us of their own free will without any more encouragement other than thinking that we are children. They pursue us, groom us, and pressure us, and we merely play along. If we don't, they will go after a real child. They do have the propensity to have sex with children. Neither I, nor the law enforcement agents I work with, have coerced anyone. The predators are not being teased or courted by us in any way. The people I work with are very careful to stay behind a line that they know cannot be crossed without tainting an arrest. We have all let many people go by the wayside simply because they never communicated with us again.

In my view, NAMBLA's definition of taboo, as well as their ridiculous assertion that they are being entrapped, is nothing more than an excuse for sexually assaulting children and getting caught. It's either "I didn't do it" or "If I did, I was entrapped."

Unfortunately, NAMBLA is not alone in their quest for communal perversion. Another organization that was created with the same apparent goals is referred to on the Internet as the female equivalent to NAMBLA, called Butterfly Kisses (www.bk-girls.org), also known as "International Female Girllove Collective" (IFgLC), a group "strongly opposed to age-of-consent laws and all other restrictions which deny women and girls the full enjoyment of their bodies and control over their own lives." They are a self-proclaimed "political, civil rights, and educational organization" that "provide[s] factual information and helps educate society about the positive and beneficial nature of woman/girl love."

The following is part of their "Introduction" page:

> Hello and welcome to "Butterfly Kisses." This web site is about and for women who are attracted to pre-teen and adolescent girls. Our primary goal is to give women and girls a tool for expressing their feelings and their love about this controversial topic, and to get people to open their minds to ideas about romantic and erotic attraction between women and girls that our society in the past has not been able to discuss openly and rationally. We also want to provide a place where women and girls can express themselves and can learn about their love in an atmosphere where they are encouraged to feel good about themselves and their sexuality.

As you scroll through the different links on the site, you are able to read various personal stories to support the contention that "Girl Love" is something healthy. One such writing was from a woman who has had a "consensual sexual relationship" with her daughter. She explained that she was separated from her husband and she and her daughter live alone together. The site, she says, "has helped her to deal with what [she] thought was a strange and un-natural relationship." She had "thought that what she was feeling was bad." Thanks to Butterfly Kisses, she does not "feel guilty or conflicted" about her sexual relationship with her ten-year-old daughter!

Further, according to their website:

IFgLC's goal is to end the extreme oppression of women and girls in mutually consensual relationships by:

1. building understanding and support for such relationships

2. educating the general public on the benevolent nature of woman/girl love

3. cooperating with lesbian, gay, feminist, and other liberation movements

4. supporting liberation of persons of all ages from sexual prejudice and oppression

Posters are available on the site that anyone can freely copy and disseminate. The poster on the next page lists "A Child's Sexual Bill of Rights."

The entire document centers around sex and advocates allowing children of any age to engage in sexual relations with anyone they choose. The fourth "Whereas" paragraph is interesting in that it states that a child who is "not allowed to express all the instinctive desires nature endowed him/her with becomes an unhappy, frustrated, anti-social being and potential criminal."

BUTTERFLY KISSES

***

The International Female Girllovers Collective

(IFgLC)

A Child's Sexual Bill of Rights:

Whereas a child's sexuality is just as much a part of his/her whole person from birth as the blood that flows in his/her veins, making his/her sexual inherent and inalienable, and

Whereas the United Nations Organization proclaimed a Universal Declaration of Human Rights in 1948, stating everyone is entitled to all the rights and freedoms encompassed in this Declaration without discrimination of any kind, such as race, color, sex, language, religious opinion, national or social origin, birth or other status, and

Whereas a Declaration of the Rights of the Child was proclaimed by UNO in 1959, but no mention was made of the sexual needs and rights of children, and

Whereas a child not allowed to express all the instinctive desires nature endowed him/her with becomes an unhappy, frustrated, antisocial being and potential criminal, and

Whereas it is time the people of the United States and their lawmakers recognise these facts of life and act accordingly.

Therefore the following inalienable rights are specifically set forth, to be implemented by appropriate legislation on a national and state level, and measures taken for the re-education of the citizenry in every part of the United States, this education to be available free to every citizen, whether school child or adult:

1. **Legal Protection** - Every child shall be legally protected in his/her sexual rights regardless of age or status as a legal minor.

2. **Child's right to his/her own person** - Every child has the right to privacy for his/her own personal thoughts, ideas, dreams, and exploration of his/her own body without any kind of adult interference, directly or indirectly expressed.

3. **Sex Information** - Every child has the right to accurate sex information and to be protected from sex misinformation as soon as he/she is able to understand this information in simple terms.

4. **Emotional growth** - Each child has the right to grow mentally, physically, emotionally, sexually and spiritually as a free, uncrippled happy person in security so he/she will be tolerant and appreciative of other individuals and their sexuality.

5. **Sexual pleasures** - Each child has the right to fully enjoy the sensual pleasures he/she may feel without guilt or shame.

6. **Learning the arts of love** - All children have the right to learn the arts of love beginning at any age he/she is able to understand, just as he/she is entitled to learn any other art or skill.

7. **Choice of a sex partner** - Every child has the right to loving relationships, including sexual, with any adult or child he/she may choose, and shall be protected and aided in doing so by being provided with contraceptives and aids to prevent venereal disease.

8. **Protection from sexual suppression** - Each child has the right to be protected from any form of sex suppression at home or in society so that in adulthood he/she will be capable of living his/her sex life according to his/her natural desires and not according to the dictates of tradition.

VISIT OUR WEB SITE:

http://www.bk-girls.org

In effect, what they appear to want us to believe is that the adult woman should have sexual control over the female child's life. In reality, we know that the innocence and vulnerability of youngsters makes them extremely susceptible to the influence of an older, manipulative adult. A simple toy, a piece of candy, or a certain look or suggestion of punishment from a relative or family friend may be all that is necessary to convince a child to try something they normally would have no incentive or desire to do. If we fall for the aforementioned argument and allow children to decide who they can have a sexual relationship with, we will have opened a Pandora's Box that would allow perverted women to malign and abuse little girls under the ruse of love.

There are a couple of other things on their site that caught my attention. One was their registration agreement terms, which states, in part:

> Membership to Butterfly Kisses is free of charge and is open to female girl lovers and anyone else who respects them. The members area of this web site is PRIVATE and is password protected to restrict access from right-wing fanatics, religious freaks, sensationalist media, fascist cops, and everyone else whose only intent is to look for pornography or harass, abuse, trivialize and threaten child lovers.

It seems like a perfectly logical reason to password protect a website. Call the well-adjusted segment of society who might abhor their behavior fascists, freaks, and right-wing fanatics. Hmm, does that mean that left-wing liberals condone their perverted activities? I think not!

In my opinion, the most interesting section on the site is where they allow people to post hate mail. The section starts off with this: "Before you read our hate mail which is largely contributed by Christian fanatics, check out how so-called Christian advocates "love" their children." The reader is then linked to the following site: http://www.nospank.net/floggers.htm, called "Flogging for God." There is a caption on the top of the homepage which reads, "FLOGGING FOR GOD: Violence toward children under the guise of religion. The poisonous pedagogy of hucksters and quacks who promote the 'benifits' [sic] of child beating." The site is filled with links to numerous articles discussing how Christians and other religious sects have abused children. I had to step back and wonder just exactly how this site is linked to the hate mail section of the "Butterfly Kisses" website. I suppose they are somehow trying to give the impression that only religious fanatics disdain what they advocate on their site. However, reading through the "hate mail" allows the reader to see in no uncertain terms that the letters are not all from "Christians" in the true sense of the word. In fact, there are many derogatory comments, and some people use extremely offensive language while offering their colorful opinions that the supporters of the site are "Sick Twisted Sub-Human F---ers," "Freaks," "sick, pinko, morally bankrupt, perverse, low life, pondskum, skunks, lower than a snakes belly, puke inducing rift raf," or "sick, mother f--kin' Michael Jackson wanna be petafillers," to name a few. Do these comments look like they came from Christian fanatics?

While the site states that the group "does not provide encouragement, referrals or assistance for people seeking sexual contacts . . . engage in any activities that violate the law," or "advocate that anyone else should do so," they make clear their disdain for "restrictions which deny women and girls the full enjoyment of their bodies and control over their own lives," and they "support the rights of youth as well as adults to choose the partners with whom they wish to share and enjoy their bodies."

There are other groups just as perverse, just as twisted, and over the top about their ideas of human sexuality and the love of children. They run rampant. The Internet has spawned a new wave of deviant activity that was once much more difficult for child predators to pursue.

Another site is called "The Neptune Link Directory," which, at the time of this writing, described itself as "a comprehensive directory of resources for all pedophiles, both boylovers and girllovers, as well as for anybody else looking for information about pedophilia and consensual child love." (See http://nld.puellula.com/Main.html.) Included on the site are several subdirectories that link the reader even deeper into the world of adult/child relationships. While at first glance some of the information may seem merely informative, it is clear that this is a roadmap into the world of deviance. For example, clicking a sub-link, http://nld.puellula.com/Directories.html, directs the reader to sites filled with various, questionable child-related information. One site, http://www.asfar.org, describes their organization ASFAR (Americans for a Society Free from Age Restrictions) as being "dedicated to protecting and advancing the legal civil rights of youth through the abolition of age-based restrictions. ASFAR fights the voting age, curfew laws, and other laws that limit the freedom of young people." (See http://www.asfar.org/faq.php.)

While that description is seemingly innocent, one need only go to the page entitled "Declaration of Principles" to see some of the underlying issues that they are focused on. For example, in calling for the repeal of various age-related laws, they suggest in Section 9, entitled "Health and Sexuality," that:

> Laws invalidating sexual consent purely on the basis of age should be repealed. ASFAR also supports initiatives to clarify the legal definition of rape to distinguish between informed and uninformed consent, where uninformed consent must be established in a court of law and not on the arbitrary basis of age. (See http://www.asfar.org/declaration.)

On the Puella site itself is a manifesto. It lists several different categories from which to choose. (See http://hfp.puellula.com/Manifesto.html#consent.) I found an interesting section under "Article 27, Chapter V: Legislation," entitled "Age of Consent." It states that the "age of consent for penetrative sexual activity shall be set at the legal age of puberty as defined in Article 14. Other forms of physical intimacy shall not be restricted for any age and no restrictions shall be made on intimacy between any persons, regardless of age differences between those persons." "Article 14: Citizenship" states "For the sake of legal clarity, the legal age of puberty should be determined as the median age of puberty in the general population, rounded down to the year."

I don't think there is a real need for me to comment on that however, I can't move on without discussing one other section under "Chapter I: Civil Liberties," entitled "Article 6: Megan's Laws," which states that "Publicly accessible sexual offender registries are a violation of the fourteenth amendment to the United States Constitution which guarantees the right to privacy and a violation of the fifth amendment to the United States Constitution, which explicitly states that no person shall be punished twice for the same offense." My comment is brief and to the point. While I'm not at all sure that sexual offender registries are truly accomplishing their intended mission, allowing convicted sexual offenders to roam freely without the "encumbrance" of having their names on a registry is contrary to the statistics that demonstrate that most often, sexual offenders will and do strike again. According to what this website espouses, these repeat offenders should be allowed unfettered access to our children under the ridiculous notion that there is some special interpretation hidden among the penumbra of privileges attached to the "right to privacy" (which, by the way, flows from certain guarantees as set forth in our Constitution). Under that premise, the "right to privacy" would, in effect, be shielding the pervert with a special coat of armor in order to keep the rest of us from knowing when one of them moves in next door. Of course, these people advocate for that! They want free and clear access to our children and they will use the gray areas of the Constitution to argue their case. I say gray areas because there is no specific right to privacy written into the Constitution. This is something that has been created by non-strict constructionist jurists who prefer an ever-evolving and flexible Constitution. I agree with those jurists; however, I do not agree with individuals who twist the goodness of our most important document to imply that it condones the unrestrained movements of sexual predators among our children.

Another interesting website is called "Pedophiles." While reading through it, I found Section 8.1, which explains their four main guidelines for pedophiles to follow:

1. Consent of both child and adult,

2. Freedom for the child to withdraw from the relationship at any moment,

3. Harmony with the child's level of psycho-sexual and physical development,

4. Openness towards the parents of the child.
   [See http://www.clogo.org/Pedophiles/index.html.]

Again, we see that consent from the child makes everything okay to these deviants. They perceive life from their own self-gratifying point of view without regard for their victims. Let me take this opportunity to introduce you to an individual who suffered at the hands of a man who most likely deluded himself into believing that a child's submission to his sick demands meant that she was giving him her consent. The girl is not the victim of an Internet predator, but the pain that a molested child suffers is the same no matter where or how they meet their attacker. These are her words:

My childhood should have been filled with fun and laughter, long days spent playing with friends outside, and the feeling that I was an invincible little girl. Instead, I have a limited memory of my life from the ages of six to about ten years old. At an age when most little girls' utmost concerns are whether or not they can watch Cinderella one more time before bed, or whether pink lacey socks match a blue striped shirt, I was worried about keeping secrets from my mommy.

I was about six years old when my mother filed for a divorce from my father. He had been abusive to her for years, but she had also become suspicious about his behavior toward me. He snuggled a little too close at bedtime and treated me like a surrogate spouse, trying to make my mother jealous. When she was out running errands, I would often end up in bed with him, although I don't recall how I got there. We had secrets and played inappropriate sexual games. I remember him saying that if I ever told my mother, she'd want a divorce and it would be my fault. I grew up feeling ashamed, scared, confused, and worthless.

Now nearly twenty years later, even though I've taken healthy steps to reclaim my life and rebuild my identity, those memories often still haunt me in the form of nightmares. I've seen several counselors. I experienced rage and hatred for my father and his actions, and when I realized that my anger hurt me more than it hurt him, I accepted the past, disowned him, and tried to make peace with my own mind and heart.

Being a survivor of child molestation has forever changed me. It affected every aspect of my personality, and for a time, every relationship I had. Because I grew up feeling worthless and dirty, I didn't have self-respect when it came to dating and was promiscuous at a young age. I didn't know I had the right to say "no" but I craved attention and affection in any way I could get it. I was bitter and depressed through most of my high school years.

If I was in a good relationship, I would sabotage it because I didn't feel worthy of love. To this day, I still wonder if I will ever trust a man enough to allow myself to fall in love, get married, and have children.

What my father did to me also affected my relationship with my mother. Even though she sensed something was wrong, I was too ashamed to tell her about it until many years later, and that made her feel as though she had failed to protect me. Fortunately, working through those experiences made my family stronger, but I know that is not always the case.

If I could ever offer any words of advice or wisdom to parents and anyone who works with children, it would be these: Always trust your instincts if you think a child is being abused or if you think someone intends to harm a child. If you can take action to save a child from sexual or physical abuse, even if it causes tension, even if it causes legal ramifications, even if it's simply uncomfortable for you—think of how that child must feel, and then do the right thing!

Those poignant words convey more than anything I could possibly describe about how a child perceives her attacker after sexual molestation. She lived it and she survived it, but not without deep scars. Sexual predators leave their mark and then move on to their next victim while justifying their actions just as those people described in this chapter. What makes it even worse is that today, sexual predators have meeting places where they can hide their faces and true identities and discuss all that is wrong with the world outside of their distorted realm of focus. They come together from every continent and talk about their "love" for children and why the laws against pedophilia and "adult/child sex" are so unfair. They are able to form bonds and gain reassurance that they are not alone. They also have links to find their way to children who have obviously been swept up in the fury of all of this deviance. There is strength in numbers, and they certainly have a lot of followers. They convince themselves and others that they are the ones who are right and the rest of us are trying to stop them from exhibiting perfectly normal, loving tendencies towards children. They call what they do "love," and I have even seen some comments on these sites to suggest that it is not considered molesting if you know and have a close relationship with a child. In other words, only a stranger can molest a child.

Along with the aforementioned links, there are also groups on various websites, including AOL, that cater to older men searching for young girls. They include such names as "Don't ask how young 4 older," described as "a place for younger guys or girls to meet older men or women we like em YOUNG, so were not asking your age, don't tell us. Were better off not knowing. :)" Another group is "Gals who like older guys come in," with the inscription "my group is about well i don't know cute people looking for other cute people im just making this group because I know there are a lot of younger girls looking for older men." Then, there is "TeEngIrLs4OldErMeN," with the inscription "teen girl who like an experienced older men, in all aspects, join then meet someone in your area, especially me, lol . . ." And, I have also come across "Younger girls seeking older men," described as a place where "any young girls that want an older man for friendship love or marriage can join," and "Older men for younger women," which describes itself as "for attractive men who would like to meet younger women for dating, relationships, and possibly more. NO PERVS PLS."

The names change frequently, but the idea remains the same. A person can post messages on any one of those sites and have them emailed to every person on the member list. Some may try to explain them away as not-so-older men looking for not-so-younger girls, but that is absolutely not the case. Having been a "child" member of all of them, I can say with complete certainty that there are several much older men on those sites aggressively searching for minor girls for the purpose of having sexual relationships.

One of the messages I received as a young teen was "You are 13? Have you been with older men? Just asking cause I'm 51, don't look my age, but . . . probably too old for you (To me, age is but a number)." Another sent three consecutive emails saying "35," "Conn.," and "How old are you looking for?" There is no question with whom he thought he was communicating. My age was listed in that profile.

The creator of the site "Older men for younger women," who included the quote "NO PERVS PLS" is someone who communicated with me thinking that I was a thirteen-year-old girl, and he still made a serious attempt to have me meet him even though he claimed to be thirty-two. In fact, when I asked him if it was cool that I was thirteen, he responded, "cooooooolllll." He also gave me his cell phone number. I can't really say anything more than that about him. I have no real way of knowing how far he would have actually gone or what his true intentions were. However, everything he typed definitely followed along with the typical grooming techniques that I have experienced with sexual predators.

There are many other avenues on the Internet by which adults seek to find children to have sex with in real time. They scope out kids and tell them lies and lure them out into the open where they can get their hands on them. No matter how hard we try, it is still next to impossible to get them all, but we do get a lot of them and they never know which one of them will be next. So, while many of them may stay under the radar, they have to be getting more and more nervous about who they are showing up to meet, to whom they are sending pornography, and who is investigating their background just by having their screen name.

They are being watched, and for every new friend they make, for every new member that one of those groups accepts onto their website, and for every new young girl they venture out to meet, there are people like me who will be waiting to take them down.

THIRTEEN

The Public Side of Pedophilia

NO MATTER HOW MUCH TIME I SPEND ONLINE CHATTING with sexual predators, no matter how many law enforcement officials form squads to go after them, there appears to be a never-ending supply of Internet predators. But, we are definitely making great strides. With the help of all of the dedicated people who have become aware of the expanding and far-reaching problem of the sexual abuse of children, we are bringing them down, one by one, and one after another. Television news programs like *Dateline*, talk shows such as *Oprah*, newspaper articles, and news reports are all discussing the issue with increasing intensity.

I watch some of the programs with great anticipation, always wondering what I will see that will be new. Unfortunately, I have not only seen it all, I have seen even worse. I am in the midst of the filth every single day, so much so that I have become somewhat desensitized to the horror factor. But, others have not. The average individual has never had any contact with a sexual predator, at least, none of which they are aware. Predators treat adults differently than they treat children. Often, parents find them charismatic or extremely dedicated individuals. But, with the large-scale exposure that the subject has been given as of late, people are seeing what these deviants are like in their natural habitats, when they are going after children.

I am glad that the subject of sexual predators is finally getting the attention it truly deserves. Only when the public is educated regarding what types of dangers await our children will we be able to diminish the capacity of child predators to work their way into our youngsters' lives. It is up to those whose job it is to protect children to make sure that these monsters cannot lay claim to one more victim. Many others are joining the crusade.

In August 2005, Dan Abrams of MSNBC's *The Abrams Report* hosted a five-part series called "Manhunt: Sex Offenders on the Loose." During each night of the series, Abrams alerted the public to some of the most dangerous predators from each state that he focused on in his report. Pictures of sexual offenders from various states were shown, along with descriptions of their crimes. The goal was to find missing sex offenders and get them "off the streets before they strike" again.

The first state discussed was Idaho, where violent convicted sex offender Joseph Duncan was accused of killing the Groene family and kidnapping eight-year-old Shasta and nine-year-old Dylan. The children were both molested and Dylan was murdered. According to the report, Duncan had already served "17 years for raping a teenage boy in North Dakota in 1980, but he had gone missing several weeks before the alleged crime spree in Idaho."

Another violent convicted sex offender from Idaho, William Lightner, had disappeared ten days prior to the report by cutting off his monitoring bracelet, and there were fears about what he would do while on the run. He had already served ten years in prison for lewd contact with a minor, before being released in March 2005. He was captured two months after the report.

One state that the report focused on was Florida, which reportedly "harbors more than 35,000 known sex offenders" and where "46 of the most serious sex offenders are missing." The state is also where children Jessica Lunsford and Sarah Lunde were both kidnapped and murdered by convicted sex offenders.

Another state discussed was Minnesota, where 11 percent of their

14,000 known sex offenders "fail to obey certain rules," such as reporting to parole officers and not using drugs.

The New York report's focus was on the parents of two different
young girls who were the victims of vicious sex crimes. The discussion
pointed to the difficulties of tracking offenders and a May 2005 statistic that out of the 500,000 nationwide registered sex offenders, 100,000
are missing.

If nothing else, the series was a great start in getting the word out
that the problem is not minimal, that it is widespread, and that something needs to be done to ensure the safety of children.

The MSNBC *Report* is not the only television segment that has
made child predators a priority. Oprah Winfrey has been a champion of
children for many years. Her efforts have consistently brought results.
She has an unmatched ability to reach the masses, and I am so glad that
she has turned her attention to this issue in an effort to help give
Americans a much-needed wake-up call. At the time of this writing,
Oprah had placed a "Child Predator Watch List" on her website. The
list contained profiles of some of the FBI's most wanted child predators. Rewards were being offered to anyone responsible for turning in
one of the predators, provided they met certain conditions. In early
October 2005, Oprah dedicated an entire show to the subject. The
words she spoke were clear and poignant:

> Today I stand before you to say, in no uncertain terms, as a mat-
> ter of fact, in terms that I hope are very certain, that I have had
> enough. With every breath in my body, whatever it takes, and
> with you at my side, and most importantly, with your support,
> we are going to move Heaven and Earth to stop a sickness, a
> darkness that I believe is the definition of evil that's been going
> on for far too long. The children of this nation, the United States
> of America, are being stolen, raped, tortured, and killed by sex-
> ual predators who are walking right into your homes. How
> many times does it have to happen and how many children have

to be sacrificed? What price are we, a society, willing to continue to pay before we rise up and take to the streets and say, "Enough! Enough! Enough!"

Oprah's audience is far-reaching, and I doubt there is one person out there who has not been touched by one of her shows. They are meaningful and timely and always leave us feeling a little bit better for having taken the time to pay attention. I am truly hopeful that her crusade against child predators hits home, that everyone who saw it took it personally and felt as though the tragedy of child molestation might possibly touch their lives, rather than that this is just something that happens to everyone else's children.

After Oprah's program aired, I assumed that the Internet would calm down a bit where sexual predators were concerned, as is often the case after an arrest is well publicized. But, there was no difference in the amount of men who reached out to talk to me. Maybe that was because Oprah's focus was not on Internet usage. The sex offenders that she discussed were convicted criminals on the run. The guys I deal with probably did not feel that they were in any danger of being caught.

During the fall of 2005, NBC's *Dateline* produced a hidden camera investigation that allowed viewers to watch the way sexual predators communicate with children on the Internet and then follow them as they showed up for a rendezvous with the kids. During their report, they stated, "Law enforcement officials estimate that 50,000 predators are on the Internet at any given moment." I often wonder just how many there actually are, considering the vast amount that I come across in just a few short hours.

The segment, repeated numerous times throughout the weeks that followed the initial airing, showed sexual predators arriving at a private house that was rented and wired by *Dateline*. Several predators showed up, one after the other, expecting to meet a child for sex. Instead, they were greeted by *Dateline* correspondent, Chris Hansen, who confronted them about their actions as the cameras rolled.

The first man to arrive was thirty-five years old, and he came expecting to meet a fourteen-year-old girl. He claimed that he was suspicious about the meeting from the beginning and only showed up just to "check it out." Another claim he made, the same as all of the other sexual predators on the show, was that it was the first time he had ever shown up to meet a child. One guy, a thirty-four-year-old, in an attempt to cover all bases in case he was caught, walked into the house and called out to the child he expected to see, telling her to say that she was nineteen years old. When she resisted, he insisted she say it, asking her if she could "read between the lines." Once confronted by Hansen, he claimed that the girl told him that she was nineteen while he was chatting with her on the Internet. Of course, the man was not yet aware that he would be faced with the transcripts of his chats with the girl. However, once he saw them, it did not shake him up in the least. He simply claimed to be an independent TV producer there for the purpose of doing research. And, when he found out that he was talking to a TV correspondent, he even went as far as to commend him for a job well done.

The show had a mix of men: one was a teacher, another a rabbi, and they all seemed like every day people—no trench coats, no dark sunglasses, no particularly deviant-looking appearances. But, their actions spoke volumes. One man even walked in stark naked. Another dropped to the floor as if to faint when confronted. Many of them thought they were talking to a police officer or the child's father until told about *Dateline*'s sting operation. Then, most ran out after realizing that they were going be part of a television program on Internet predators. During the two and a half days that the sting operation continued, the *Dateline* reporter confronted eighteen men. *Dateline* has continued to produce more of these segments in different parts of the United States.

Since the story was run numerous times, it was the topic of many conversations. I found that most people had not previously been aware of how very easy it is for a sexual predator to reach a child. It shocked them to hear that many of the men who showed up were productive members of society, some with wonderful reputations; that is the part that must be instilled in people. We need to stop blindly trusting those people we think are the most likely to keep our children safe. It is a hard fact to accept, but it needs to be said that sexual predators are people who do everything they can to be near children. They are often the ones we entrust our kids to every day. We must reevaluate our feelings about all of the dedicated souls who spend much of their time focused on the activities of our children.

We also have to be careful that our own actions are not inappropriate in any way. It is a shame that things have come to this point, where a well-meaning teacher cannot give a comforting hug to an injured child, or where a person who volunteers to help children may be looked at as though they have an ulterior motive. Even someone who may mistakenly wander into the wrong place is likely to suffer consequences. For example, WABC-TV reported that a woman was ticketed in a New York City playground under a law that prohibits adults from sitting in the area without a child. The law is meant to keep pedophiles out. The woman claimed to have been waiting for an arts festival to begin nearby and said that she did not see the sign that was posted at the entrance. I am not disputing her claim, and the description of the incident certainly made it look as though the police may have taken the situation a bit more seriously than was necessary. However, the fact is that sexual predators frequent places where children hang out, places like playgrounds. If you are going to make the mistake of walking into the wrong place at the wrong time, especially under those circumstances, be prepared to suffer the consequences. After all, how do the police know who is a sexual predator and who is not? Predators do not have marks on their foreheads or signs that would make them easy to identify. Nobody should be allowed to simply walk away without being scrutinized.

I know that my attitude seems harsh, and if that woman was innocent of any wrongdoing, it's a shame that she was being penalized for

THE PUBLIC SIDE OF PEDOPHILIA

inadvertently walking into the playground without seeing the sign. However, I spend my days dealing with sexual predators. As a matter of fact, as I write, I am being instant messaged by several of them who see that my Teen2hot4u screen name is online. I have seen thousands of pictures, I have talked to numerous men *and* women, and I am aware of what many of them are like and what their professions are. Nobody is above suspicion, especially if they are near children. It is sad that those of us who have good intentions have to change our behavior due to the rampant predatory activity in our society, but that is just the way it has to be. Nowadays there is no excuse for any questionable behavior to be permitted around children.

Aside from television programs, there are other avenues by which information can be obtained regarding child predators. There is a very informative website (http://www.12.familywatchdog.us/) which allows users to plug in their home address to find out if a sex offender lives nearby. Not only does it show the area where a sex offender resides, the user is able to get the offender's name and address as well as their criminal record. Not every state was available yet at the time of this writing, but most were on the list.

Another site, the United States Justice Department's "National Sex Offender Public Registry," can be found at www.nsopr.gov. By entering your location and clicking on the map, you can find sexual predators in your neighborhood. The site also lists the names, addresses, and criminal records of offenders.

Some jurisdictions have laws or are in the process of passing legislation aimed at making it difficult for a convicted sex offender to reside in certain areas. Pedophile-free zone laws, many modeled after drug-free zone restrictions which are aimed at keeping drug dealers from doing business in areas where children are found, are cropping up in various states.

During the summer of 2005, Michigan State legislators passed a bill prohibiting sex offenders from working or living within 1,000 feet of schools and made all school employees subject to criminal background checks. A former law restricted them from living or working within 500 feet of schools.

In New Jersey, a number of different communities passed somewhat similar legislation. However, theirs was limited to where sex offenders reside rather than including the criminal status of school employees.

On November 1, 2005, one New Jersey community enacted a law that prohibits sex offenders from living within 1,000 feet of schools, and 2,500 feet of recreation areas, playgrounds, and parks. On November 9, 2005, another New Jersey community enacted legislation prohibiting sex offenders from living within 2,500 feet of playgrounds, daycare centers, recreation areas, and schools. A third New Jersey community passed a law on November 10, 2005, that prohibits sex offenders from living within 3,000 feet of playgrounds, daycare centers, and schools.

New laws such as these are cropping up all over the country. In June 2006, Suffolk County, New York, legislators enacted a law that prohibits convicted sex offenders from living within one-quarter mile from schools, daycare centers, and playgrounds.

After researching the Michigan, Florida, and New York laws, I believe that part of the Michigan legislation is imperative in that any person working with children should be screened for criminal involvement. While pedophile-free zones seem like an appropriate way to regulate how close sex offenders can reside to specific areas, it seems to me that there is something strategically lacking in the idea. Restricting sexual predators from living in certain neighborhoods will not guarantee the safety of the children in those communities. For one thing, the assumption is that sex offenders are all registered and their whereabouts are regularly monitored. However, there are three flaws with that premise. First, many sex offenders move to an area without registering. Second, there are many dangerous sexual predators who have not yet been caught and therefore, are not on any registries. And third, there are only a handful of people out there who are responsible for monitoring thousands of registered sex offenders, which makes it virtually impossible to keep track of all of them. Thus, they may be living in close proximity to or within the restricted areas and still have complete access to children.

Another problem that I see with pedophile-free zones is that keeping a predator from residing in an area does not prevent one from hanging around in one. So, he or she may live 5,000 feet or one-quarter mile away from a school and still walk down to the play yard, the park, or the recreation area every day and prey upon children.

Finally, the law suggests that children are most vulnerable in areas near schools, playgrounds, recreation areas, and daycare centers. While it is true that these are the places where sexual predators are most likely to find an abundance of children from which to choose, lest we forget how many kids have fallen victim to these predators in malls, front yards, walking down the street, at the beach, in their own homes, in the homes of friends and relatives, in church, in school, at the doctor's office, on the Internet, and many other places that have absolutely nothing to do with regulating where a sexual offender resides. Passing these laws are noble efforts, but the true benefits do not appear to have been well thought out. People do not want to live next door to a sex offender and I do not blame them. But, the truth is there are more sex offenders who have not yet been caught, than those who have and are listed on registries.

None of the Internet predators that I have been involved with had ever been caught before for committing sexual acts against children. Many were reputable, upstanding members of their communities, the kind of people you think you would want living next door to you. So, while the legislation is a good start, there needs to be more strategic planning to protect children.

I recently read about some of the solutions that one county in New York is utilizing. At this writing, legislators in Suffolk County were considering several pieces of proposed legislation to put even tighter restrictions on the movements of sexual predators. One resolution requires notification to victims and/or their legal guardians by the probation department if a sex offender disappears from supervision. Another pro- posal prohibits Suffolk County departments and contractors from facil- itating the placement of more than one sex offender in a single place of residence. This most likely came in response to a finding that there were numerous clusters of sexual predators living in various neighborhoods around the county. A bill was also introduced that would require deputy sheriffs to verify the whereabouts of sexual predators by periodically visiting their residences, while another requires that county, town, and village elected officials be notified when level 2 and 3 sex offenders move into their communities. Also up for consideration was a law requiring landlords to register with the probation department and receive training before renting to multiple sex offenders. Other measures were being introduced. These are well-crafted solutions that came about because people paid attention to what was happening in their communities and recognized the dangers that sexual predators create when they are near children.

Another method of keeping track of sex offenders is called the Global Positioning System (GPS), which is a satellite tracking device used in many states, including Florida's criminal justice system since 1996. Florida has recently made it mandatory for convicted sex offend- ers to wear the tracking devices for life. Wisconsin's State Assembly passed legislation on November 9, 2005, requiring the most dangerous sex offenders to wear the GPS for the rest of their lives to keep track of their locations, and it requires the state's department of corrections to track the most dangerous child molesters for at least twenty years after their release from prison.

I hope their technology is better than what William Lightner was wearing when he cut his off to escape the system. While some civil rights activists see lifetime GPS as a violation of a person's civil liberties, it must be remembered that the recidivism rate for sex offenders is extremely high. These people are not just criminals in the sense of somebody doing what they want and getting away with it. This is about a serious addiction and compulsion. So, what do you do with someone who has already had a few convictions for child rape? Either monitor them for life or put them away for life. I choose the latter option.

As of this writing, approximately ten states have passed or are attempting to pass legislation making GPS monitoring mandatory for certain sex offenders. One thing to keep in mind is that the GPS bracelets or anklets only reveal the location of the person wearing them. The information may not be transmitted every second, but rather a certain number of times per day, leaving gaps in monitoring. Also, the system only picks up the sex offender's location, not their actions. So if they are in an unrestricted area molesting a child, the system will not reveal that.

Another interesting twist to the GPS system is that parents are purchasing them in the form of wristwatches and bracelets to track the whereabouts of their children through the Internet and by telephone. Some of the devices cannot be removed without an alarm going off, and some have panic buttons that connect directly to 911. While questions have been posed regarding the privacy issues of children, I would venture to say that the youngest sector of our society should be considered the prime targets for these devices and there should be no debate about whether or not a parent or legal guardian has the right to know the whereabouts of their minor children. Keeping track of kids may be one of the most worthwhile uses of GPS and one of the best ways to ensure their safety.

The Walt Disney Company just came out with a wireless cell phone service that allows parents to control their children's cell phone usage. Among other things, there is a GPS tracking system that allows parents to locate their child's whereabouts, as well as a feature that makes the parents or other family members' calls to the child a top priority. In other words, the parent or family member's call will automatically cut off any other call the child may be on. Once again, none of these features will guarantee that we know what the kids are doing or what someone else is doing to them.

This is all still in the infancy stages and there are other, more pressing concerns that go with this discussion. The most important aspect of all of the above restrictions and devices is the fact that people are paying attention to the problem and they are sending a very clear message: *Sexual predators beware!* We are no longer going to sit by and let someone else worry about the problem. We are on to you, and we will not allow you easy access to our children. You will have to go through us and you will not succeed.

However, along with the vast publicity, the informative websites, the ever-evolving laws, and the latest tracking technology, the danger to our children still exists. So, the real change has to begin with us in the messages that we send to them.

The most important protective and preemptive method that can save the majority of children from child molesters is knowledge. Knowledge is power, and power is what will protect them. Many of the kids who end up in the grasp of a predator have walked into a bad situation, whether by being duped by someone offering to do something nice for them, by someone claiming to need help, or while thinking they are going off to meet another child when, in reality, they are going to come face-to-face with an adult and be trapped somewhere alone with them. So we have to offer them knowledge that is understandable and crystal clear.

Some of us may actually be putting our kids in danger by the contradicting messages that we send. We tell them not to trust strangers. Yet, we drop them at ball fields with coaches we may have never met; we allow them to stay after school because, after all, they will be with their teacher, a person who has made the selfless sacrifice to give the child extra help; we send them to dance lessons, scout meetings, play groups, daycare centers, friends' homes, malls, movie theaters, ice skating rinks, parks, parties, beaches, and even doctors' offices without making sure that they are able to recognize when they are in danger. We teach them not to take candy from strangers, but on Halloween, we often make exceptions, especially if it is in our own neighborhood, where sexual predators may lurk or reside. And while we tell them not to even *talk* to strangers, we make an exception there, too, for police officers or other representatives of authority. However, sexual predators have jobs in every profession. There *are* no exceptions; they are white-collar professionals, blue-collar workers, and unemployed individuals. It's impossible to tell sexual predators from the rest of the population. They are everywhere. They can get to your children from every angle.

We need to revamp the way *we* think in order to teach our kids how to change their own way of thinking and stay safe. Instead of picking out a group of people to whom our children can turn when they are in trouble, such as police officers, we need to simply and openly teach children *how* to know where to turn. They have to be trained, in effect, to use their own intuition about people, but it is imperative that they use it in conjunction with the information that we have provided to them. Their intuition, by itself, at such a young age can get them into trouble if they do not have a frame of reference to use with it. Predators can easily gain the trust of a child, instill in them a feeling of security, and often lead them astray by convincing them that they are mature enough to make their own decisions. That is why we need to give children, starting from a very early age, the vitally important information to help them take the power away from predators. Children have to be made aware that predators can and will approach them in broad daylight, and on the Internet, anywhere at anytime. But, at the same time, we do not want to make them paranoid; they need to be alert and resourceful.

If we can instill in our children the need to be completely aware of their surroundings on a much higher level than we generally do, then it is a start. If we can go beyond the "don't talk to strangers" lecture and get into the "even our friends and family may do or say something inappropriate and you need to tell on them" talk, then we are making more headway.

If we let children know at a young age that people older than them cannot always be trusted, that someone may try to talk to them about things like "secrets" and "special friendships," and that children need to tell on them, then we are making some progress.

If we explain openly and honestly that there is nobody that can be crossed off the list of people to follow the rules about, then we might just get through to them.

Kids are resilient. They are smarter than we think. Giving them the tools to protect themselves at an early age is wise, because it will come naturally to them as just another lesson in life. Waiting until something bad happens to them or their friends is not the time to share the information. I realize that it is hard to imagine instilling thoughts into their young minds like *you never know who you can trust*, but if it is done appropriately it will make a clear impression.

We teach children to respect and trust their elders, and that is still a good premise. However, I also believe that elders must earn the child's respect and trust. Children should not be sent out into the world assuming that an adult is always trustworthy. They should be taught that there are certain things that are totally inappropriate and that nobody, not even their parents, has the right to cross those lines. It is a hard situation with which to deal. I know that firsthand, having had that simple conversation with my own son. I also had the experience with "Uncle" Frank and I was too ashamed to tell my mother. I only wish that someone had the foresight back then to talk to me about the dangers of sexual predators and the importance of telling on them. But, things are different today, and although the kind of lecture I'm talking about may seem overwhelming, it is something we need to discuss with our children just as we teach them to take baths, brush their teeth, dress warm in the winter, do their homework, look both ways before crossing the street, and many other little tidbits of information that we offer to them as parents.

We also need to give them specific boundaries. Don't allow your children free reign on the computer, no matter how trustworthy *they* are, because sexual predators are extremely cunning. Keep the computer in a central location in your home and put safeguards on it in order to know what your child is doing. Also, having your child's password is essential when you are dealing with a minor who regularly uses the Internet. I know these suggestions sound harsh. You don't want your children to feel that you don't trust them, but this isn't about trusting them. It is about protecting them from an element of society that is so perverse, so manipulative, and so intrusive, that each and every day kids fall prey to their advances. Remember that when a child meets a stranger in a chatroom, he or she is actually meeting them right under your nose, inside your home, maybe even in their bedrooms. This is where your child is supposed to be safe. This is where you least expect them to get into trouble, and today, it is the easiest place for a predator to reach out and grab them. Diligence is the key, because there are thousands of predators just waiting for the chance to make your child their next victim.

Everyone asks me how I deal with it—talking to predators all the time. They wonder how I can stand them. At the same time, they are fascinated. They ask what predators are like, what they say, and what they do for work. They want to know how predators are able to get children to believe them and how they are able to convince children to come out from behind their computers to meet them. They don't understand why kids are so naïve and gullible, and they assume that the parents of those children who do willingly meet with a sexual predator probably haven't taught their children well and most likely don't care about their kids the way they do. They also assume that predators are sleazy, easy-to-spot creeps who hover in dark alleyways waiting to pounce on unsuspecting children, but they have the wrong impression.

There are all sorts of deviants with all different fetishes and addictions, and after a few years of doing what I do, it has become easy to spot each and every one of them on the Internet. They all have one thing in common. For the most part, they all belong to an exclusive little club. All the cybersexers say the same thing. All of the phone sex perverts say the same thing. All of the slave masters say the same thing. All of the submissives say the same thing. All of the sexual predators who want to venture out to meet a child say the same thing. They are not unique. Most are not even creative. They are a bunch of deviants who cannot make their way in a normal world, so they create one of their own where it is legal and acceptable to have sex with a child.

Sexual predators have no place in a society that protects children from what they have to offer. Their rationalizations, excuses, and blatant put-downs of the legal and social systems by which we live just don't cut it. They can gather up all of the other deviants and create clubs with fancy names and fraternity-like groups where they can congregate on or offline and commiserate about how terribly society treats them and how unfair laws against having sex with children are, and it won't make a tiny bit of difference; they are soulless, conscienceless, selfish people who couldn't care less about anyone but themselves, and they prove it every time they say something obscene to a child, every time they send a picture of their genitals to a child, every time they moan and groan and describe to a child what they are doing to themselves, every time they discuss what they want to do to the child, and every time they leave the privacy of their computers to go out and meet a child for sex.

We need to take action. Thankfully, federal laws are getting tougher. Under the Protect Act of 2003, convicted sexual predators faced a minimum mandatory sentence of five years' imprisonment and a maximum of thirty years on the enticement charge that most of the predators that I have identified have been convicted under. The coercion and enticement law can be found in the United States Code, Title 18, Section 2422(b). Those predators who traveled interstate to have sex with Lorie and Julie, such as Corso, Patel, and Brand, have been charged under United States Code, Title 18, Section 2423(b). Then there was Hamilton, who was charged with enticement, but also with transporting a minor in interstate commerce with intent to engage in sexual activity, under Section 2423(a), because he bought Lorie a bus ticket to Ohio.

Now, due to the recently enacted Adam Walsh Child Protection and Safety Act of 2006, the Protect Act of 2003 has raised the minimum mandatory sentence for the enticement charge to ten years, with a maximum of life. So, we are making progress.

But, while laws are changing, so must we. There is no other way to protect our children. Proactive parents create safer environments for their children. That is not to say that children who have been molested have bad parents or parents who are not proactive. Sometimes, there's nothing we can do to protect our kids. Often, kids just do things because they think they are smarter than their parents, and sometimes, kids act out because they are hardheaded and want to prove that they can make good decisions all by themselves. And sometimes, they are so totally manipulated by a child predator that they don't even realize that they are being sucked into a web of deceit. But, in the end, the blame can only go where it truly belongs—on the predator, the person who needs to be punished and taken off the street and put away so no other children can be hurt.

The ultimate responsibility for the pain that is created when a molester goes after a child belongs to the molester. They have no excuse. They can claim they are mentally ill, that they were molested as a child, that they are lonely, depressed, and immature, that they really love children and only want to show them that love, that they were entrapped, that they were only going to lecture the child they showed up to meet, that they thought the child was really an adult, that they never did it before, and that they were in the wrong place at the wrong time, but it's all nothing more than stories, excuses, and justification for their sick, crude, cruel, and disgusting behavior towards children.

I talk to them every day. I hear their words, I see their chats, and it is all the same. Internet predators are pathetic insects who hide in their homes and offices and prey upon innocent children like swarms of bees looking for honey. They have one goal, to satisfy their own insatiable appetite for children, by any means necessary. They will convince a child to lie to their parents, to cut school, to sneak out of the house, to travel far to meet them, to give out their phone numbers and addresses, and to trust them enough to have sex. It is unimaginable that there are so many sexual predators, yet even more unimaginable that so many children fall prey to them. The key is to get to the children before the predators do.

When children talk to a predator, it strengthens the predator's addiction. It is the same as handing an alcoholic a drink or a drug addict a drug. Until children are savvy enough not to react to the advances of predators, they will still be susceptible to becoming victims. And, to keep that from happening, we need to start with the basics. We have to teach them how to handle themselves on the Internet, because we cannot stop them from signing onto it. They may do it at a friend's house, at school, at the library, or even an Internet café.

One of the most important pieces of advice that kids need to hear is that a predator has the ability to find them using even the smallest amount of information that the youngsters give out on the Internet. It does not seem feasible to young minds that revealing their first name and describing a few hobbies can be dangerous. It is. For example, while chatting with a person they don't know, which is often the case, the conversation may go something like this:

```
Kid4kid:      hey im joey
Teen2hot4u:   im lorie
Kid4kid:      hey lorie how old r u
Teen2hot4u:   im 12
Kid4kid:      cool im 13 where r u from
Teen2hot4u:   ny where r u from
Kid4kid:      cali what grade r u in
Teen2hot4u:   7th u
Kid4kid:      8th i like baseball what do u like to do for fun
Teen2hot4u:   i play softball
Kid4kid:      wow i bet u r real good I play first base what about u
Teen2hot4u:   i'm catcher
Kid4kid:      sometimes we play at my school the Calverton middle school
              but sometimes we play at other schools where do u play
Teen2hot4u:   we play at my school ps42
Kid4kid:      my games r tues an thurs when do u play
Teen2hot4u:   wed an sat
```

Kid4kid: wow r games r at 4 on tues an 4 on thurs wut bout u

Teen2hot4u: well the wed game is at 4 an the sat game is at 10

Kid4kid: I guess u get done with school the same as me like 3

Teen2hot4u: no I get done at 2:30 an when I got a game, I hang out on the field practicing til it starts

Kid4kid: our uniforms r so cool we got a pic of a tiger on the pocket an there yellow an blue an we r the cal cubs

Teen2hot4u: my uniform got a pic of a bird on it an its red an white an we r the cardinals

Kid4kid: wow i like that I bet it looks cool with ur number on it mine is 23

Teen2hot4u: yeah it does my number is 4

Kid4kid: I was in ny last year visitin my cousin for Christmas maybe u no him he lives in Brooklyn an his name is steve davidson

Teen2hot4u: no silly ny is a big place an I live in merrick anyhow so I don't know anyone in Brooklyn.

Kid4kid: oh yeah so u got any bros or sis

Teen2hot4u: no jus me an my mom

Kid4kid: I got two bros an a big dog u

Teen2hot4u: no animals :(my mom wont let me

Kid4kid: to bad my dog is cool sometimes he walks me to school do u walk or take a bus

Teen2hot4u: I take a bus

Kid4kid: must be cool not havin to walk an carry ur books I only live a block away so its no big deal

Teen2hot4u: I live bout 12 blocks away

Kid4kid: wow thats far I hope u never miss the bus lol I bet it gets cold in the winter waitin for it to come

Teen2hot4u: yeah it does but sometimes we can go into the grocery store on the corner to wait cause the mans real nice an he gives us hot choc

Kid4kid: that's cool it must be a big store to hold all the kids on the busstop

Teen2hot4u: no its jus a lil one mr jones owned it when I was only a lil kid

	my mom says an anyhow theres only 2 kids waitin with me for the bus
Kid4kid:	mr jones sounds real cool I wonder if we have the same grocery stores here
Teen2hot4u:	I don't think so cause poppy's foods is jus here I think
Kid4kid:	k so is ur mom a pain like mine
Teen2hot4u:	I guess
Kid4kid:	mine is always home when I get here an sometimes I wish she worked like my dad so id have some privacy u no
Teen2hot4u:	my mom works so shes never home when I get here like until we eat dinner
Kid4kid:	cool*

That chat seems innocent enough, one where a child who has been warned about giving out last names, addresses, and any personal identifying information might feel safe that she has not revealed too much. But, take a deeper look. It is clear that Lorie has put herself in danger, because she probably didn't realize how far she had gone with what she said. Lorie told Joey that she is twelve-years-old, in seventh grade, that she's a catcher on a softball team called the Cardinals, and that she has the number four on her uniform, which is red and white. She told him she plays her games at her school, PS42, on Wednesdays at four and Saturdays at ten, and that she lives alone with her mother in Merrick, New York. She has no brothers, sisters, or animals, and she takes a bus to school, which is about twelve blocks from her house. She also said that she stands alone with two other children in front of Poppy's Foods waiting for the bus to come.

That is more than enough information for a predator to find Lorie. He knows where her school is, where her bus stop is, and what time

---

*The screen name Kid4kid and the names Steve Davidson and Joey were created for the purpose of the above chat and are not meant to represent any real people who may have ever, may currently, or may someday use those names on the Internet.

school lets out when she isn't playing softball. More importantly, he knows when and where she plays ball, what her uniform looks like, and what the number is on the back of her shirt. He also knows that she spends all her free afternoons at home, alone. Any half-way intelligent adult could find Lorie, and the odds are that someone who spends that much time fishing for information lives a lot closer than he claims. He is also probably a lot older than thirteen. The conversation is typical for a sexual predator who wants to venture out of the house to find a girl. He skirts the issues and beats around the bush, making questions so innocent and typical, just like what a kid would ask, that Lorie does not even realize how much information she has offered. It happens all the time. There are horror stories about how predators have followed children home from schools and ball fields and attacked them in their own homes, knowing that they would be alone there for several hours, and the kids had no idea how anyone knew where to find them.

This is an epidemic of enormous proportions. Pedophiles, sexual predators, child molesters, and whatever else you want to call those monsters who take advantage of children, are sick people. No matter how long they stay in prison, no matter how much help they receive, no matter what they say or do, they are not going to be cured. They will carry the burden for the rest of their lives, which is why it is highly unlikely that they will ever own up to the fact that, laws or no laws, it is morally and socially wrong for an adult to have sex with a child!

I sit here at my computer every day. As I have written this book, I have chatted with sexual predators. I try to do both, sometimes deferring to one or the other when necessary. So, in the background of my mind, between the lines of this book, are experiences, very real experiences with very real sexual predators. There is never a day when I am not contacted by one, two, three, ten, or more of them. They are a click away from any child, and I try to be that child. I let them continue to chat with me so they don't chat with a real child, but just as I can chat with a number of different predators at one time, they, too, can chat with several different children at one time. I cannot do much more than what

I do. I will not cross the line under any circumstances. I will not give any one of them an excuse to get out of being held criminally liable for their disgusting behavior.

As for how I feel about my work, I keep in mind that the means do justify the ends and I find solace in that fact. If by my actions I am able to save another child, or perhaps dozens of children, from a lifetime of torment, that alone is enough justification for me to continue. I do not enjoy communicating with predators. My greatest wish is that I would sign onto the Internet and find that my work on here is no longer necessary, that nobody wants to go after children anymore. There is no pleasure in what I do with the exception that I take predators off the street. I remove them from their natural habitats and reissue them into a world where they become the prey and the predators are all around them just waiting for a chance to pounce. It is the cruelest irony I can bestow upon them.

I plan to continue working with the FBI for as long as they will allow me to in an effort to keep sexual predators away from children. I cannot stand by and watch adults take advantage of our youngsters, convincing them that they are special in order to manipulate them into having sex; to build up their self-esteem, only to ruin the rest of their lives with nightmares of molestation and rape; to take away the innocence of their youth and replace it with the fear of being loved; to shame and guilt them into keeping the dirty little secrets that predators force upon them; to use their young bodies in such ways that they make sex a frightening and horror-filled experience, so that they cannot have normal intimate relationships as adults; to close their innocent eyes to the beauty of the world and leave them with the ugliness of the sick minds of those who call what they do "love."

The ball is now in your court. You can choose to run with it, you can pass it along to someone else, or you can drop it. But know this: Only when we all work together to protect children will we be able to stop these monsters in their tracks, one predator at a time, once and for all.

Epilogue

I F YOU TAKE ANYTHING AWAY FROM THIS BOOK, PLEASE LET it be the courage to win the fight against sexual predators. They succeed through silence and secrets, and we must break the silence, tell on them, and pursue their prosecutions through legal means. I know this is a difficult concept, especially for victims and their families. However, it is the only way that we can take them off the streets and away from children.

I am not saying this lightly. Coming forward and revealing your identity is frightening. Victims have enough to deal with without worrying about public opinion. There is also a fear factor. I know about that. When I first began to write this book, I wasn't sure how I would tell my story or whether I would reveal my own identity, although I did plan to use the predators' real names. Otherwise, the book wouldn't have the same impact. I thought about using a pseudonym in order to protect myself from anyone seeking to retaliate against me for having turned them in to the FBI. In spite of having my identity revealed in the courtroom, I felt that my exposure there was limited to a small group of people who might put more of their focus on the defendants than on me. My only real fear was of the incarcerated predators and their families.

Though I had finally made the decision to put my name on *Exposed*, I hadn't quite convinced myself that it was wise, due to safety concerns. Then, on October 23, 2006, Matthew (Tempoteech) Brand's appeal was discussed in an article in the *New York Law Journal* and the Court's decision was published in the same paper three days later. My name was revealed several times throughout both publications. To my knowledge, it was the first time that my name was printed in connection with one of the many sexual predator cases I had been involved with during the past four years. Having my name revealed at the same time that my book was about to go to print was a sign to me. I don't believe in coincidences, so I felt that I was doing the right thing, not only by revealing who I am, but more importantly, what I do and why I do it. It is my mission to let as many people as I can know about my story and understand the importance of coming forward, not only as concerned citizens, but also those who have been victimized by sexual predators. It is only by raising our voices in unison as loud as we can that we will stop allowing the predators to go free. This is the example that we must set for our children. Speak up and speak out! Never keep the secrets of those who hurt us. Never think that the secret protects us, because it doesn't. It haunts us and eats away at us and it protects the predator. Be brave and be strong and let your voice be heard. You are not alone.